# Market Power and Business Strategy

## In Search of the Unified Organization

DAVID JOSEPH MORRIS, JR.

# Q

QUORUM BOOKS
Westport, Connecticut • London

**Library of Congress Cataloging-in-Publication Data**

Morris, David.
    Market power and business strategy : in search of the unified
organization / David Joseph Morris, Jr.
        p.   cm.
    Includes bibliographical references and index.
    ISBN 1–56720–045–1 (alk. paper)
    1. Strategic planning.   2. Organizational effectiveness.
I. Title.
HD30.28.M6479    1996
658.4′012—dc20          95–50742

British Library Cataloguing in Publication Data is available.

Library of Congress Catalog Card Number: 95–50742
ISBN: 1–56720–045–1

First published in 1996

Quorum Books, 88 Post Road West, Westport, CT  06881
An imprint of Greenwood Publishing Group, Inc.

Printed in the United States of America

The paper used in this book complies with the
Permanent Paper Standard issued by the National
Information Standards Organization (Z39.48–1984).

10 9 8 7 6 5 4 3 2 1

When we leave this world we will not be recognized for what we have taken, but rather, for what we have given to others. This book is dedicated to the United States and to all those who have made us what we are today and what we will be tomorrow.

# Contents

# Figures

# Preface

When I began the journey that led to the writing of this book, I had no idea that there existed any way to think about the world other than the post–World War II American approach. My conversion to a broader understanding began to occur when I realized that knowledge, skills, and attitudes (KSA) were easily combined and that the KSA gained in one area could be transferred to all others. I initially recognized this through a determined effort to learn multiple trades. After completing several accelerated evening courses in a variety of pursuits, not only did I possess the knowledge to perform many skills, I possessed an unanticipated insight: it all overlapped. The great illusion was that each skill was distinctive, but I discovered that essentially they were the same.

When I later chanced on a book called *The Way of the Samurai* by Yukio Mishima, I realized that hundreds of millions had taken this same path. The philosophy of their society encouraged it, and those who achieved this insight were considered enlightened. I then found myself far more capable of predicting the behavior of Western and Eastern corporations based on these philosophical underpinnings. As an associate professor of marketing, I began to organize my courses into two worldviews: the pluralistic (or linear) with its strategic business consequences and the unitary (or circular) with its business consequences.

This book is written for the student and the teacher, for those who work hard every day and want to compete in a global marketplace and win. KSA are everywhere, and, as I tell my students, opportunity is not out there somewhere, but under our noses. Opportunity presents itself in the people that we meet every day. They all have stories connected to one another and to ourselves. I have had a successful radio show *Live the Journey* that reinforces this understanding for me each week. We are all teachers. We teach others through our countless actions each day and through the choices that we make a million times in our lives. This book will help the reader with the choices that are directed at outperforming com-

## Figure 1
## Operating System and Resources

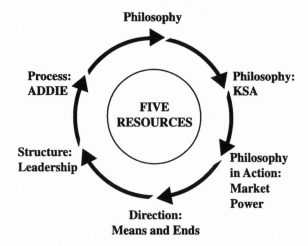

Philosophy

Process:
ADDIE

Philosophy:
KSA

FIVE
RESOURCES

Structure:
Leadership

Philosophy
in Action:
Market
Power

Direction:
Means and Ends

petition in business.

This book has seven modules, not chapters, because chapters imply a linear approach to learning and strategy. The reader can begin anywhere and read in any order. The ideas are drawn from many disciplines. I tried to include any ideas that I believe to be helpful in pursuing a unitary philosophy to gain market power.

The first six modules (figure 1) consist of a comparison of separating and combining operating systems. The "Introduction (Philosophy)" module outlines the two worldviews and their impact on all aspects of life. Both Western and Eastern philosophies and their relations to business operating systems are outlined. The module "Philosophy: Knowledge, Skills, and Attitudes" connects KSA to the philosophies of separating and combining. "Philosophy in Action (Market Power)" outlines the common operating system of market power. The "Direction (Means and Ends)" module focuses on the common direction for the organization. "Structure (Leadership)" applies a leader/trusted-follower model. "Process (ADDIE)" follows, with a discussion of a common process throughout the organization. These six modules outline a universal strategic operating system. The last module— "5Rs" (Marketing, Human, Physical, Intangible, and Financial Resources)—is then applied to previously developed modules, combining operating system. It outlines the available marketing resources to attain market power. The key to this book is that the same operating system transfers to all resources. This will streamline your thinking and improve your performance as a strategist. It is no longer appropriate to visualize members of the organization as particular specialists. In conclusion, "Final Thoughts" is a discussion of the application of the ideas put forth in the book.

We have a great deal of work to do in the United States to recover from the extremes of separating and its impact on our lives. Many nations have been unwilling or unable to come together even in times of great peril. My hope is that the

United States will be up to the collective challenge. This book not only attempts to identify the issues but puts forth specific actions.

This book may challenge many strongly held beliefs. If that is the case, please bear in mind that the best way to learn is to avoid such tired and unproductive arguments as "my ideas are better than your ideas," "my culture is better than your culture," "my philosophy is better than your philosophy," "my operating system is better than your operating system." If you get into this type of argument, you may never be able to get past your own philosophy to a point of understanding that is possible. It is more productive to weave ideas into a broader philosophical framework. Exit one system and enter another. Do not try to overlay but instead become a part of a different philosophical world. Then you will be able to create your own combinations. When we learn to enter the minds of our competitors, we will be able to face the Chinese, Japanese, Koreans, Germans, and indeed all others.

Because of this alone, this book is not a duplication of every other book that tells us that we are in trouble and then gives a couple of checklists of actions to be taken. This book is also not a "let's ask the top companies and top names how come they are so great" to ensure that the book sells. These formula business books may be nice, light reading, but their solutions are often oversimplified. As suggested in a popular mass-market business publication, many American managers are now walking around their companies but few are outperforming the Japanese or the Germans.

Examples are drawn from everyday experiences as much as possible because the answers are in those experiences. There are great role models for us all in every town, on every street, and in every family. Build on them by incorporating them into your KSA. Find your own solutions, teach yourself. Use others as guides, not final authorities. Combine and simplify to achieve a purpose.

# Introduction (Philosophy)

The United States is involved in a historic clash of philosophies. Today, more than at any other time in history, with the exception of the incursions of Alexander the Great into the East and of Genghis Khan into the West, these philosophies are challenging each other with clarity. The United States—as the archetype of the Western-based philosophy of separating—is challenged by Japan and its Eastern philosophy of combining. The United States and the Yankee traders have enjoyed the dominant position in this battle for centuries. The Western philosophy of separating, referred to herein as "pluralism," is linear, and it has been taken to such extremes in the United States that Americans are unable to compete in the modern world marketplace. Eastern philosophy is "unitary" or circular, and is proving to be a formidable alternative to the recent Western approach.

The search for a philosophy with which we may live our lives has been a universal quest of mankind. Many nations and groups of nations have failed to develop a philosophy of life that could ensure their long-term survival. They have risen and fallen everywhere on earth because, it is hypothesized, people within each society believe that they have the mandate of heaven. No matter what they do, or do not do, all will be fine, for they have been given a special mandate to be successful. This leads to a lack of interest in incorporating the knowledge, skills, and attitudes (KSA) that are outside of the accepted norms of their society. When other KSA are introduced, these societies have had a difficult time at best assimilating the ideas into their philosophical systems. This has led to the constant redrawing of the boundaries of groups into nations. Tolerance and intolerance seem to be parts of the legacy of every generation. The dream of an individualized, universal, secular philosophy has failed. There is no evidence that it has ever succeeded, and yet it still dominated unchallenged, until very recently, in the United States.

The United States has attempted to make business a science with the belief that our pluralistic interpretation of a scientific approach will ensure success and prosperity. Since World War II, Americans have justified their pluralistically derived operating system with the mistaken belief that the war was won through just such principles. In actuality, the United States emerged victorious from the war because society worked together for a common purpose. In wartime, Americans applied all their resources to achieve this end and were able to outperform the competition.

This success has driven America to separate all aspects of society from business activities while all its competitors have continued to combine resources. After World War II, those Americans who had accomplished the successful war effort would have been unable to believe that destroyed competition would ever rise again to any significant economic or military level. Since Russia was part of the winning side, Americans believed that the threat must come from that country.

American business in the postwar period was more than willing to share all its commercial success with the defeated nations. The United States believed that its astounding commercial success was due to the postwar model of separating and not to the war model of combining. The competition did not make this strategic change in philosophy and continued to build on its ancient philosophies of combining.

The success of a corporation depends on the ability of its employees to organize in order to realize market power. "Market power" is defined as the use/employment of organizational capacity to block existing and potential competitors from access to targeted markets. This does not suggest that market power is the most important factor in business; rather it is the KSA that people in a business apply to adjust to environmental alternatives that determine success or failure. Members of organizations must continue to combine their actions to respond to their ever-changing competitive environments. For an organization, it is the choice of the combination of actions which are derived from available resources which ensures continuous survival.

Resources such as marketing, human, physical, intangible, and financial (the "5Rs") have no value to an organization until they have been applied to an operating system to achieve market power. The operating system and the concept of market power remain constant. Direction and resources change. Western business theory and practice continue to emphasize the role of resources while neglecting the importance of a philosophically derived operating system. This resource-driven pluralistic model of the West is manifested in the functional organizational design. The functional approach has been a successful organizational configuration under past competitive environmental conditions, but it is no longer considered the best way to attain and sustain market power.

Those who have advocated the functionalist view in the past still continue to emphasize the importance of one particular function over another. Neofunctionalists have carried on this theme by promoting quality, cycle time, cost reduction, entrepreneurship, best practice, statistical processes, world-class management, and reengineering. Both the functionalist and the neofunctionalist persist in an adherence to a single-solution linear philosophy.

## PLURALISM VERSUS UNITARIANISM

There are two central philosophies from which business has evolved. The first approach is termed *pluralistic*: the dividing and separating of all actions into a linear representation. The second philosophy that impacts business is *unitary*: the combining of all actions into a circular representation. Western business theory and practice, particularly in the United States, have embraced the pluralistic philosophy. Non-Western business theory and practice, as adopted by the Japanese, have incorporated the unitary philosophy. Both philosophies remained relatively isolated from each other until the 1950s when the U.S. government opened its markets to Japan after the Korean War. Since that time, the American pluralistic model has proven to be little match for the Japanese unitary approach to business.

Fundamental change must occur if Americans wish to respond to present environmental conditions. The pluralistic and unitary philosophies have impacted every aspect of life within their respective societies. For most Westerners, it is difficult to believe that actions assumed to be fundamental to their lives are driven by the presence of one of these all-encompassing philosophical constructs. These frameworks overlap across national, cultural, racial, and religious boundaries. They have affected the way we view life and death, time, family relationships, education, language development, science, and business.

Business theory and practice mirror the philosophical norms that have been developed by a society at large. The role of business education has been to provide formal mechanisms such as the master in business administration (M.B.A.) to transfer these national philosophies to the next generation. This has been done with little if any consideration of possible alternatives. Once these norms have been set in a young mind, it is difficult later to accept, at any level, the value of alternative perspectives. The self-assurance of these particular positions remains beyond the point of personal and even national disaster. Many people and nations have chosen destruction over change.

The misguided belief of many Americans that the Germans and Japanese have changed their philosophical foundations and copied the United States after World War II is unsubstantiated. When the colonial power of the United States was no longer a threat, German and Japanese business theory and practice moved back into their old fundamental belief systems. Thus it can be argued that these nations were changed very little after World War II because the change was forced from the outside. Although American public relations may have emphasized these changes as a justification for both military and political expenditures, history will view them as cosmetic at best.

The great American business myth of the last fifty years has been that the Germans and the Japanese have copied the U.S. model, and therefore, all Americans have to do to compete is to continue to do what they have done in the past and perhaps just improve on quality. The accomplishments of both the Germans and the Japanese have been used by many American academics to justify changes in business practices based on a misinterpretation of evidence. For example, such academics have attributed the success of the Japanese in business to a lack of hierarchies. They characterize the Japanese system as one where all individuals work together with little or no supervision from above. The consequence of this

disinformation for American management is the belief that it is most advantageous to reject hierarchies when organizing a business to compete with the Japanese. This could not be farther from the truth. The Japanese have been and continue to be one of the most hierarchical cultures on earth.

It has been part of American political philosophy for two hundred years to be
against hierarchies in government. The argument was put forth against business
hierarchies before Japan was ever considered to be a competitor. In a quest to
avoid political hierarchies, many Americans have attempted to destroy business,
military, religious, and family hierarchies.

The reason for this type of American behavior is that each philosophical framework (pluralistic and unitary) and its subgroups view the actions (both positive
and negative) of others as a justification for their own behavior. To understand
performances from another philosophical position, a person must often exit an
entire system and enter another way of thinking. The concept of hierarchy is different when formulated through another philosophical construct. To try to overlay
one precept on the other will only lead to erroneous conclusions. These conclusions may be acceptable to those who do not wish to change, but they will not be
accurate representations that will assist in outperforming competition.

Sun Tzu, a Chinese military strategist of twenty-five hundred years ago, advocated that people should know themselves and know their competitors. Sun Tzu
called these competitors "enemies." To do this, you must think as your competitors think, you must become your competitors, you must see yourself through
your competitors' eyes. American businesspersons have not considered it necessary to understand their competition for many reasons. America's success in World
War II, its long-term isolation, its ever-expanding internal markets, and its abundant natural resources have given Americans a sense of invincibility (a "mandate
of heaven"). China suffered from this same overestimation, and because of this, it
has endured a long-term decline. China failed to incorporate Western thinking
into its own operating system.

## CULTURAL IMPACT OF PHILOSOPHY

The pluralistic and unitary views of life have had an impact on the perception
of life events, the calendar, family, education, mathematics, language, causal relationships, science, system theory, and business. Some have suggested that the human brain takes on a physiological form relative to the culture in which it is developed. There is no doubt that individual examples can be cited that differ from the
dominant direction of society. The rugged individualism of a man like Soichiro
Honda in the Japanese car industry or the collective behavior of the Mormons in
the United States could be considered by some to be outside the dominant philosophy that drives the larger culture.

However, when you identify Honda as a rugged individual, do not try immedi-
ately to overlay that behavior on the pluralistic philosophical framework. Honda
achieved that individualism within a unitary culture that many in the West would
put forth as impossible. Honda's individualism is nothing like that of a Henry
Ford, a Lee Iacocca, or others who evolved as part of a pluralistic philosophical
framework. We are all a part of an overall philosophical formulation of the broader

society.

The Irish in the United States are different from the Irish in Ireland. They will continue to be different as long as they are influenced by the larger American culture. St. Patrick's Day means very little to the Irish in Ireland. Although they have a parade in Dublin, it is filled with Irish Americans from Boston who have come to recreate their Irish-American festival in Ireland. The American Irish also view themselves as having a right to influence Ireland. Their wishes are not always the same as those of the people of Ireland.

The contrasts between world philosophies, as discussed in this book, are far different from those between the American Irish and the Irish in Ireland. It is the difference between those (generally from Europe) who have been influenced by one worldview and those (generally from Asia) who have been influenced by another. This discussion does not exclude other sections of the world as examples of these philosophical alternatives.

Those in the West who have been influenced by varying degrees of pluralism have not considered the unitary view because of its perceived linkage to pagan religions. Western intellectuals have been working hard for centuries to separate religion from areas such as science, government, education, business, and the law. To embrace another worldview that does not seek to separate different disciplines would be counterproductive to their long-term argument.

The strongest justification for their lack of interest in the unitary approach has been the Western linear contention that Eastern people are in an evolutionary state and that once they get enough education, they will adopt Western insights. The groups in the West in the past that have seemed interested in a unitary approach included a few intellectuals and the disgruntled fringe of society. What has been more important for the West has been to expose Easterners to Christianity, smash their idolatry, and bring them into the next century. This crusade, which lasted four centuries, has been halted with the success of the Japanese and their economic conquest of world markets.

These markets had been the reserved domain of Europeans and Americans for centuries. With the economic conquest of the West, the influence of Asian religious and philosophical thought may also be a motivation and catalyst for Asian nations to expand into the West. How this will evolve, most of us will live to observe. The following modules select different cultural and philosophical domains and demonstrate how they have evolved from the broader pluralistic and unitary philosophies. The objective of this comparison is to lay the philosophical groundwork that can lead the reader to three conclusions: (1) differences do exist between the two worldviews; (2) these differences show how an operating system is created or evolves; (3) Americans, too, must again unify to compete.

## LIFE EVENTS

### Pluralistic

*Christianity, Judaism, and Islam*

The pluralistic view of life's events is linear, fragmented, and segmented. Individuals are born; they move through childhood and young adulthood; they marry, raise families, and retire; finally, they die. Consequently, under the impact of the pluralistic approach, Christians believe that they are judged to determine if they will go to heaven, purgatory (in some cases), or hell. Heaven, purgatory, and hell will reflect the type of life that the person lived while on earth. Those who repent for their sins, will be ensured their positions in heaven. Later, they will be reborn, on the Day of Judgment, the time of the end of the world when God will come to judge the living and dead.

Judaism does not recognize heaven as a reward and hell as a punishment for actions that one has done in this life. Heaven is represented more as a world to come. Heaven and hell play little part in ritual and teaching. The person atones for sins that have been committed against others and is judged by God and the community. The asking for forgiveness is directed at the person who has been wronged and not at God. Islam recognizes paradise and hell. People go to paradise or hell based on their deeds in this life. At the end of the world, there will be a Day of Judgment.

Normative Christianity and Judaism represent God in the masculine form as the creator of humankind. In Islam, God, or infinity, has no sex. Infinity is considered shapeless and formless. Infinity was always there and will always be there. The infinity can create any form by intending to create it and saying the word "be." This is how the first human, Adam, was created. In Islam, the human is not created in the image of the infinite. Nothing that the creator creates resembles the creator in any form. Infinity, or God, is separate and above both humans and nature.

The relationship between humans and God is clarified and administered institutionally in Judaism and Christianity. In Islam, this relationship is defined as that of the master with the master's creation. The Holy Qur'an is the last revelation sent to humankind through the last Prophet, Muhammad (son of Abdullah).

The individual may be brought into the faith ceremonially, as with baptism in Christianity. At about thirteen years of age, the Christian youths become members of the church at confirmation. At the age of thirteen, Jewish boys are bar mitzvahed and Jewish girls are bas mitzvahed. The purpose of this ritual is for the youth to show a capacity for leadership in the service. The bar-mitzvah boy has to prove to the congregation that he is literate in the scriptures. In Islam, every child is born into the Islamic faith. There is no formal ritual of induction. Muslim boys and girls at puberty are required to perform the five daily prayers and fast in the month of Ramadhan. Once they begin to earn a living, they are required to give yearly compulsory charity *(zakat)* to the needy. If they can afford it, they are required to perform a pilgrimage to Mecca once in their lifetime.

The Christian is married in the church, the Jew in the synagogue, the Muslim in a mosque. At death, the Christian is brought to the church for a ceremony; the body is taken afterward to the graveyard for another ceremony. The Jewish individual has a ceremony in a funeral home and then at the cemetery. The Jewish family and friends are to mourn for seven days (Shivah) and to reflect on how the remaining people will live with the loss. At the end of the seven days, they are to return to work and learn to live without the dead person. Each year, the person is remembered at the anniversary of their death at a Yahrzeit, or the recital of the Kaddish. This includes the lighting of a memorial candle or lamp. The Muslims have prayers at the mosque and graveyard and then return home for mourning.

The Muslims believe Jesus (Son of Mary) is the Messiah and that he did not die on the cross, but was lifted up by God, with both his body and soul intact. Although the Muslims do not believe in the divinity of Jesus they do believe that Jesus will return to the earth as a follower of the Prophet Muhammad to cleanse the world of the Antichrist (Dajjal). Dajjal is a one-eyed monster, who will be given the power by God to perform miracles, to prove that right is wrong and wrong is right. The Muslims believe that Jesus will appear in a mosque in Damascus at the time of the dawn prayer. He will then declare himself to be Jesus (Son of Mary) and will proceed to burn a cross to indicate that he did not die on the cross. He will also slaughter a pig to convey that he never permitted the eating of pork. After Jesus (Son of Mary) cleanses the world of the Antichrist, he will die a natural death as a human.

The religious tolerance among these faiths at the social level has been minimal for centuries. This is not true at the theoretical level where there is much overlap. This individualized religious intolerance has also been directed at all other faiths. Christianity, Judaism, and Islam have rejected non-Western faiths, and Christianity and Islam have adopted a missionary component to convert the "nonbelievers" to their beliefs. Each of these Western faiths postulates that its particular religion is sufficient and that there is no reason to combine. In fact, they do not encourage one belief system to be mixed with another. Each is separate, distinct, and unrelated to the others. It would be exceptional if a person were to be baptized as a Christian, bar mitzvahed as a Jew, married as a Muslim, and buried as a Buddhist. Multiple religious and nonreligious configurations, however, are not uncommon in Japan where faiths can be combined.

It is difficult to discuss religions because of the variations that occur. The three major Western faiths have a great deal of overlap, but their individual missions generally have been to emphasize the differences among them. These religions, when viewed as one conceptual system, have encouraged an underlying philosophical commitment to pluralism or separating for thousands of years (see figure 2).

## Unitary

The unitary perspective of the Orient has similar life events, but at death, the individual may be reborn. The four stages of Hindu life are student, householder, forest dweller, and renouncer. This process of life, death, and rebirth continues for an indeterminate number of times during which the *atman* (loosely equivalent to the Western Christian concept of "soul") undergoes a variety of life experiences. This circle of life and death continues until the *atman* is released from this earthly bondage to become one with the Infinite. This event is referred to as *mukti* or *moksha* in Hinduism and *nirvana* (although different) in Buddhism. The Infinite is beyond human understanding or expression and is beyond any symbol or representation of God. All that is known and unknown will return to become one with the Infinite. Every single thing, when rejoined with the Infinite, becomes absolutely indistinguishable from all other things.

## Figure 2
## Life Events

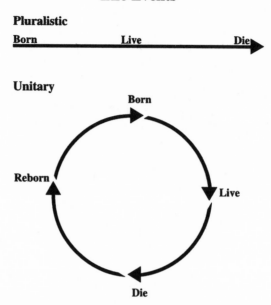

**Pluralistic**

Born                    Live                    Die

**Unitary**

Source: *Marketing Theory and Practice: A Unitary and Pluralistic Approach* (West Haven CT: University of New Haven Press).

### Hinduism

There are sixteen Hindu rituals from conception to death. The upper castes of Hindus (priest, warrior, and trader) have a ritual called *upnayan samskara*. However, those of the lowest caste, *Shudra*, are forbidden by scripture to have this ritual or to wear the sacred thread, *yagynopaveet*, across their shoulders. Millions in India have been working for centuries to eliminate the concept of the untouchability of the *Shudra*. Because the Hindus believe in the perpetuation of life after death, they de-emphasize celebrations of birth and anniversaries in favor of the sixteen rituals.

According to Hindu mythology, the departed *atman* of the deceased wanders for thirteen days before it either enters another body or attains *mukti*. Therefore, after the dead body has been cremated—preferably on a riverbank—there is a thirteen-day period for mourning and prayer for the departed *atman*. On the thirteenth day, there is rejoicing, usually in the form of a grand feast celebrating the birth of the deceased. Another mythology of Hindus states that the River Ganges (*Ganga*) descends from and then returns to the heavens. Consequently, a typical Hindu who hopes to go to heaven desires to be cremated on the bank of the Ganges. Heaven and hell are part of Hindu mythology, although neither is the final attainment. The final attainment is only in the state of *mukti* after a multitude of cycles of births and rebirths.

## Buddhism

Buddhism, as is well known, derived from Hinduism as a reform movement. Consequently, it has retained many tenets of the latter: there is the ritual of cremation as opposed to burial and the belief in the cycle of birth and death as opposed to the Western belief in only one life. Being a reform movement, Buddhism has done away with the Hindu caste system, particularly the untouchability of the lowest caste. Furthermore, emphasizing the principle of *karma*, Buddhism has shortened the cycle of birth and death for the attainment of *nirvana*. According to Buddhist belief, based on his or her righteous deeds, a person can attain *nirvana* in a single cycle. The concept of dependent origination avoids the issue of the permanence of a soul and puts forth the concept that actions are derived from previous actions. The impact of all our actions moves beyond our life.

Buddhism did not flourish in India, its country of origin, because the reform movement failed to convert the Hindus. The flexibility of Hinduism enabled it to incorporate Buddhist beliefs into its philosophy. In Hinduism, a person can seek his or her own individual salvation; therefore, Buddhism as a separate belief system was unnecessary. Buddhism has a missionary component, and its teaching has been very successful in many other parts of Asia. It has evolved into two distinct schools: *Mahayana* ("big boat," or universal, salvation) and *Hinayana* or *Theraveda* ("little boat," or individual, salvation).

The Japanese have incorporated *Mahayana* Buddhist philosophy into their culture through the Indian and Chinese approach called *zazen* from *za* ("sitting") and *zen* ("meditation"). *Zazen* has encouraged scholarship, art, and poetry in Japanese culture. With a view to emphasize compassion for fellow beings and to de-emphasize the individual ego, the Buddha enunciated the concept of "dependent origination": the material world manifests the relationships within and between all things. Every action in life is representative of every other action. All elements are linked and intertwined.

This is why the Japanese practice *koan* in their monasteries. A *koan* is a statement, puzzle, or riddle given by the abbot on which the novice is expected to meditate—for example, "What is the sound of one hand clapping?" It is everyday life and the performance of each task that reveal the interconnections of all things. Each action represents all other actions and each has equal value. In the end, it can be noted that both the Buddha and his followers have neither affirmed nor denied the concept of God or the First Cause of the Universe on the premise that finding the cause and the cure of human suffering is more important than speculating on the metaphysical issues. For example, it is not unusual for the Japanese to subscribe to many faiths at the same time because of their unitary approaches toward life. All faiths and philosophies can be combined in any configuration that the individual prefers.

## Shinto

The Shinto religion considers the supreme ruler, or emperor of Japan, the direct descendant of the Sun Goddess. The chronicle of the history of the Shinto religion is recorded in two books: *Kojiki* and *Nihonshoki*. These books, written in the seventh century, represent an oral tradition that may be thousands of years old.

The Imperial Sun Successions, embodied in Emperor Akihito, represents a single unbroken line that includes all the Japanese people. Those that follow Shinto believe that the Japanese are the divine descendants of the gods.

Shinto has a hierarchy of *kamis*, which rules the destiny of human beings before their births, during their lifetimes, and after their deaths. Each *kami* has a different sphere of influence and control, such as wind, fire, longevity and the harvest. Upon death, the believer becomes a ghost whose role is to influence and assist the living. Particular trades or crafts have their own gods. Shinto workers in modern Japan perform on their job according to these traditions and rituals. In Shinto, the living are governed by the dead. The influence of the dead on daily action is profound. The living are observed by the dead at all times in their life. The living have an obligation not to forsake or cause the dead any shame through their behavior.

*Author's note: The author does not suggest that his discussion of religion is more than superficial. This normative discussion is intended to show broad influences on our lives. Separating or combining has evolved from these foundations.*

## THE CALENDAR
### Pluralistic

Western calendars are linear. The Christian Gregorian calendar begins with the birth of Jesus Christ. This solar calendar refers to all events before that date as B.C. ("before Christ"), whereas those that come after are A.D. ("anno domini," "the year of the Lord"). The years B.C. are considered to go back to the time of the creation and Adam and Eve. Those who wish to use the Christian calendar but not the B.C. or A.D. have incorporated the designations B.C.E. ("before common era") and C.E. ("common era").

The Hebrew calendar also begins with the creation of the world and the descendants of Adam and Eve. This calendar is lunisolar, meaning it incorporates both the moon and the sun. In the Gregorian year 1996, on September fourteenth, it will be 5756–57 in the Hebrew calendar. The Islamic calendar begins with the "Hegira" (forced flight) of Muhammad from Mecca to Medina, in the Gregorian calendar A.D. 622. The present year in the Islamic calendar is a lunar approach— on approximately May 18, 1996 it will be A.H. 1417 (the A.H. stands for "anno Hegirae," "the year of the "Hegira"). These three calendars extend to the end of time or to the coming or second coming of the Messiah to earth. People of each faith view their own calendar as unique, separate, and linear (see figure 3).

### Unitary
*Chinese Calendar*

The lunar Chinese calendar is represented by a circle divided into twelve-year cycles. Each twelve-year cycle begins with the year of the rat and ends with the year of the pig. Twelve-year cycles are combined into five groupings, or sixty years, a sexagenary cycle, which represents one lifetime. Each sixty-year grouping is then given a special name to distinguish it from other sixty-year cycles. A period in time, for example, may be the year of the goat in the fourth cycle. The

# Figure 3
# Calendar

**Pluralistic**

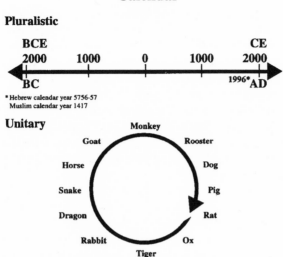

* Hebrew calendar year 5756-57
Muslim calendar year 1417

Source: *Marketing Theory and Practice: A Unitary and Pluralistic Approach* (West Haven CT: University of New Haven Press).

Christian-calendar year 1996 begins a new sixty-year cycle in the Chinese calendar. The new year begins between January 21 and February 19. The Chinese also had a calendar that began with the emperor's reign and ended with his death. This type of calendar is still used in Japan. China also has a linear lunar calendar that starts with the Legendary Period. Applying a linear representation to the Chinese calendar, 1996 (the year of the rat) is the year 4694.

## Japanese Calendar

The Japanese begin their calendar with the emperor's reign and end it with the emperor's death. They have had 125 emperors, which is the longest unbroken line of succession in the world today. Japanese emperors are believed to be descended from the Sun Goddess. The date that has been generally given for the goddess's ascension to earth is 660 B.C.

The emperor was considered a living god until 1946, when Emperor Hirohito was forced, during the U.S. occupation, to renounce his imperial divinity. Each emperor names his reign with a theme. Emperor Hirohito's reign (1926–1989) was *Showa*, or "Shining Peace"; Emperor Akihito's reign (since 1989) is *Heisei*, or "Achieving Peace." When an emperor assumes the throne, the event is considered a new beginning. Debts are forgiven, and those imprisoned for past crimes are released from jail. The Japanese have also adopted a Western calendar as a means of organizing time. The Chinese and Japanese can easily adapt to multiple calendars, but their general, long-term view of life fits into their circular calendars. Their system for telling time is repetitive and circular.

## FAMILY
### Pluralistic

In a society that separates, the relationships among family members are ones that encourage individual autonomy. Father, mother, children, and grandparents do not have clearly defined or understood roles. This creates a family power vacuum that may be filled by any individual or group of family members. In many cases, these roles have been turned over to others outside the family.

Day care takes the responsibility for the preschool education and the nurturing of the very young; schools educate the young; churches dispense religious training; and the legal system disciplines. The skill of making a living is no longer provided within the family. It is left to higher education, trade unions, and the business community to train the young for their lifework. It is unnecessary for a family to pass its profession or skill on to its next generation. The young feel no obligation to do the same type of work that their parents did.

Much of the family's time and energy is devoted to resolving conflicts of role clarification. The grandmother is no longer required to assist in raising the grandchildren. The mother has little particular responsibility in teaching the young. The father does not have to teach his son a trade. Because traditional roles have been dissolved, older and younger members of the family are caught in a power struggle to gain, hold, or regain power.

With other outside specialized organizations assuming these roles, family members are left in a vacuum. From a pluralistic perspective, this makes sense because the family had incurred too much responsibility in too many areas. It is more efficient to let other specialists assume responsibility within their particular areas of expertise. Family members who attempt to adhere to traditional roles and maintain a more inclusive participatory set of responsibilities are scorned by society and by other family members, particularly the young, as being out of step.

As the individual grows older, his or her power and prestige within the family begins to decline. The older family members are often considered a burden to be tolerated or turned over to specialists who house, entertain, and care for them. The children are under no obligation to assume responsibility for their elderly parents. Older family members often fear that their children may put them in nursing or retirement homes. Their value to younger family members is questioned, and conflicts can occur between grandchildren and grandparents if they perceive each other as competing for family resources. Family obligations are defined and redefined from generation to generation from an individual perspective. Little if any formal obligations of roles apply to any particular family member.

### Unitary

In a unitary society, family relationships are clearly delineated from generation to generation. The relationships are derived from Confucian philosophy or some equivalent. Power is explicitly defined and transferred from mother to daughter and from father to son. Individual autonomy is replaced with obligation to the family, the community, the nation, and the world. This obligation extends to past and future family members. Respect for and obligation to those who have gone before and those that are to follow are required. Grandparents, parents, and children have clearly defined and understood roles and obligations. The members of a family are aware of their roles and what is required to perform successfully in these roles. They learn their roles from birth and possibly even from previous births.

The first son within an immediate family becomes the leader of his family. He is responsible for his brothers and their families. He is responsible for any sisters who are not yet married. If his father is unable to lead or has died, he is responsible for his mother. It is the obligation of all family members to assist the family leader in any way they can. If the oldest son dies at a young age, then it is his son who assumes the role of leader. It is the obligation of the entire family to aid in his development and education.

The bulk of the family's wealth is transferred to the oldest son. The oldest son is asked to oversee decisions regarding his brothers' children on marriage, career selection, and education. These decisions are made with the entire family's welfare in mind. For example, if one family member is already a doctor, the desire of another family member to become a doctor may be repressed in favor of a different, more "useful" direction, such as taking over the family business. These decisions are made in the interest of the family's future security and balance.

A daughter is not considered a long-term asset of the family. When she marries, she becomes a member of her husband's family and is placed under the tutelage of her mother-in-law. Her obligation is to have children (preferably male) and prepare them for responsible family membership. The mother-in-law is a powerful figure in her daughter-in-law's life. It is her responsibility to see that the daughter-in-law performs her family obligations.

This relationship between mother-in-law and daughter-in-law has not always been without strife. If it becomes too unbearable, the husband and his family side with his mother against his wife. Generally, the family in which the wife grew up would not welcome her back, so she has to adjust and wait her turn to be the mother-in-law and rule over her son's wife. However, not all mother-in-law/daughter-in-law relationships are painful. The daughter is aware of her obligations from birth. Family stability and security are the main motivations of all members. They are achieved through a Confucian system of well-defined roles that are passed on from generation to generation in a never-ending circle of past, present, and future family members.

## Confucius

The *Analects* records the dialogues of Confucius (551–479 B.C.) with his pupils. The key ideas put forth by Confucius are *jen* and *li*. The concept of *jen* represents the virtuous relationship between humans. If one treats people with *jen*, life will be harmonious. Kindness, gentleness, and civility are virtues to be pursued as a part our daily actions. To understand and practice *jen*, one must respect and love all of humankind. *Li* describes the rules that a civilized person must embrace. Confucius believed that *li* will save a society from turmoil and lawlessness. *Li* is accomplished with ease when one has *jen*. *Confucius*, just as the Buddha, did not discuss religious doctrines but instead advised to focus on the affairs of humanity. All must practice filial piety. These relationships are well defined and understood by all within the society. The family is a microcosm of the nation—when the family is in order—all society is positively affected.

## EDUCATION
### Pluralistic

Education in the United States is conceived of as an individual's birthright. It is one of the key means by which a society improves the standard of living for its next generation. All members of the society must contribute to a free public education from kindergarten through high school and to a subsidized higher education.

In the United States in particular, few standards of performance deny the individual the next level of education. The individual decides which career path to take and which field to study. Job access at the end of this process is not a consideration. It is expected that if one prepares for a particular career there will be enough jobs within that area to support these new entrants. Little if any government and business guidance prepare the young for the actual jobs of the future. If students are unprepared for available jobs within the organization, then the organization has to train or retrain them. Education and the future intellectual obligations of society are separate.

The curriculum is linear and lockstep with subjects taught as specialties. Little if any attempt is made to integrate these subject areas. In an example from my own life, only after college did I realize that all the different time lines that I was taught in each specialized area such as history, art, and music overlapped. What happened in science has not been integrated with what happened in history or English. Not until I had finished my Ph.D. was I able to synthesize what happened in the West with what happened in the East. Such synthesis is not even an issue in American education at any level.

For the past century, the educational system in the United States has embraced the theory of identical elements. The theory is based on the belief that the best benefits come from an education that prepares the learner for a specific job or task. Thus, American higher education offers such programs as business, engineering, tourism, and fire science. Specialization is also apparent at the elementary and secondary levels: many specific courses and programs are added to the curriculum each year.

### Unitary

The purpose of education from a unitary perspective is to prepare family members to assist in the survival and prosperity of the family, the community, the nation, and the world. Education is not a birthright of every member. The education of family members is grounded on Confucian philosophy in Asia. The first son is to receive the attention and resources of the family because he is to be the future leader of the family. The family has control and influence over the career paths of its members. In school, family members are expected to perform for their family. Those who have lived before and those who will come in the future are dependent on the present generation. Nonperformance is considered a bad sign for a family's future survival.

Women generally have not been given access to the same type of education as the men because their roles in society are understood to be different. The distinctions between the roles that men and women will play are clear. Education reflects these distinctions and attempts to reinforce these roles. For example, Japanese women have equal access to a college education, but their education differs from men's. The women focus on education in relation to family needs within the home, whereas the men focus on education for a job outside the home. Having the responsibility of teaching the next generation of the family is not to be taken lightly. Raising a family is a respected and important role in the society.

The teacher, therefore, holds a highly respected and important position within the community. In the classic unitary concept of teaching, the student comes to learn from the master. The master takes responsibility for the development of the student. The teacher transfers "understanding" to the student over a long period of time. The student makes the effort to learn. The student who underperforms is faulted and viewed as a disgrace to the family.

The educational philosophy that has influenced the development of a curriculum that fits into a unitary model is the theory of mental discipline, which advocates that the student study the classics of the culture and civilization. It is not the specific subjects of study that are the issue, but the disciplining of the mind that comes from study. The student is expected to be put through a rigorous program of study. It is through this rigorous discipline that the student is prepared for life. The teacher is valued for the contribution he or she makes to this process. Within this value system, universal insights are gained through discipline.

## MATHEMATICS
### Pluralistic

Western numbers are derived from a mathematically linear system. Roman numerals move in a progression starting with the number one. They were used in Europe until the tenth century. They are built on seven symbols: I, V, X, L, C, D, and M, whose Arabic equivalent are 1, 5, 10, 50, 100, 500, and 1,000, respectively.

A numerical symbol following one of equal or greater value adds value. For example, "III" represents "3" because "I" (1) is followed by a symbol of equal value, "I," and another of equal value, "I"; therefore, the three "I's" are added.

A numerical symbol preceding one of greater value is subtracted from that value. For example, "IX" is "9" because the symbol of greater value is the second number; therefore the "I" (1) is subtracted from the "X" (10).

When a numerical symbol is between two of greater value it is first subtracted from the symbol to its right, the remainder then being added to the preceding symbol. For example, "XIV" is "14" because "I" (1) is subtracted from the "V" (5), which equals "4," which is then added to the "X" (10) to make "14." The Roman system had no zero, and thus the use of larger numbers was kept to a minimum.

### Unitary

The number system known as Hindu-Arabic was introduced in the West by the

Arabs. This numerical system introduced the concept of zero. The numbers are built on the repetition of nine digits with the addition of a zero or zeros. There has been disagreement in the West on the naming of the numbers. For example, Americans call the number 1,000,000,000 a "billion," whereas the British call the same number a "milliard." The British number for "billion" has twelve zeros.

One of the most significant advantages of zero is that it allows the minus to be a reflection of the plus. This characteristic is an amazingly rudimentary mathematical concept in which to express complicated applications. The zero helped business and science flourish. People had not been able to create systems for barter or trade, but the addition of zero made the process more universally acceptable because zero combined the concepts of positive and negative.

The concept of zero was conceived in a culture that viewed the universe as a repetitive process of birth, life, death, and rebirth. The abstraction of the Void or the Infinite, which reflects the absence of all things, is also incorporated within zero. Balance between opposites (*yin* and *yang*), which are viewed as two sides of the same coin, is well-embedded in Oriental philosophy. Plus and minus or binary numbers are mirror images of the same thing. (*Yin* and *yang* are discussed in more detail in the Causal Relationships section of this module.)

## LANGUAGE
### Pluralistic

Western linguistics have evolved from Greek atomistic philosophy. It has been a general assumption that language should be organized in a well-defined structure. Language is composed of small units that can be combined according to certain rules. The fundamental view of the West is that language should be approached as an abstraction. When abstractions are not able to duplicate reality, exceptions to the rules are formulated. Meaning is connected to such categories as nouns, verbs, prepositions, adjectives, and adverbs. Meaning must be precise and must be the same for all users. For example, the meaning of the word "compute" has changed and evolved to meet the changes in the application of the word. Such usage then requires a new formal definition.

Grammar does not allow for presumptions about audience. Units or categories are arranged in patterns as sentences. Once in a sentence, these units assume another function. For example, a noun in a sentence becomes a subject or an object. Sentences are then categorized into the abstractions of simple, compound, and complex sentences. Sentences have rules that must be followed in order to place classes of words such as nouns or verbs. Each sentence can be diagrammed and taken apart, and if it does not have the appropriate components in the correct order, it is considered to be grammatically incorrect. Some words can have multiple meanings depending on whether they are used as nouns, adjectives, or verbs. The concept of abstracting language by dividing words into categories and then creating a system of rules for combining them is Western. The belief that these rules then create an order to language reflects a cultural drive toward specific meaning. This meaning in a low-context culture (such as the American culture) is not dependent on the context in which it is communicated. "Low context" means that the context in which communications occur are not important. Meaning is in the words that are communicated, not in the context in which they are given. Western thinking in all areas has followed the model of creating abstractions and then determining rules to describe those abstractions.

A universe is created that reflects this particular philosophy. From these abstractions, rules and processes are developed that mistakenly are presumed to ensure the same meanings for everyone. Each discipline then attempts to define precise meanings to describe its own particular abstractions. Each discipline searches for those attributes it can apply to separate language into clearly delineated meanings. Interpretation is clearly defined so that the members of a particular group can transfer meaning among themselves in precise language. Meaning, from the pluralistic perspective, is in what is spoken and not in its context.

## Unitary

Eastern linguistic tradition has evolved from a unitary perspective. Abstractions are not clearly defined. It is the role of the receiver to interpret meaning beyond the spoken word or words. Meaning is indirect, and formal language avoids offending either the sender or the receiver. There is no attempt to organize literal translations to a word or group of words. Meaning is fluid and ever-changing. For example, an entire thought may be transferred in just one word. A statement that conveys meaning need not have the formal structure of a sentence. A combination of words also may have no literal interpretation, but its meaning is found outside the logic of the stated words. The Japanese language has a formal structure that differs from that of Western languages. It employs a subject and/or object followed by connecting words that end with a verb or action word. The Japanese avoid using the words "I," "me," and "you" in writing and speaking. It is considered impolite to use these words to describe actions or circumstances. The person would say "cold" rather than "I am cold." There is no reference to the self: the reference is understood without having to be stated.

This exclusion of any reference to the self is in accord with Confucian philosophy and the attitude of affirming one's obligation to others. This unitary belief is represented in the formulation of language. The concept of silence or absence of words is the key to understanding Eastern language. It is through this silence that one is opened to meaning. It is in the movement beyond words that meaning is found. Language does not have a precise word or group of words that can be understood by all senders and receivers. Meaning is veiled by what is literally being stated.

To understand meaning, one must know the sender and the context in which the statement is communicated. Asian culture has been considered "high context," where meaning resides in the specific communication. A declaration between friends may not have the same meaning when it is repeated in a more formal setting.

The concept of silence in the language as a reflection of meaning is the same as the abstraction of the Void in Hinduism and Buddhism; as the linking of past, present, and future families; and as the zero in math. Interpretation is defined through the absence of words. Each member determines meaning in a unique context. Meaning is conveyed by both the spoken and the unspoken.

## OM

### Pluralistic

The concept of *om* or *aum* has no direct equivalent in Western society.

### Unitary

Eastern meditation has incorporated the concept of *om*, or *aum*. The sound of *om* is repeated as a representation of the universe. This is called a *mantra*, or the repeating of a statement to gain internal understanding. *Om* is made up of the vowel sounds that can be made through the opening and closing of the mouth. It is believed that the sound of *om* incorporates all the sounds that can be made through the opening and closing of the mouth. The sound of *om* is repeated over and over again to assist the person in connecting with the infinite. As the "m" ends, there is silence before the "o" begins again. A person repeats the sound while sitting in a meditation posture. When a Buddhist monk moves his hands in a circular motion while mediating on *om*, the motion represents the repetition of the cycle of life, death, and life. The silence in the sounding of *om* is an illustration of the Void. Silence brings everyone back to the same ultimate position of nothingness.

### CAUSAL RELATIONSHIPS

*Author's note: In the following discussion of causal relationships, specific philosophers of the pluralistic school are identified, whereas the unitary philosophy is approached more generally. Because unitary societies have many fascinating philosophers, interested readers are encouraged to pursue other sources of such study. Many in the West attribute the success of Western science—followed by military and business superiority—to its specific approach to cause and effect. The unitary East has not separated science, human, and nature. The concept of karma extends the relationship between cause and effect beyond the life of the individual. The relationship is balanced in yin and yang and, thus, is different from the one presented in the Western linear model. This should not suggest that innovation and discovery have not been a part of Asian culture, but simply that the focus has been on unifying rather than separating God, humans, and nature.*

### Pluralistic: Philosophers

*Francis Bacon*

The philosophy of Englishman Francis Bacon (1561–1626) has had a profound impact on Western thinking. Bacon was concerned with the principle of induction and the methods for collecting facts about nature. He proposed that knowledge in the world should be acquired and explained through observation derived from experimentation.

Bacon believed that human beings can control nature through knowledge, but that traditions, mores, and customs prevent humans from achieving such an understanding. Humans, he said, need a scientific methodology to protect them from false idols, because these idols have been a poor means for the acquisition of proper knowledge. According to Bacon, it is through the study of the sciences—when separated from theology—that humans will reduce suffering. He believed that knowledge is power. In the West, Bacon's work led to the discussion that separated God from humans and nature.

## René Descartes

The French scientist and philosopher René Descartes (1596–1650) conceived of the human as an entity that thinks. Through the act of thinking, an individual finds the realities of the self. The senses of the body confuse, whereas the mind alone enables the individual to understand nature. These qualities must be described through a method. Problems are broken into parts. The parts are then reconfigured into a whole by applying logic. Logical proofs are derived from geometry. Descartes's separation of mind and body moved the West in a direction that still has a profound influence on our lives. One of Descartes's most often quoted statements is *"cogito, ergo sum"* ("I think, therefore I am").

## Thomas Hobbes

English philosopher Thomas Hobbes (1588–1679) recognized the importance of mathematics in understanding the laws of nature. Humans are mechanical beings, and anything thought or imagined is measurable. He believed that the human is made up of particles that move in accordance with laws of nature through space. Hobbes divided all knowledge into two categories: natural and civil. Natural deals with the laws of particles, whereas civil is concerned with the relation between the sovereign and his or her subjects. The state, or Leviathan, is an overarching force, or power, that controls or restrains the actions of the individual. Each person, Hobbes explained, is afraid of the other person because the other person represents the threat of death. Peace is achieved by humans delegating all authority to the state.

## John Locke

John Locke (1632–1704), also of England, maintained that humans are born with a clean slate (*a tabula rasa*) and that ideas are acquired through experience. These experiences are formulated by either reflection or sensation. Locke argued that universal agreement is not a sufficient form of evidence because individuals are not cognizant of their underlying cause. Knowledge acquired by the mind is limited to what we experience in the world. For example, there are no inborn ideas of good or evil. Therefore, human pain or suffering is evil. Society should then be driven by the pursuit of pleasure. This is in contrast to the Eastern concept of *yin* and *yang*—that views human pursuit as a balance between opposites such as good and evil.

## Isaac Newton

English mathematician and philosopher Sir Isaac Newton (1642–1727) searched for a scientific explanation for the existence of God. It was Newton's belief that the universe was created by God as a rational orderly system. If Newton could unravel this God-created ("First Cause") system, then he could prove that God exists. Newton's research had the full support and backing of the church. He envisioned a universe that runs like a huge divine clock. In such an orderly universe, the movement of planets could be predicted.

Newton never rejected the concept that the universe was divinely created and inspired. To him, the First Cause of all actions was God. It was God who caused all living and non-living things to perform their specific functions within this grandly designed universe. However, at this time, scientific inquiry began to challenge seriously explanations that the church had determined to be divinely inspired. There had been earlier inquiries that challenged the position of the church. German astronomer Johannes Kepler (1571–1630) believed that the planets revolved around the sun in an elliptical orbit, and Italian astronomer/physicist Galileo Galilei (1564–1642) hypothesized about the distance that a body falls in relation to its descent.

At first, these differing perceptions of the universe were rejected by the established societal structures as acceptable worldviews. The organized position had far greater market power in which to block competitive ideas from access to markets. Newton's discoveries, however, gained acceptability within England, largely because Newton was a force within the establishment and he had position, wealth, and power. Henry VIII (1491–1547) had challenged the authority of Rome and had established the Church of England in 1533. This led to a political and religious reform movement that tolerated new ideas, especially those that challenged the authority of rival Rome.

To his chagrin, Newton's work became a catalyst for a small group of individuals who, to gain power, were interested in neglecting God: they searched for causation without First Cause. They separated science and religion. Their energies were focused on the development of practical experiments and functional machinery. Their efforts enhanced the productivity of the British worker and began the Industrial Revolution. The British navy capitalized on this productivity and conquered three quarters of the world. It brought back much wealth to the homeland for centuries. Science, by then encouraged by the British Royal Society, was seen as the advantage that enabled Britain to achieve its world position.

After World War II and the American successes, science reached the status of a savior. All of mankind's problems could now be solved through science. Once the causes of the problems are determined by experimentation, solutions can be found to alter the negative effects. Thanks to science, human beings can do anything: conquer disease, poverty, hunger, and war.

The key result of the Western understanding of cause and effect after Newton was the distinct separation of scientific explanation from religious interpretation of the universe. Western science began to rely on a causal framework where cause precedes effect: thus, "if A, then B." The religious position was defended against the scientific explanations of the universe. Nevertheless, it began to decline while the scientific stance ascended.

Western organized religion took the position that what it believed was based on faith and that its explanations of the universe had to be taken literally. The church defended the existence of a First Cause and reaffirmed that God created the universe in His image. Although many attempt to combine them, science and religious beliefs are generally at odds unless the issue of First Cause is resolved. A society that encourages pluralism does not require a synthesis between religion and science. In such a culture, both can exist as separate areas with little requirement for overlapping and search for unity. To unify them would require that each appropriates at least some of the other's philosophical assumptions.

## David Hume

Scottish historian and philosopher David Hume (1711–1776) argued that nature could not be used to prove the existence of God. Science does not yield truth because truth is impermanent. Cause and effect is only a habit developed by humans. According to the Newtonian thinking of the time, the universe is conceived of as a great machine that works together in harmony; this machine's design also applies to human knowledge and, when combined with a similar models in the natural world, gives evidence of First Cause. Hume criticized this proposition because it can be argued from either the affirmative or the negative. Actions may just be the results of chance occurrence. Buddhism, puts forth the concept that present action is derived from moral choice. Everything impacts everything else.

## Karl Popper

Austrian philosopher of science Sir Karl Popper (1902–1994) suggested that the method for testing in science should not be inductive but deductive. It is the role of science to falsify claims not to verify them. Science as an activity is differentiated from other activities because science employs empirical falsification. A scientist should put forth theories and then logically test those theories. Propositions that cannot then be verified can be falsified. This was far different from those that saw science as the inductive process of theory building.

*Author's note: There are many more Western philosophers that probably should have been added. One should explore Western philosophy in much more depth to begin to understand from whence a great deal of our thinking has evolved. I particularly like the audiotapes provided through The Teaching Company. They are a great place to start. (1-800-858-3224)*

## Unitary

The Eastern view of cause and effect is different from that of the West. God is not conceived as an incarnation of the First Cause of the universe. God is the person's last barrier before the Void. After God, comes the Infinite for which there is no name. Within the earthly realm of time and space a cause may be influenced by past lives. What occurs within this life is affected by what has occurred in a past life. This force known as *karma* is generated from the cycle of birth, life, death, and rebirth, a cycle that continues until the individual is liberated and released. This disengagement is called *nirvana* in Buddhism and *moksha* in Hinduism. When something happens to a person, one does not ask—as would be typical in the West—"What was the cause?"

In a pluralistic society, each action is viewed as having a separate identifiable cause. If the cause is unknown, it is generally believed that science will reveal it someday. However, a cause is understood differently in a society that believes that a cause may be related to experiences in a past life and that the present experiences are somehow a continuation of the earlier experiences. This is one reason why Hindus, for example, appear to be unmoved by the plight of those around them. They believe that the life they are living is predestined and that all humans live in order to gain a particular experience. In an earlier life, the pauper may have been an emperor.

## China

The Chinese, and indeed those of most Asian cultures, have been influenced by the philosophy of Taoism. This belief system is based on the balance between opposites in the universe: the *yin* and the *yang*. Moving back and forth, each is the beginning of the other. The symbol for *yin* and *yang* is a circle divided into two sections, black and white. In the black section there is a small white circle, and in the white section, a small black circle. These small circles are representative of the beginnings of one within the other. For example, although male and female are opposites, the male has some attributes of the female, and the female has some attributes of the male. They are not separate, distinct, and unrelated, but are two sides of the same coin. Other obvious opposites are day/night, hot/cold, young/ old, and life/death. The list is endless. Causation is viewed as the movement and balance between these opposites. If the body is ill, it is considered out of balance, and once it is brought back into balance, the body will be healed. Balance is effected by many variables that often require more than a single solution. To restore wellness, individuals may need to balance any number of personal factors, such as their diets, their circulation (as with acupuncture), and their relationships at home and/or work.

## India

The Hindus believe that an individual's future is predestined by his or her past *karmas* (sum of one's actions). However, such a destiny may not be realized within one life cycle. After many cumulative righteous deeds during various life cycles, one may attain redemption—*moksha,* or what the Buddhist call *nirvana.* All religious systems view redemption as the ultimate goal of mankind, but for Hindus and Buddhists in particular, it is the righteous cause that produces one's destiny here and hereafter.

## SCIENCE
### Pluralistic

Western science has divided and subdivided scientific inquiry into distinct fields of specialization such as physics, chemistry, biology, botany, and zoology. These fields have been subdivided into distinct areas of inquiry. For example, a physicist may specialize in particle physics, astrophysics, atomic physics, subatomic physics, or Newtonian physics. This continual subdividing of fields into narrower and narrower areas of investigation has been a trend that probably started with the Greeks twenty-five hundred years ago.

The success of the United States in World War II encouraged modern scientific specialization. The U.S. government funded scientific research in both the public and private sectors as a means of solving all the problems of mankind. The social sciences, responding to this change in policy, began to imitate the scientific model by subdividing their disciplines into more and more areas of specialization. The fields that did not or could not adopt this scientific model were considered of a lower status.

Fields such as history, English, foreign languages, philosophy, fine arts, and music were devalued because they did not profess to be scientific in nature. Engineering, the hard sciences, psychology, and business education expanded. Business education in the United States, responding to the criticism that it was not scientific enough, began to move in that direction with great success. Business and science were linked. Americans concluded that if they were successful in business, it was because they were the best in science, and business was a science; business, therefore should concentrate on subdividing into narrower and narrower areas of specializations.

Western science is based on what has been called the scientific method: inquiry and experimentation. The scientific method, as a process, can be experiment-specific or applied as the same method no matter what the experiment. For centuries, the scientific community, has been debating the issue of a correct process or method for scientific discovery. Is there one optimal method that should be used when conducting experimentation?

The Western scientific community, in addition to dividing science into fields and subfields, has applied distinct methodologies when conducting experiments. The tendency has been to move from a recognition of the problem to a conclusion in varying steps. Each step also has its own definition and special terms. The scientific community has neither embraced nor adopted a single set of steps with a precise definition of each step. This has contributed to the separation of all sciences: each science now speaks a different language describing a different process. As scientists become more specialized, they tend to incorporate both the specific content of their field and the unique process or processes that apply to their discipline. This has led to a situation where the solutions found in one science are not applied to problems in another. Discovery and application of scientific information are considered separate areas of pursuit.

## Unitary

Since the seventeenth century, the Western paradigm has influenced science in the East. Although Eastern science did exist, it cannot be directly compared with the Western model. It is a Western simplistic view to reject the existence of a science in the East because of the particular way science has evolved in the Western world. In the East, science as with all aspects of life, is not separate from metaphysics or Eastern philosophy. God, humans, and nature are intertwined in an endless circle of birth, death, and rebirth. The need for science to accomplish certain objectives is not as pressing in a culture that has a non-Western understanding of death. If death is a process of movement through the experiences of many lives, the value of using science to prolong life diminishes.

The recent debate in the United States concerning a person's right to die is a cultural reflection of the value put on a single life as an unrepeatable experience. Unitary cultures do not view death as the linear end of life; therefore, the right to die is not an issue. Eastern science is not applied in the same fashion nor to accomplish the same ends as that of Western society. From a unitary standpoint, everyday actions manifest the spiritual. Many Western scientists, especially physicists beginning with Einstein, have been coming to the point of understanding where they are, asking the same spiritual questions that have been asked and answered in the East for thousands of years.

The answer to these questions is that all is linked and connected and all is one. Throughout the twentieth century, Western scientists have been searching for a unified field theory. To date, they have identified the components of this theory to be the weak force, the strong force, electromagnetic fields, and gravity. Modern physicists are trying to combine quantum physics with these four components. The aim of their quest is to combine and unify, not to separate. If they are successful, this "new" theory will alter the West's understanding of science.

From a unitary perspective, the issue of a scientific method applicable in all experiments or unique to a particular experiment is unimportant. This should not negate the existence of a common underpinning to all actions. But it is through the experiences of life that one finds the collective oneness of knowledge. The value of any discipline, be it a science or nonscience, resides in the individual understanding that it makes possible. The particular discipline that leads to that understanding is not important.

Unlike pluralistic philosophy, the unitary does not perceive one action to be more valuable than another. All actions lead to the Void, or nothingness. Once insight is gained, all actions combine into a common action that cannot be taught or described. Scientific method within a unitary culture would tend to combine processes used in a single discipline and those shared by many disciplines because all aspects of the culture combine into a well-defined circle. Theory and philosophy are merged with the particular representations of that theory or philosophy, and they are universally linked and connected. Theory in the East does not represent a particular division or subdivision of any field of human or nonhuman endeavor as it does in the West. Instead, theory and philosophy are one and the same. Science and philosophy are one; nonscience and philosophy are one; the single scientific method and multiple scientific methods are one; the discoveries and applications of science are combined as one.

## SYSTEM THEORY
### Pluralistic

The West has attempted to incorporate a unitary perspective with the abstraction of system theory. It is generally believed that Ludwig von Bertalanffy started this movement in 1939 with his book *General System Theory*. There are supposedly two types of systems: an open system and a closed system. The open system interacts with its environment, the larger system of which it is apart. The interaction represents the exchange of energy or information. The closed system has no interaction with the external environment. The model used to describe an open-system theory is input ⎯⎯⎯⎯→ process ⎯⎯⎯⎯→ output, with a feedback loop from the environment into the system. Information is received from the output and then feeds back to the input.

For example, a temperature gauge or thermostat in a house is set at seventy degrees. As the temperature drops to sixty-nine degrees, the furnace is activated. The furnace goes on and stays on until the temperature hits seventy degrees, and then it shuts off. As long as the temperature remains above seventy degrees, the furnace remains off.

System theory advocates that all organizational components be interrelated and integrated. The organization as a whole works to survive within a larger system. System theory had its first broad impact in the 1950s and 1960s. After that initial thrust, the school of system theory that evolved began to decline in popularity for three reasons. First, the concept of unifying was alien in Western culture. It would require a change in the way the society was structured. Few were willing to accept such change at the time. Second, those in system research did not do the research required to create systems and subsystems that would assist in this transition. It is one thing to suggest unity and another to create models that help individuals and organizations accomplish that goal. Third, system theory could not gain enough momentum to break functional boundaries. Each functional group recreated the system's concept within its own field, with little interest in or understanding of the linkages between its field and other fields.

### Unitary

In the East, system theory—or the idea that all is linked and connected—did not begin in the late 1930s but has been in place for thousands of years. The evolution of entire cultures and subcultures has been based on the belief that all aspects of life are connected. Thus, they could be easily adapted to the concept of system theory. Research directed at the unifying of all systems would not be alien. Models and methods contributing to this process are encouraged. The linkages within and between fields is sought after as an outcome for organizations. The input ——→ process ————→ output model with a feedback loop is not applied as a unifying foundation. There are other life process models. The input ————→ process ————→ output can be configured within the unitary organizational structure. But instead of being envisioned as a straight line with a feedback loop, it has been represented by a circle with feedback as a part of all three components. An even closer representation of an Eastern perception of a system is to illustrate feedback as the same as zero, silence, or the Void. When this is done, the interpretation of system theory becomes very different from the Western version. Each field is conceived as a system linked to all other systems. The boundaries within and between systems are abstractions that separate and that have no meaning beyond the convenience of the moment. To understand one event is to attempt to understand them all. This understanding does not have to be expressed, but once it is gained, the individual will create his or her own connections. System theory describes one process that can lead the individual to insight. It is not the single solution as its Western advocates may have determined. It is another representation of the ultimate insight.

### BUSINESS
### Pluralistic

Pluralism, or separating, has been the foundation for the development of Western social institutions. There are seven potential power centers within society: government, business, education, religion, military, family, and the individual (see

## Figure 4
## Business

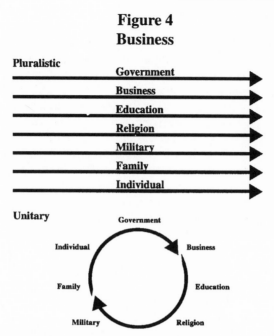

Source: *Marketing Theory and Practice: A Unitary and Pluralistic Approach* (West Haven, CT: University of New Haven Press).

figure 4). In American society, for example, each center works as a separate power nucleus that attempts to shift the resources of the other six to benefit its position. Each center works toward its own ends with little if any interest in combining forces with the other centers for a common purpose. Alliances do exist, but they are for the purpose of coalition of power within a particular center or centers. One center is always attempting to seize power from another. This continual power struggle may not be in the long-term interest of the nation.

*Business and Industry*

Business and industry have been overcome by government policies favoring the growth of the government sector. Government in the United States began this ascension after the passage of the Sherman Antitrust Act in 1890. The act was passed in order to destroy the perceived grip of the railroads on the transportation of agricultural products. Since its inception, the U.S. government has systematically dismantled and punished any business enterprise considered to be too big or too powerful. During World War I, large industries were put under the control of the government to prevent them from profiting from the war. This did not occur during World War II, perhaps because of the perceived invincibility of the enemy and the critical need for productivity. After World War II, the U.S. government returned its crushing restrictive policy toward business. Its justification for this policy has been that big is bad for all sectors except the government and that the best way to assure the lowest possible price for the consumer is to break up economic concentrations. The Department of Justice continues to employ thousands of lawyers for this purpose. National resources are not diverted into the businesses of the future. In the United States, business is supposed to be successful without the assistance of government. The reality is that business has to be successful in spite of government.

## Unitary

The unitary perspective views the same power elements differently. Government, business, education, religion, military, family, and the individual combine their resources to achieve a common national purpose. All groups are valued for their contributions.

### Business and Industry

Each unitary resource is applied to achieve a present or future purpose for the entire society. Government, education, religion, military, family, and the individual work to improve the business environment of the nation. Government, laws, and regulations are not put in place to control and hinder business. They are created to assist and encourage business growth. Neither big nor small business is either good or bad. Both must work together for the good of all. The organization of business is based on what the nation wants to accomplish. National resources are diverted into new areas of growth while resources are contracted from those areas that are not to be expanded. The power centers decide cooperatively which business areas will grow and which will decline, a decision derived from an analysis of present and future market conditions. Once the decision is made, all sectors of the society move in that direction. Actions are taken to achieve a collective purpose.

## SEPARATING AND COMBINING

Two world philosophies have been identified: pluralism (separating) and unitarianism (combining). These philosophical foundations have an impact on all aspects of our lives: the calendar, family relations, education, math, language development, causal relationships, system theory, and business. These two philosophical underpinnings are the foundation of an operating system. Resources are then applied to a circular or a linear operating system. These resources are organized far differently when derived from one philosophical foundation or another. It has been difficult at best for the West, especially the United States, to embrace the possibility of another worldview that may have value to any group in the modern world. Americans thought their role was to teach and not to learn. The Japanese, in contrast, thought their role was to learn and not to teach. The Japanese learned and continue to learn, while Americans know little about them. Americans constantly search for separate snapshots of the picture. The Japanese have no interest in changing our understanding of them.

## PHILOSOPHY (KSA)

The West has separated its knowledge, skills, and attitudes, while the East has combined its KSA. The scientific method that has a grip on Western thinking encourages endless separation. KSA are divided and subdivided with little interest or reward for the slightest combining. The position of most businesspersons in the West is that one can either separate and protect, or combine and lose. The East has viewed combining as an indicator of those who are enlightened, and each person works to combine the actions of each day into the unified structure of his or her life.

## PHILOSOPHY IN ACTION (MARKET POWER)

If one believes that there are different philosophies that affect the behavior of entire cultures, then the lives that the people in those cultures live are their philosophies in action. The West has taken the colonial position for centuries that the East was there for the West's convenience. The West, claiming its own mandate from heaven, believed that any resistance from the indigenous peoples of Asia would ultimately be viewed as the unfortunate consequences of the Asian's philosophical "unenlightenment." Westerners assumed that any and all aspects of Asian peoples' lives must be brought to the Western philosophical position.

The common unifying philosophy in action for the corporation is market power. All resource areas are driven by market power assessment and analysis rather than by the individualized philosophies in action that dominate in functionalized corporate America. The unified organization works together for a common purpose. Functions become resources that are applied to move the organization on a clearly defined direction. Market power is the underlying combining philosophy that drives decision making.

## DIRECTION (MEANS AND ENDS)

From a unitary view of direction, it is far more advantageous to drive an organization in a single common direction. Resource allocation is then a means to achieve that end. Organizations in the United States start with the resource areas that have power in their own right and then try to fit that power into many purposes. Actions become the self-interest of each functional power center. The common interest of the firm is superseded by the individual functional interest.

## STRUCTURE (LEADERSHIP)

Organizational structure in a unitary organization is derived from a tribal model of leader, trusted follower, and support staff. We all assume all three roles many times in the same day. The ability to shift roles leads to the reward of further responsibility. American business schools have rejected the tribal model and consider it not only an artifact of the past, but an actual threat to America's quest for individual achievement. The tribal model, however, is the dominant model in most of the world. Instead of accepting the tribal model and improving on it, American academics have rejected it and have worked to debunk its impact. The problem is that it is the model that is actually in place under the illusion of the separating model of organizational structure. The force of the U.S. government has worked to destroy the tribal model, while America's competitors and their governments encourage the form. Pluralists want to change this structure to respond to each situation. The past is rejected as a separate disconnected activity in the pluralistic worldview, but it is embraced within a unitary worldview.

## PROCESS (ADDIE)

In a pluralistic universe, process changes with each new situation and content area. Functional areas have developed their own separate processes for their separate actions. These processes are described by applying different steps and different languages to describe those steps. An organization may be unified at the process level when the same process is applied to all resources. This same process has the same terms and the same definition for each term. Analysis, design, development, implementation, and evaluation (ADDIE) is the process that is recommended in this book. This does not mean that each step in the process could not be called something else.

The concept is that the steps, no matter what they are called, have to be consistent throughout the organization. This ADDIE process accomplishes several important unifying activities. The transfer of KSA is accomplished because the process barriers are reduced. Those interested in quality have begun to talk about process, but they have missed the point. They want to hold a common process only in their unique area of quality. This is a big step over other, multiprocess functional areas in the West. The quality people have yet to understand the difference between quality and process. Quality is a part of the evaluation step in ADDIE.

## 5RS (MARKETING, HUMAN, PHYSICAL, INTANGIBLE, AND FINANCIAL RESOURCES)

The concept of function in the West has separated resource areas into smaller and smaller power centers. These centers have become isolated and move in their own directions to their own ends. Their market power has been unchallengeable within the borders of the United States. Within a unitary organization, functions are eliminated, and they are conceived of as resources. Resources are to be applied to achieve an end.

## THIS BOOK IN A SENTENCE

Combine and simplify to achieve a purpose.

## SUGGESTED READINGS

Bacon, Francis. *The new organon.* Ed. Fulton H. Anderson. New York: Macmillan, 1960.
———. *A selection of his works.* Ed. Sidney Warhaft. New York: Macmillan, 1988.
Bodde, Derk. *Chinese thought, society, and science.* Honolulu: University of Hawaii Press, 1991.
Borthwick, Mark. *Pacific century.* Boulder, Co.: Westview Press, 1992.
Capra, Fritjof. *The turning point: Science, society, and the rising culture.* Toronto: Bantam Books, 1982.
Cleary, Thomas. *The Taiost I Ching.* Boston: Shambhala, 1986.
Cohen, David, ed. *The circle of life rituals from the human family album.* New York: Harper Collins, 1991.

Confucius. *The analects (lin yu)*. Translated by D. C. Lau. New York: Penguin Books, 1979.

Descartes, René. *Discourse on method and meditations*. Translated by F. E. Sutcliffe. London: Penguin Books, 1968.

Deutsch, Eliot, ed. *Culture and modernity: East-west philosophic perspective*. Honolulu: University of Hawaii Press, 1992.

Hayashi, Shuji. *Culture and management in Japan*. Tokyo: University of Tokyo Press, 1988.

Hearn, Lafcadio. *Japan: An interpretation*. New York: Macmillan, 1904.

Hesse, Hermann. *Siddhartha*. New York: New Directions Press, 1951.

Hobbes, Thomas. *Leviathan*. Indianapolis: Bobbs-Merrill, 1958.

Hume, David. *An inquiry concerning human understanding*. Ed. Charles W. Hendel. New York: Macmillan, 1955.

————. *A treatise of human nature*. Ed. Ernest C. Mossner. London: Penguin Books, 1969.

Hunt, Shelby D. *Modern marketing theory: Critical issues in the philosophy of marketing science*. Cincinnati: South-Western, 1991.

James, William. *A pluralistic universe*. New York: Longmans, Green, 1909.

Muller, Max F., *The institutes of Visnu*. Translated by J. Jolly. Delhi: India, Motilal Banarsidass, 1986.

Kalupahana, David, J. *A history of Buddhist philosophy*. Honolulu: University of Hawaii Press, 1992.

Kuhn, Thomas. *The structure of scientific revolutions*. 2d ed. Chicago: University of Chicago Press, 1970.

Magili, Frank, N. ed. *Masterpieces of world philosophy*. New York: Harper Collins, 1990.

Martin, Richard C. *Islam: A cultural perspective*. Englewood Cliffs, N.J.: Prentice-Hall, 1982.

Mawdudi, Abul A'la. *Towards understanding Islam*. Message Publication, 1986.

Ono, Sokyo. *Shinto: The Kami way*. Rutland, Vt.: Charles Tuttle, 1986.

Ross, Nancy W. *Three ways of Asian wisdom: Hinduism, Buddhism, Zen and their significance for the West*. New York: Simon and Schuster, 1966.

Suzuki, Daisetz T. *Zen and Japanese culture*. Princeton, NJ: Princeton University Press, 1989.

Suzuki, Shunryu. *Zen mind, beginner's mind*. New York: Weatherhill, 1983.

# Philosophy:
# Knowledge, Skills, and Attitudes

All we have to trade to be successful in employment is our knowledge, skills, and attitudes (KSA). *Businesses* do not sell products and services; *people* organize into what we call a business to sell products and services. The type of organizational structure selected and the ability of an individual to work singly and collectively within that organizational structure determines the success of the enterprise.

The previous module pointed out that different people take different approaches to the most fundamental aspects of life. The operating system that the majority of us have embraced has been selected for us from birth by our larger culture. We are, essentially, our culture's children. To change the dominant direction and worldview of the culture into which one was born is difficult and not necessarily rewarding. Individuals who try are not always honored by their culture, and more often, they are punished and sometimes even killed for their efforts. Only some—like Abraham Lincoln, Mahatma Gandhi, and Martin Luther King, Jr.—become highly celebrated for their courage, foresight, and sacrifice, reminding us that societal change is often the salvation of the society.

In a culture where opposing points of view are not allowed to compete, any agreed-upon position is sufficient to attain success within the boundaries of that culture. For example, the fields of management and marketing in the United States can continue to publish strategy books that in no way consider the strategies that have been developed in opposing cultures. The histories, religions, and philosophies of other cultures have been excluded in the United States from the American business education market. These cultural differences have not been allowed to participate in the debate. This exclusionary system does well only until foreign competitors are allowed to enter U.S. markets, bringing their own rules, regulations, and philosophies.

Exclusionism has proved a further disadvantage to Americans when they wish to enter an overseas market and find they have to adopt the rules, regulations, and philosophies of another culture. The ideal situation for any organization is when its competitors are forced to play by its rules. However, when each of two distinct organizations is allowed to apply its own system, either system may dominate the other. If this occurs, then the philosophical position of one culture will win and that of the other will lose. This situation may put the business enterprises of an entire nation at risk of extinction. Those willing to acknowledge their own vulnerability will wisely ask, "Do we continue on our familiar course until all is lost, or do we adjust our knowledge, skills, and attitudes?"

Businesses' activities have evolved within the larger environment and culture that influence employees, customers, communities, and nations. The United States has had a special challenge since World War II because of internal cultural diversity. Individuals from different cultural backgrounds often work within the same organization. This has created a variety of business subcultures. Americans tend to profess that this cultural diversity in business has been a strength. In contrast, most industrialized nations—such as Japan, China, Korea, and Germany—each considers its cultural *uniformity* a fundamental strength. These two positions are neither true nor false. What matters is what each nation wishes to accomplish, and what means are optimal to attain that end. (This is explained in more detail in the "Direction" module.)

## THE PLURALISTIC AND UNITARY APPROACHES TO BUSINESS

The thesis of this book is that an underlying philosophy creates an operating system that drives the actions of people who have combined to form a business. Business actions can be explained by placing them into this larger philosophical

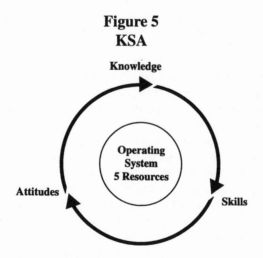

**Figure 5**
**KSA**

framework. These philosophies cross national, cultural, religious, and racial boundaries. The two major philosophies affecting all mankind are pluralism (or separating) and unitarianism (or combining). Every business in the world has evolved within one of these two philosophical frameworks. People who have separated into a business with a pluralistic philosophical foundation create an environment far different from that created by people who have adopted a unitary philosophy. Whereas a pluralistic framework considers knowledge, skills, and attitudes as separate, linear, and unique, a unitary framework considers them combined, circular, and unified (see figure 5).

## Pluralistic

### Knowledge

From a pluralistic point of view, knowledge is defined as data, information, and facts. Within a pluralistic society, a particular power group—an educational power structure—controls and dominates the appropriation of knowledge. Educational institutions generate and distribute knowledge for the society. In the United States, those from about age five through adolescence are turned over to acquire this knowledge. Most, if not all, of the courses given to students in this system emphasize the teaching of the knowledge of the subject area. There is little effort in a pluralistic society to encourage the application of this knowledge to achieve different aims. Unfortunately, all the knowledge in the world is worthless to a business employer if it cannot be applied to achieve a purpose. A straight-"A" student can still become an ineffectual employee. Knowledge alone is an insufficient measure of a person's value to an enterprise.

The acquisition of specific knowledge of what is taught or not taught is culture bound. From the early 1900s, the United States has embraced an educational philosophy that has attempted to focus on the teaching of specific knowledge to achieve optimal transfer to life and work. The knowledge taught has become so specialized that the student has been forced to learn a great deal about highly defined subjects. Social rewards have been directed at the specialist in all fields of endeavor.

In a pluralistic society, specialized knowledge is archived in libraries where a great deal of information is available to anyone in the society. Knowledge is cataloged and stored for retrieval. The purpose of libraries is to collect and build knowledge for those who wish to find what has been said in the past and what is now being said in each specialized area. Although a pluralistic education teaches the means of acquiring and assembling specific knowledge concerning a particular area, it does not teach anyone how to perform in a job. However, it is the specific knowledge of how to do a job that has value to others: it is, after all, what generates the paycheck.

For centuries, corporations could rely on success in school as a criterion for hiring; however, this is no longer true because the institutions that control knowledge cannot agree on acceptable standards of performance. In school, grades have little to do with what has been learned or not learned. American businesses now hire raw material from the U.S. educational system and then spend hundreds of millions of dollars each year teaching their employees the simplest requirements.

Business in the past has focused on the teaching of specific jobs to a broad knowledge-based workforce. Now, businesses have a workforce that is unable to read, write, or socialize at the most minimal levels. Even more frightening to corporate leadership is a disregard for learning among American youth; a large number of students have dropped out of high school, whereas others have viewed learning as nothing more than a ticket to get a better job. They go to school but learn very little, if anything, for their effort. Incongruously, and quite unfairly, the ultimate responsibility for training and retraining too often becomes that of the employer. In spite of the cost involved, the employer may be forced to pay for the employee's on-the-job socialization, called training and retraining, or face fines and legal actions.

The educational system in the United States is not preparing the future workforce of the nation with individuals who are able to function in the corporations of the future. American businesses may no longer be viable competitors in foreign and domestic markets. Throughout history, many nations have lost their positions. After World War II, European and Asian countries suffered temporary loss of competitive position. The British, Greek, Egyptian, Babylonian, and Roman Empires are examples of those who encountered long-term loss.

Those individuals who are in the skills and attitudes areas do not utilize much, if any, of the knowledge that the knowledge areas have accumulated. Specific information becomes trapped in the knowledge domain. Those in the skills and attitudes areas do not incorporate much of the accumulated knowledge within their daily thinking. The knowledge areas continue to accumulate information for their own ends and persist in teaching many subjects that are obviously unsuccessful in practice.

*Skills*

Skills are the practical talents that enable an individual to apply knowledge to attain a particular purpose. The skill areas in a pluralistic society are controlled by unions, and accrediting and licensing agencies. These institutions prevent others from achieving access to the information and thinking processes required to do a particular job. To maintain a highly selective entry system, long and stringent educational requirements are demanded before trainees are given access to perform the skills actually required to do the job. Once these useless rites of passage are completed, members must be continually updated (actually taught how to do the job) to adapt to changes.

Little that goes on in law, medical, or business schools has to do with what is actually performed on the job. Knowledge gained in these institutions is of secondary interest to present members of these professions. It is the long educational requirements for entry that help protect the fields from becoming flooded with competitors. The control of the flow of those who may or may not participate is of primary importance to those who hold present positions. This situation is pervasive in a pluralistic society and only changes in times of war when a profession becomes critical to the survival of the nation.

Large corporations, too, have made the mistake of including educational degrees in their criteria for job advancement. Many creative and productive people are not given the opportunities to advance in the corporation because they lack the appropriate credentials. These people, if given the opportunities, may work much harder than those with credentials. The reason such credentialism exists is that, as a group, those with the formal educational background tend to perform better. But this selection process has eliminated many with less education who would have benefited the entire workforce. Consequently—much to the detriment of big business—countless numbers of creative and industrious Americans are among the "undereducated" who either find a niche in small business or become virtually lost in the employment shuffle.

Skill attainment is not always ensured unless someone is able to get a license. Licensing has been used successfully to control the number of people who have special skills. It is not within the educational institution, however, that one becomes licensed to perform a particular job. Examinations are run by those in the professions and not by the knowledge people (schools) whose implied role it is to prepare the future employees for those professions. When they finish school, the would-be doctors, lawyers, barbers, accountants, nurses, and the like., cannot work unless they take the appropriate tests. If they work without having passed the requisite tests, they can be punished by law. Where, then, does the power to determine job access lie, in the knowledge areas or in the skill areas?

Those in the skill areas incorporate little of the knowledge and attitude areas in their decision-making processes. Many of them describe those in the knowledge domain as ivory-tower professors who have no concept of reality. And they tend to fear the attitude domain because it represents the influence of family and religion even though families used to control the skill areas. Those in the knowledge domain are attempting to enter the attitude domain by teaching courses on ethics that are often in direct conflict with the values of family and religion. They have, of course, done this in the past: it is their job as defined by society, but the conflict has never been so obvious.

## Attitudes

In a pluralistic society, attitude has been considered the domain of religious institutions and the family; there is little formal inclusion of attitude development and support in the knowledge and skill areas of the society. One can have the job knowledge and the skill to apply that knowledge yet fail miserably in the area of attitude.

How many times do we come in contact with someone who has the knowledge and the skills to perform the job, but because of attitude, he or she cannot do the job? I have given many students "A" grades in marketing, although they have miserable attitudes toward life, work, themselves, and others. Student's grades in the knowledge environment (i.e., college) reflects their knowledge of marketing, not their skills or their attitudes in relation to marketing. I have tried to stress the importance of attitude in class. The results have been only moderately successful. One college course does not often change a person's attitude toward life.

One's attitude does not seem to be linked to one's level of educational and professional attainment. Many highly educated people have poor attitude development. In any given situation, a person or a group of people can have any of three attitude responses: positive, negative, and neutral. It is not uncommon for an individual to become easily characterized by his or her attitude. Many individuals are extremely predictable and their "response to choice"—positive, negative, or neutral—emerges in virtually every circumstance.

Those attempting to maintain positive attitudes are more likely to succeed in business. Attitude alone, however, will not ensure success in business. Many business people with negative attitudes are successful, but, almost certainly they usually have other disciplinary characteristics that gained them market power.

The decline of the importance of family and religion in the United States has created a situation where the media, through advertising and program selection, have attempted to develop the attitude component within the pluralistic society. Many major corporations—including automobile, soft-drink, and beer manufactures—rely heavily on television advertising to promote their products. But how many TV commercials portray hard work as a positive, or even a necessary virtue? Very few, in contrast to those that create attitudes that devalue the concepts of hard work and the postponement of satisfaction. Much of the advertising industry has succeeded in instilling attitudes that have helped to displace family and religious values.

Advertisers have proved it is possible to sell a sophisticated computer system by associating the product with a character who represents buffoonery and ineptitude, but when all those purchased computers reach their destination, one fact will supersede all others: whether they use computers or not, many individuals will work hard and many will hardly work. The issue is not diet cola or a personal computer. The real issue is attitude. Any company can put a soda machine and a computer in every office, but without changing the prevailing attitude within, it will likely be unsuccessful as an international competitor. When assessing attitude development, it becomes clear that material values are insufficient substitutes for family and religious values.

## Unitary

From the unitary perspective, knowledge, skills, and attitudes are circular and interrelated; thus they are applied in combination to achieve a common purpose. No single group assumes undisputed responsibility for knowledge while another dominates skills and a third controls attitudes. It is undesirable that one of them, independently of the others, achieves recognition in one area.

### Knowledge

People who have embraced a unitary view have a great respect for knowledge acquisition as a part of their daily lives. Historically, the transfer of knowledge occurred within the family or tribe. This structural relationship was critical for transferring knowledge from one generation to the next. It was and still is the obligation of the teacher (master) to pass on what he or she has learned to the next generation. It is the responsibility of the students to prove themselves worthy of receiving the master's knowledge.

Students demonstrate their determination to their teacher through years of hard work and study. Although the student initially understands the specialized knowledge pertaining to only a particular area, the goal is to use that knowledge as an opening to a universal understanding. The transition to the role of master does not occur until the student links the specific knowledge to all other KSA. Insight is gained through the exact duplication and modeling of everything taught by the master.

This non-Western system of rote learning has been misunderstood and thought of negatively by many Americans, who argue that this learning technique discourages creativity in students and indeed the entire society. The value of rote memorization, however, is different when this learning is practiced in a unitary rather than a pluralistic framework. Rote memorization, according to the unitary view, leads to a breakthrough in understanding, a breakthrough that in the West is called "creativity."

Unitary and pluralistic cultures do not employ the past in the same ways in order to gain insights. The unitary East perceives creativity as an extension of the past. The pluralistic West perceives creativity as a break with the past. Western society stresses personal experimentation and the questioning of the masters' teachings as the most effective methods of gaining insight. This may be one reason that the number of history courses in American universities continues to decline. The past is not, in Western thinking, considered a means to understand the present. The past, present, and future remain separate in the West.

The unitary teacher/learner relationship attempts to open the student to the better understanding of all, whereas the pluralistic teacher/learner relationship focuses on a particular discipline. In a unitary culture, the masters apply the insights gained in a particular discipline to all aspects of their daily lives. If knowledge is not applied or represented in daily action, it can be concluded, then, that the knowledge has not been acquired. One does not select an order of importance where the knowledge of A is more important than the knowledge of B: both A and B make the whole person.

Knowledge acquisition at the national level is a critical part of the process of a "market power assessment" (see the Direction module). This is especially true for the Japanese. Their knowledge is assembled and coordinated by one particular government agency. The Ministry of International Trade and Industry (MITI) collects information for the purpose of making decisions concerning the entire Japanese economy. All available information is centralized and assembled for this purpose. The concept of knowing for a nation requires that data, information, and facts to be collected and cataloged. In a pluralistic society, knowledge is only a step in the decision-making process that may or may not be incorporated into the skill and attitude areas. From a unitary perspective, all KSA are combined to achieve a national purpose.

*Skills*

Skills represent how one applies knowledge to achieve a purpose. The concept of skill may be broadly interpreted to include all actions. For example, the Japanese do not differentiate between daily actions and skills. Each action is to be done with the same dedication and commitment as every other action. This philosophy is founded on Buddhism, where daily actions are the spiritual. The material manifests the spiritual. In this way, each skill is linked to all other skills because they all represent a devotion to daily action. The most common actions deserve the same undivided attention as seemingly more significant actions. There is no hierarchy of actions in terms of the effort that should be given to each. They are to be studied with enthusiasm and require great discipline to accomplish. Although actions can be prioritized in terms of the tasks and subtasks that are needed to be done, the best effort should be put forth in performing each task and subtask.

As people's knowledge of life improves, so do their skills. Skill is a reflection of the person's knowledge and attitude. The individual's performance of each skill reflects the KSA of those who have come before him or her and those who will come after. For example, as a teacher, I am a reflection of my teachers, the past generations of my family, community, and nation. I am also a reflection of my students, my children, the future of the community and the nation. No one action is more representative of the inner person than another. All actions combined are the reflections of the person.

The Japanese believe that to strive to achieve perfection in a particular skill is inappropriate, because in so doing, all other skills must suffer. For example, it would not be to a person's advantage to be considered a great marketing professor, because the concept of marketing is too limiting. By focusing too much on marketing, the professor would be sacrificing the larger body of KSA that could have been gained from broader understandings. The marketing professor should incorporate KSA from many areas, not just marketing. These KSA may give some insights into marketing because, being derived from more than just one area, they have more breadth and depth.

Marketing is only an opportunity to break through to a universal insight. It is the dedication and the determination to study. Marketing is only one of thousands of actions that will get us all to the same place.

*Attitudes*

Attitude represents how people as individuals and as a collective react to knowledge and skills. In a unitary environment, attitude is not separated from knowledge and skills. One acquires knowledge, skills, and attitudes at the same time. Knowledge and skills are reflected in the attitude that the person brings to all activities. Each person is linked to all others in a never-ending circle of birth, life, death, and rebirth. This reinforces the person's responsibility to others, including those who have lived and those who will live. With this responsibility comes the realization that a person's life must become a spiritual representation of other lives. This requires hard work and dedication (in all actions) to family, community, and nation. A negative attitude is unacceptable because each action represents more than just the individual performing each action. Perhaps, negativism is the individual's ultimate self-destructive act.

**CONCLUSION**

In a society, such as the United States, that separates its knowledge, skills, and attitudes knowledge is the domain of the educational institutions. Skills are controlled by licensing agencies and unions, whereas attitude has been the domain of the family and religion. The media, through advertising, is challenging the family and religion in defining attitude. The separate centers of power derived from KSA have little overlap and hardly influence each other. Because KSA are the fundamental underpinnings of all actions, they explain and predict phenomena. Cultures create their own particular worlds by organizing their own distinct KSA. In so doing, they either combine or separate. Those from the combining philosophy and those from a separating philosophy will have different perceptions of the same set of resources. These two philosophies have generally remained apart from one another, out of the range of conflict, but they are now competing in the world economic arena for the control of the same markets. The challenge to those adopting one or the other philosophical position is to adjust and change in a never-ending strategic battle to achieve their ends. Superior resources, military power, and geographic position have been past attributes that have given nations economic domination. Many have succeeded in spite of themselves by historical accident, by being in the right place at the right time.

It must be strongly emphasized that government, business, education, religion, military, family, and the individual are all responsible for the plight of American business. A change will occur only when knowledge, skills, and attitudes are unified to block competition. The downward business spiral will continue until this is understood and appropriate action is taken. The history of the twentieth century is replete with nations (including the United States) that have chosen war as a solution rather than make the harder decision, to improve the economic stability of the nation through peaceful means.

## SUGGESTED READINGS

Churchman, C. West. *The designing of inquiring systems: Basic concepts of systems and organization*. New York: Basic Books, 1971.

Senge, Peter M. *The fifth discipline*. New York: Doubleday Currency, 1990.

# Philosophy in Action
# (Market Power)

The concept of what constitutes a theory or even the abstraction of a theory itself is rooted in one's philosophical foundations. The quest in the West—since the sixteenth century—has been to search within both the social and the hard sciences for theory-based explanation and prediction. This book attempts to bring the theory-based system under control. A theory cannot exist outside of a philosophical domain. It is the underlying operating system of the members of a group or culture that explain and predict action.

Theory evolves from these philosophical norms. Science has attempted to create the world as we want the world to be. When science no longer is perceived as useful to a society, it will be changed or replaced. Science did not discover itself. A small group of people organized and designed a system for looking at the world, and they called that system "science." Science was to be beyond culture, the final authority for humankind. Most studies in the sciences and social sciences reveal the acceptable norms of a society rather than an unbiased observation of the world. The higher the statistical significance, the more a conclusion has been embraced.

Western pluralistic scientists established the concept of science as a methodology that divides itself into more and more distinct subdivisions. This methodology has directed the development of Western science. Western success in the military, medical, and technological areas enhanced an Occidental view of the importance of science. As the West declines, the concept of science will change to reflect more of the dominant Eastern unitary philosophical position. The scientific community will face the same dilemma that the business community now faces.

It is easier to suggest that, the Japanese are successful because they copied Western business practices. It is much more difficult to suggest that a rethinking of Western business fundamentals is required. This rethinking will force a change in the way those in the West perceive the entire concept of business. Western scientists will ultimately face this same challenge as they continue to be outperformed. In the process, they will continue to believe that the Japanese have copied them until they, too, go out of business.

American scientists have yet to realize that they have been playing out a worldview that has separated Western philosophy and science. The philosophy of science has been one of separating with the exception of physics, which has been searching for a unified theory. Those in science, particularly in the United States, have been functioning in isolation from the rest of society. The U.S. military has supported their efforts since the beginning of World War II. The returns of the last fifty years of science have been less than outstanding. Britain in the seventeenth century could boast more advancements in science than Americans can since World War II.

Western Christianity began to reject the influence of scientific prediction and explanation because the church had proposed a different explanation of the universe and man. The church embraced science as long as it was viewed as a means of identifying the First Cause. Religious (particularly Christian) institutions chose to fight Western science and viewed it as a threat to their fundamental authority. They were unable to share their authority with a competing philosophy. Although Islam and Judaism evolved from the same philosophical foundations as Christianity, they did not reject science as a threat to their authority. For reasons beyond the scope of this book, these faiths had less problems with the sharing of authority and did not view science as a competitor to their religious control. This could have been related to the issue of general providence versus particular providence.

When Islam and Judaism separated God, humans, and nature, they had less difficulty than Christianity in calling the study of God "theology" and the study of humans and nature as separate "-ologies." The Christian Church ultimately recognized the different views of science, and both science and religion have lived in an uneasy truce for less than one hundred years.

When a society that prides itself on its adherence to the principles of its science sets up its business enterprises, it will organize the business management on a scientific foundation. This model for Western business has evolved from a philosophical foundation of separating. The principle of a philosophy as a foundation for the behaviors of a society is just as true for people that combine and unify as for those who separate. The concept that business has evolved from scientific principles alone would not be considered worth discussing in a unitary society because science would be considered too limiting. Business, like other domains, is linked and connected with all human activities.

If this is true, then theory becomes an outgrowth of the dominant philosophical foundation of a society. A better representation of this underpinning may be termed "philosophy in action." The foundation for explanation and prediction is not theory as proposed by Western science. The Western concept is founded on the misunderstanding that theory somehow represents a foundation that is not encompassed by any presupposed belief system.

This concept is simply false. Everyone responds to the universe from his or her different perspectives, and that response has never been universal in practice. Scientists from different cultures do agree, but they can agree only on a particular representation of a world. These representations are never without a foundation even if the person, the source of the representation, is unaware. A separating scientist is a different scientist from a combining scientist. That they may agree does not necessarily prove that their explanation is correct. They both can be incorrect.

Once the concept of separating or combining dominates a particular group, its philosophy of how the universe should be organized is allowed access within its society. This philosophy then determines how the group's world is organized. The Western attempt to portray science as an unbiased observer and predictor is also an outgrowth of a separating philosophy. It is just as correct to assume that God is the unbiased observer. The concept of science, however, is transformed when it is placed in a unitary society. Therefore, it is all philosophy in action.

## PLURALISTIC

Each organizational function has its own unique theory that drives its particular area. The search is for the distinguishing attributes of that function. Marketing, as a functional area, is driven by customer needs and wants. All of the organization is viewed through the perspective of the customer. Marketing proponents believe that for an organization to be successful, it must first identify what customers need and want and then respond, at a profit, to those needs and wants. Those in the marketing function believe that if this is done correctly, the organization will prosper.

Human resource development, as a functional area, is driven to maximize internal human resources. For an organization to be successful, it must select, train, and upgrade the people working for it. If this is done correctly, it will prosper. Human resource professionals believe that all employees want to do a good job and that if they are managed and motivated correctly, the organization will prosper. Physical resources, as a functional area, are driven by a cost/benefit orientation. The cost and benefit of each action are compared. This comparison is sufficient in determining the success of a company. Intangible resources are protection-oriented. For a firm to be prosperous, it must protect itself from both internal and external challenges through the legal and regulatory system within its nation of residence. Financial resources are focused on the maximization of stockholder wealth. The organization that is to prosper must return the greatest profit possible to its shareholders.

Marketing, human, physical, intangible, and financial resources each has its distinct theory that drives its actions. Subsets or components of each one of these areas (viewed as separate functions) continue to be influenced by the particular theory that is supposed to drive that unique function. For example, if those in marketing propose that price is a subset of the marketing function, price would be determined by the needs and wants of customers rather than to maximize stockholder wealth or cost/benefit which would be driving other functions. In actual corporate practice, price may be under several functions, each with its own theory to apply. There is no consistent, agreed-upon theory for the tasks and subtasks called pricing. In this environment, several functions with their underlying theories compete to determine how a product should be priced. Because the decisions reached are inconsistent, they do not help to achieve a common purpose.

## Needs and Wants of Customers

The marketing concept is an American ideal: an organization should identify and fill the needs and wants of customers at a profit. The terms "needs" and "wants" have different definitions. Some define a "need" as food, clothing, education, sex, and medical care and a "want" as a particular, food for instance, that a customer may desire. We all need food, but we may want a McDonald's hamburger. Those who follow this philosophy argue that marketing helps create these wants, whereas the needs are always there. These wants are created through the application of the marketing mix or the "4Ps": price, product, promotion, and place.

Others in marketing apply Maslow's "Hierarchy of Needs" to define a need. For them, these needs are manifested in wants. However, both definitions of needs and wants apply the marketing mix. These four factors in various combinations, based on different definitions of the terms "needs" and "wants," make up marketing as a separate function. Marketing professionals in the United States generally agree on the underlying theory of needs and wants but disagree on how the terms are to be defined. This type of controversy does not arise in the field of science but in that of philosophy.

## Maximize Human Resources

Some corporate managers believe that the ideal firm maximizes its human resources. These functional members believe that it is the role of the firm to help develop each person within the organization to his or her fullest. This is done through the selection, training, and upgrading of all the members of the firm. The term "maximize" has no clear definition to follow for those within the function of human resources. Maximize can mean many things to many people within the same department. Each can be working to select, train, and upgrade, employing his or her own definition of maximize.

## Cost/Benefit

The function within the firm that is directed by the philosophy of cost/benefit examines all circumstance in terms of the cost in relationship to the derived benefits. All undertakings are placed under this template. Cost is generally interpreted as economic risk. This may vary from person to person and department to department. The cost factor of any action is easier to derive than is the benefit. There is no clear definition of what constitutes a benefit—or who is the object of the benefit. Some think that it is society that benefits, others that it is the world, and still others believe that it is the stockholders of the company.

## Protection under the Law

Those interested in the protection of the corporation under a legal umbrella are concerned with the influence of the legal system. Companies are and always have been vulnerable to the legal actions of the environment where they operate. Laws, stated and unstated, must be accounted for when an organization offers a new product or service. Firms approaching new international ventures must consider different legal systems. Proponents of protection advise that a firm should not venture into agreements or contracts without having a legal position that ensures success.

## Maximize Stockholder Wealth

Some in finance advocate that an organization should focus on the price of its stock; thus, all should work for the greatest return on the stock. Many corporations link executive bonuses to the price of their stocks. This practice has come under criticism because employees feel that executives are laying off workers to bolster stock prices. Many also believe that the financial function has influenced many executives to destroy the future of their companies just to increase personal, short-term wealth. The linking of executive bonuses to increases in stock price is understandable if the financial function in the organization serves to maximize stockholder wealth. This underlying theory of maximizing stockholder wealth is much more definable than the other four theories of needs and wants, maximizing human resources, cost/benefit, and protection under the law. However, its implementation may not always represent the best underlying theory for an organization to follow in order to survive and prosper.

## Vision, Strategic Intent, Mission

The corporate vision, strategic intent, and mission have been determined to comprise the most important, if not critical, first step in the development of Western strategy. The company informs its employees of what it considers its vision and what it wants to be. Each employee is expected to apply this vision as a road map to enhance his or her daily performance and actions. A firm may spend hundreds of thousands of dollars to inform its employees of its vision. Their involvement in the development of this vision is thought to increase their commitment to it. The idealized expression of this vision is written in what is called a mission statement. This statement then appears in as many places as possible to continue to reinforce and instill this ideal in all employees.

### *Levitt Mission Model*

Much has been written to justify the mission statement as a beginning step in the strategic process. The article most quoted to justify a mission statement is the one by Theodore Levitt, "Marketing Myopia" (1960). It is one of the most popular articles that has ever appeared in the *Harvard Business Review*. Readers for thirty years believed that this article traced the development of the railroad and film industries in the United States. The conclusion drawn from Levitt's history is that the railroad and film managers were myopic because they failed to respond to new technologies: of transportation in the railroad industry and of television in the film industry.

The management's inability to identify the shift and then respond to it were supposedly responsible for the near destruction of many American industries. The article recommends that the railroad managers should have envisioned themselves in the transportation business and the film managers should have expanded their vision into the entertainment industry. Both had failed to identify and respond to their customers' needs and wants. If these myopic managers had a clearer understanding of the mission of their businesses, they could have avoided the near destruction of their companies.

*Drucker Mission Model*

In the early 1950s, Peter Drucker was one of the first writers to call for a mission statement. Levitt's article clarified Drucker's earlier thinking about the development of a business mission statement. Drucker maintained that only a clear definition of the mission of an organization makes possible realistic business objectives. The business mission is the foundation for priorities, strategies, plans, and work assignments. Structure follows strategy, and strategy determines the key activities to be performed in a given business. Strategy requires knowing what business one is in and what business one wants to be in.

*Kimball Mission Model*

According to David Kimball, a company's mission should be linked to the written mission statement. Unfortunately, some organizations hesitate to state their missions in formally written documents because they are reluctant to reveal their true missions. They believe that if competitors gain this knowledge, the competitors will have market power. Kimball's study found that the stronger the organization's sense of mission, the higher its level of profitability. Although the link between having a written mission statement and enjoying increased levels of profits is not as strong, organizations are finding that it is valuable to have a written mission statement. This statement enables them to communicate formally six basic components, which, according to Kimball, are customers, vision, values, employees, quality, and stockholders. These components were determined to be the most important in a survey of 119 executives of the New York Chapter of The Planning Forum. The executives indicated that other components should be added into the company mission as well as a written mission statement on an as-needed basis. Although the executives in the Kimball study agreed on the importance of a company mission, they did not indicate how strongly they agreed on its importance as compared to the other elements used in designing strategy. Thus, this study does not support the notion that a company's mission is the most important step in the designing process. Even though a company's mission is important in developing strategy, it alone will not guarantee success. A company's mission might have been enough to guarantee success in previous decades when organizations existed in a very mechanistic manner. However, because of the current economic situation and the requirement for speed in decision making, a company's mission is no more important than other externally oriented strategic elements, such as an external environmental assessment, a strategy implementation, or an evaluating strategy.

## *Pearce and David Mission Model*

John A. Pearce and Fred David are also proponents of having a written mission statement. An effective mission statement defines the fundamental and unique purpose that sets a business apart from other businesses of its type and identifies the scope of its operation in product and market terms. Pearce proposed that the components of a mission statement include customers, product/services, philosophy, self-concept, public image, location, technology, and concern for survival. In 1989, David compared seventy-five firms with a formal mission statement and 106 companies without a formal mission statement. He found no statistically significant differences in terms of profitability.

## UNITARY

All organizational functions are driven by the application of the organization's particular philosophy. When the philosophy unifies, all resources are driven to combine. This occurs only when each resource area applies its attributes under the influence of the same philosophical assumption. This requires that marketing, human, physical, intangible, and financial resources be applied to the same philosophy. (These resources are discussed in greater detail in the "Resources" module.)

The unitary approach rejects the concept of theory and substitutes for it a philosophy in action because a philosophy rather than a theoretical science formulate actions. The First Cause is a philosophical concept, not a scientific one. This avoids actions of functional areas founded on separate worldviews under the justification that science is developing unbiased, scientific theory. That each functional area bases its actions on a different set of principles, which it calls theory, reflects the underlying worldview of separating. This goes beyond the findings of those working within the function. The findings for which one searches reflect one's underlying philosophy. One could argue that the stronger the statistical findings, the more solidified the philosophy within that culture.

This underlying philosophy where each function searches for its own independent theory is called pluralism. Therefore, a theory has to be based either on separating or combining. The field of physics searches for a unified field theory to predict and explain phenomena. Although this is called the search for a unified field theory, from the unitary perspective it would be just as easy to conceive of it as a search for a scientific foundation. In this example, philosophy and theory attempt to describe the same occurrence. The West, adhering to pluralism, has not considered the possibility that when thinking of science, it is describing a philosophy.

Is there one philosophy in action that can unify the organization? Perhaps there are thousands, but as long as all participants agree any one philosophy in action as their driving philosophy, it may be sufficient to unify their organization. The challenge is to find one agreeable philosophy in action that encompasses all resources. Marketing would adopt such philosophy if all resources had to be driven by the needs and wants of customers; however, finance would adopt it if all resources were driven to maximize stockholder wealth. Members of each functional area would like to have the theory driving their area also drive all others.

The adherence to this internally competitive functional system has created an environment where different functional areas have come in and out of vogue. Each gets its chance to take the lead because of the failure of the other functions to perform well during a certain period. In spite of the failure of a functional area to perform well, its members often continue to embrace their function's theory and to sabotage the areas assuming a temporary dominate position. Western functions have been unable to give up their underlying separate theories (philosophies).

Although finance has been dominant in the West for several decades, now it, too, has failed to secure the future for the organization. Marketing, human, physical, and intangible resources suggest that their particular theory (philosophy) will make an organization successful against competition. However, from a unitary perspective, no one functional area alone can give the organization all it requires to overcome competition. Many scholars have attempted to unify the functions by applying a common theory from another field: biology provides survival of the fittest, utilitarianism the greatest good for the greatest number of people, and supply and demand and market forces are from economics. Scholars have rejected a common philosophy in action which could unify their work because they fear the loss of functional power. The underlying competition between functional theories has interfered with the organization's ability to succeed.

## Survival of the Fittest

"Survival of the fittest" is a concept derived from Charles Darwin's theory of natural selection and survival. A particular attribute of a species allows it to survive and reproduce. Those who apply this concept to business argue that a company survives because it adapts better than its competition to the environment. They believe that if a company fails to survive, then it deserved extinction. Survival of the fittest is a fundamental law of nature that holds true for business.

This philosophical foundation has an influence on the attitudes of Western corporations. It is reflected in the belief that if a new product fails, then it deserved extinction. Since Western thinking has no philosophical concept of rebirth, there has been little interest in bringing a product back from the dead. Westerners have generally been more interested in starting over with a new venture rather than in resurrecting a project that has failed in the past.

## The Greatest Good for the Greatest Number of People

The utilitarian philosophy of John Stuart Mill (1806–1873) and Jeremy Bentham (1748–1832) advocates the principle of utility. Every person works toward and promotes the greatest happiness for the greatest number of people. All people seek pleasure and avoid pain. Pain is always bad and should be circumvented whenever possible. The intention of an act is not the measure of success or failure but the avoidance of pain. An act aims not at success or failure but at the avoidance of pain. This philosophy has had an influence on the direction that organizations should follow. An extension of this philosophy is the proposal that people should have fun and enjoy their work. Work and life should be without pain. An organization has the duty to cause as little pain as possible to the greatest number of people. If it is responsible for causing pain, the greater society may intercede to reduce that pain.

## Supply and Demand

The concept of "supply and demand" is derived from the field of economics. The concept states that as supply decreases, demand increases, and that the reverse also is true: as the demand goes up, the price will go up until others find or invent alternatives, and then the demand goes down. The role of government in this process is to make sure that everyone plays fairly so that no company can create a monopoly. In a monopoly, a company or group of companies can control supply and demand. Those who have monopoly can charge as much as they wish for their products. In the United States, it is believed that federal sanctions against monopolies will ensure the lowest possible prices for the consuming public. It is the government' responsibility to guarantee that no company or group of companies can form a monopoly. Resources that are not applied to achieve a present or future purpose are without value.

## Market Forces

The concept of "market forces" is based on several firms interacting at the same time with the consumer. This model assumes independent actions on the parts of buyers and sellers. Consumers confront the supplier and then, through their interaction, both determine a price. Those who advocate the approach of market forces profess that a free market should be mutually exclusive: the buyers and sellers act alone. Workable competition favors the sellers because it guarantees their success.

## Market Power

From a unitary point of view, the philosophy in action that drives all the resources is market power. "Market power" is defined as the use/employment of organizational capacity to block existing and potential competitors from access to targeted markets. The concept of market power is not unfamiliar in the United States. It is discussed extensively in the structure of industry literature in the field of economics. The problem with the research and discussion in the United States is that market power, for political and philosophical reasons, has been considered bad. Selected companies that have attained market power are in violation of the law of the land and are to be punished. The effort of American economists has been focused on making market power something negative within specific industries. This reasoning is unique to the United States.

In January 1992, while President George Bush was on his tour of the East to protest the unfair use of market power or barriers to entry of American goods to Japan and Korea, the Australian farmers were protesting the unfair trade barriers of the United States against their agricultural products. Americans have been told so often that they have a free-market economy that many actually believe it. The United States has the distinction of being the only nation that, under the guise of a free market, selectively discourages concentration of resources to the detriment and often the destruction of its own industry. This means Americans will let the

Japanese ravage their automobile industry but not their agricultural industry.

The important question for Americans is not whether market power is good or bad, but why has the government allowed the automobile, machine-tool, shoe, electronics, and other industries to be devastated. The argument put forth is that if other nations can produce a better quality product, then they deserve to get the business even if it drives American firms out of business. The answer to this argument is that the philosophy of pluralism has been taken to extremes. Each area is acting in its own self-interest and not in the interest of the nation as a whole.

The way the game is now played is far different from the way young Americans are taught in school. There is little evidence Americans are schooled in how to be good businesspeople. If a master in business administration (M.B.A.) degree is an indicator of business understanding and ability, then Americans should be light-years ahead of the rest of the world. Instead, one could show that the rise of the pluralistic M.B.A. has coincided with the decline of American business. We now require a unitary M.B.A.

Americans think their political philosophy is best, they naively insist that they have the mandate of heaven, and, therefore, the Japanese, Germans, and everyone else should open their markets to the United States. The vast majority of countries never have opened their markets to free trade, and they never intend to do so. Every nation functions in its own self-interest. Markets are opened because it is in the self-interest of a nation to do so. There are two ways to force a nation to open markets when it is not in its own self-interest: one is the threat of military force, the second is economic force.

Since the 1950s, Japan has been successful in using economic force to gain market share in the international arena. The United States has been successful in opening markets by following the military component developed after the British model. The Japanese are newcomers to the game, but they have been extremely adept since the late nineteenth century. Much of their success can be attributed to the fact that they adopted the model of the British, who have been the long-term masters of international trade.

Until 1945, the Japanese in their drive to colonize used the model of military force. They failed because they underestimated the British military power and Britain's ability to bring the United States to the rescue. After their failure in World War II, Japan began to emphasize economic force while Britain and the United States continued to emphasize military force in an effort to stop the spread of Communism. During this time, Japanese and German success in the economic force area has been unparalleled. This success has been supported and nurtured by the U.S. military force.

*Colonial Model to Attain Market Power*

Although the following example is from the automobile industry, the strategy has been the same in all other conquered industries. Step one is the most important: encourage the targeted nation to become economically dependent on your nation. This can be done by lending or giving food, military protection and supplies, development money and loans, medical supplies, and technology. In exchange, you ask to help develop the resources of that nation by opening up selected markets so that the now debtor nation can begin to repay its obligations. The aim is to begin to make the nation economically dependent on your nation. Step two is to destroy existing and potential competitors in targeted market areas. This can be done in many ways, but Japan has done it to the United States by selling its products below the cost of production of American competitors. This is achieved through government and/or consumer subsidies in the home markets. The choice is higher taxes or higher cost of products for your own nation until you achieve market dominance. For example, suppose the Japanese and Americans can both produce a car for the same price, $5,000, and there is a $2,000 markup to the consumer. You then block access to your markets so that you can raise the price of the car to $9,000. This allows you to charge $5,000 in your competitor's market. The price ends up to be below the cost of production of the competition. As competition improves efficiencies, you continue to raise the price in your home market so that the price can be lowered in the offshore markets. No company can win this competition from a business supported by a nation.

If the competitor nation wishes to retaliate, they may apply military and economic threat. Another strategy is to shift resources to the opposition parties or power centers. In the United States, for example, if the Republicans do not support Japan, their resources and influences will flow to the Democrats. A drop in the financial markets right before the next major election could easily embarrass the Republicans so that the Democrats would be swept back into office. Do the Republicans know this? Of course. Would the Democrats do the same if they had the chance? Of course. Saving General Motors or getting reelected—which of the two do you think they would choose? The U.S. president is surely intelligent enough to hold the Japanese at bay if he is supported by the American people. That support will require a great deal of pain.

These principles hold for any business enterprise. The force of law given by government is the most desirable for a nation's business enterprises in their quests for market power. When a government understands its role to be the destruction of business in its own nation, that nation ends up with a large number of poor and exploited citizens.

*Kingston on Market Power*

Market power cannot be attained and sustained without the assistance of government. According to William Kingston of Trinity College, Dublin, Ireland, there are three types of market power: capability, specific, and persuasive. All three have their roots in positive law. Kingston defines "market power" as the capacity to exclude others from entering a market.

Capability market power is the investment in productive assets that enables a firm to dominate a market. According to Kingston, the market power of capability stems from laws regarding joint stock companies and limited liability. This enables a corporation to assemble enough money and to protect the owners from personal liability. If you have the money and KSA (knowledge, skills, and attitudes) to purchase the expensive equipment to produce a product or service and your competitors do not, you have capability market power.

IBM had capability market power with its mainframe computers. They were expensive to produce and required a large, highly trained workforce. Once competitors in the computer industry were able to produce the same type of computer with less capability, IBM lost its market power. Its former capability market power has now become its liability. The supposed adherence to the customer that IBM has bragged about has had little to do with its actual success. Even IBM admits it, at this time. IBM's present problem is that its management still does not understand why it was successful and, therefore, cannot duplicate its previous success.

Specific market power is given by some identifiable ordinances of the government. These may be patents and other forms of licensing. A patent gives its owner the exclusive right to a product for a given number of years. This time frame changes from nation to nation. The drug companies, for example, are allowed exclusive rights to sell their patented drugs for predetermined amounts of time. This enables them to recover their investments in research and development and make a profit. Without this form of market power, pharmaceuticals would quickly become a commodity as competitors enter the market. These competitors would then have avoided the initial cost of bringing the product to the market and, therefore, would have market power.

Persuasive market power, according to Kingston, is gained when the organization is protected by trademark and copyright laws. This is an investment in the changing of consumer preferences. Kingston's view of persuasive market power is limited to the area of advertising. This type of market power gives the organization the ability to unmake a market.

Although I agree with Kingston on the fundamental principles of market power and am in debt to him for introducing me to the concept, I believe that my application is much broader than Kingston's. I view market power as a unifying philosophy in which the entire organizational capacity is combined to block competitors from access to targeted markets. Kingston views market power as having its roots in law. For me, organizational capacity is much broader and includes law. All actions have their roots in philosophy.

### David Morris on Market Power

The philosophy that drives market power is unitary. Market power results from unifying knowledge, skills, and attitudes. Because the application of that philosophy directs the entire organizational capacity, it is termed philosophy in action and not theory. Others have attempted to base organizational theory on law, as in the case of Kingston, or on science, as in the case of those who advocate a Western philosophy of science approach. Still others insist that business is an art. However, business is the outcome of the underlying philosophy that dominates a society. Business is based on a pluralistic or unitary foundation. Thus, all capacity is either separated or combined. When the dominant philosophy separates, each functional area develops its own theory. The question becomes what makes marketing, human, physical, intangible, and financial resources unique and different rather than similar.

The search for a philosophy in action involves discovering those attributes that unify marketing, human, physical, intangible, and financial resources (the "5Rs"). As these resources are combined to block competitors from access to targeted markets, the firm or nation is applying market power to achieve a collective purpose. Separate functional areas now become resources, not competing philosophical centers. These resources are applied to achieve a purpose.

## Market Power Driven

Market power as a philosophy in action drives both the organizational means and ends. (For an in-depth analysis of means and ends, refer to the "Direction" module.) Market power driven is defined as the gap between present and desired market power. Every organization has a present capacity to achieve a purpose. Capacity is derived from the organization's present means and ends. An organization is never static. Each organization can do two things: either advance or decline. The measurement of this advance or decline differs.

### *Tyndall on Market Power Driven*

According to Bruce Tyndall, professor of mathematics at the University of New Haven, the measure of that advance or decline can be assessed through market share. Market share is considered a fixed measurement, and organizations gain or lose market share against competition. The respective rates of gain or loss are significant when comparing companies. Ford and General Motors, for example, have both lost market share, but General Motors has lost it at a greater rate than Ford. According to Tyndall, this is founded on each company's capacity to learn and unlearn. Therefore, Ford has learned at a faster rate than General Motors.

While both Ford and General Motors have unlearned the car business, Toyota, gaining market share, has learned the car business. Learning and unlearning are derived from the unifying of knowledge, skills, and attitudes (see the "Philosophy: Knowledge, Skills, and Attitudes" module). Loss of market share represents a loss of market power because the combined organizational capacity of Ford and General Motors has been insufficient when compared with Toyota's. This decline will continue until Ford and General Motors relearn the automobile business at a faster rate than Toyota.

### *Means and Ends and Market Power Driven*

The identified gap in market power may require a change in both organizational and indeed national means and ends. There are three possible combinations of means and ends: the organization can continue to pursue the same means and same ends, it can apply the same means to different ends, or it can apply different means to different ends. To identify this gap, the organization must assess where it is now in order to better determine where it wishes to go (see the sections on "Market Power Analysis" and "Market Power Assessment," in the "Direction" module).

## MARKET POWER DRIVEN

Theodore Levitt's undisputed view of the history of the railroad and film industry (discussed in "Vision, Strategic Intent, Mission" in the "Philosophy in Action" module) remained unchallenged for thirty years. Almost everyone seemed to take at face value the hypothesis that the railroad and film managers were just unequipped to respond to a changing marketplace. A more accurate view of the history of the railroad and film industry is that both attempted to move into new markets but were blocked by U.S. government regulatory policy.

When I returned to the original documentation I was able to demonstrate that the U.S. government had blocked access to the new markets. The whole foundation for strategy taught in business schools in the United States has been built on the false assumption that major industries failed to identify and move to new markets. The reason put forth was that those in management misunderstood the visions or missions of their businesses and that they had failed to respond to the needs and wants of their customers. According to this misconception, these allegedly myopic managers deserved their fate. That fate has been more government regulation.

The question that has to be explored is why this oversight occurred and why it still continues? After reading my 1990 article "The railroad and film industry: Were they myopic?" the proponents of the "myopic managers" theory agreed that the history was misrepresented, but they often countered that, although the original examples used were wrong, the idea was still correct.

The reason for this misunderstanding is that Americans have believed since the 1930s that government is and should be a balancing force to control evil business. These industries had been powerful, and they and others were accused of causing the Great Depression, and it was now the government's role to curtail that power. Government would not enhance or encourage business but instead control it. The government put forth an idealized business environment where several competing companies drive down the prices. The prevailing sentiment was that diabolic businesspeople had destroyed this nation, and they had to be controlled by honest government. A company falters because it has failed to respond to its customers, not because the might of the government is destroying the industry. The U.S. government destroyed the railroads, and now, under the illusion of maintaining the unrealistic concept of free trade, it has destroyed the automobile industry and the machine tool industry. It is well on its way to destroying the information industry.

## Market Power and Japan

Japan has been applying market power for centuries. Japan denied access to its markets during the three-hundred-year Tokugawa shogunate. This came to an end in 1868 with the fall of the shogunate and the installation of the imperial Meiji government. The imperial position was that Japan would be opened to the outside world—particularly, the West—in order to acquire the military and economic power to prevent the overrun that had occurred in China. China, and indeed most of Asia, had been plundered by the West. The French, Germans, Dutch, Americans, Russians, and British had opened Eastern trade by force of arms.

To counter this colonization of Asia, the Japanese set up a two-tier system: one internal and the other external. The internal system would employ as many people as possible, whereas the external system would apply all available resources to gain market power in the international markets. The best and brightest of Japan would be focused on the external.

In the 1890s, Japan introduced the *zaibatsu* (industrial and financial conglomerates) form of business. The *zaibatsu* were turned over to ruling families. Each family had control over a different aspect of the economy. The four *zaibatsu* were Mitsui, Mitsubishi, Sumitumo, and Yasudo. Absolutely no internal competition was allowed for any of the *zaibatsu*: they were virtual monopolies.

At this same time, the United States passed the Sherman Antitrust Act to destroy monopoly. The Japanese monopoly system was increased in the 1930s with the addition of such military *zaibatsu* as Nissan, Nihon Chisso, Nihon Soda, and Showa Denko. In the occupied Japan of 1945, Supreme Commander of Allied Powers Douglas MacArthur dismantled the *zaibatsu*, but this decision was overturned for political reasons, and the *zaibatsu* were modified and reinstated under the new designation of *"keiretsu"* ("enterprise groups") in 1952. With the advent of the Korean War (1953), Japan became a military supplier and regained its industrial position. At the end of the Korean War, to maintain Japan's economic stability as a buffer against Communism, the Americans opened up their markets to Japanese products. During this time, the U.S. federal antimonopoly forces were breaking up American companies while the Japanese government continued to encourage and support monopoly.

## Market Power and Other Nations

Like most nations, Japan, Korea, Germany, France, Taiwan, Great Britain, and the Netherlands have applied market power for thousands of years. Although the nations of Western Europe, along with the newly independent nations of Eastern Europe and the former Soviet Union, may appear to be breaking up in certain respects, they are attempting to unify as a trading bloc. The Germans have their *kartels*, the Koreans have their *chaebol*, and the Taiwanese have *da chi yeh chia*. These are all forms of monopoly power given to the business enterprises of a nation.

The world is dividing into several distinct trading blocs. Canada, the United States, Mexico and, I believe, Great Britain will make up one bloc. The British will have a difficult time as members of a European Community led by Germany. The European Community may bring in more members from Western and Eastern Europe.

Russia may attempt to develop a trading bloc or move into the European Common Market. In creating their own economic community, the Russians face a major difficulty at this time: they do not have the military or economic power to lead it. The European Community and the United States are not going to let Russia develop its own bloc. Japan is again attempting to develop a bloc in Asia. All over the world, many other blocs have been formed to attain and sustain market power for the participating nations. Each is viewed to be in the best interest of the participants.

## CONCLUSION

A fundamental change in the philosophy that drives organization theory is necessary for the United States. From a pluralistic perspective, theory continues to separate disciplines or functions. Each area has its own unique theory, which describes that particular area. Marketing resources are concerned with the needs and wants of customers; human resources attempt to maximize human resources; physical resources take a cost/benefit approach; intangible resources search for protection; and financial resources want to maximize stockholder wealth. Each of these resource areas are then expected to work in harmony toward achieving multiple purposes. This separation of disciplines continues even within functions. For example, the field of marketing has divided itself into macro and micro. Each searches for its own distinct theory to describe marketing. The separating is endless as each function continually divides and subdivides in an effort to develop a theory for more and more specific applications. Terms like "needs" and "wants" are defined differently. This continues to lead to confusion and separating.

Unitary philosophy requires that all functional areas adopt the same theory and the same definition of terms. This requires that the marketing, human, physical, intangible, and financial resources ("5Rs") have the same philosophical underpinning. This is called "philosophy in action" because the entire organization is grounded on a unitary philosophy. This philosophy rejects the notion that scientific explanation and prediction is unbiased. Therefore, from a pluralistic perspective, there is no such thing as theory unless the theory is that those who follow that philosophy will separate. It is the philosophy of separating that is driving the organization, not the many separate theories present in that philosophy.

Although it is possible to employ almost any common philosophy in action to unify the organization, market power has been recommended because it reflects human nature. Market power is the blocking of competitors from access to targeted markets. Resources are then applied in any combination to achieve market power. Marketing is no longer driven by the needs and wants of customers but by blocking competitors from targeted markets. Therefore, one sets a price to block competition, one advertises to block competition, and one develops products to block competition. The same is true of human resources: one hires to block competition, one trains to block competition. Physical resources, such as land, buildings, and equipment, are acquired and maintained to block competition; intangible resources are applied that benefit the firm in blocking competition. Organizations can effectively use their financial resources to block competition.

## SUGGESTED READINGS

Abegglen, James C. *Kaisha: The Japanese corporation*. New York: Basic Books 1985.
Baldwin, William L. *Market power, competition, and antitrust policy*. Homewood, Ill.: Irwin, 1987.
Drucker, Peter. *Management*. New York: Harper & Roe, 1974.
Chalmers, Norma. *Industrial relations in Japan*. London: Routledge, 1989.
David, Fred R. How companies define their mission. *Long Range Planning* 22 (91) (1989): 90-97.
Dietrich, William S. *In the shadow of the rising sun*. University Park, Pa.: Pennsylvania State University Press, 1991.
Halberstam, David. *The reckoning*. New York: Morrow, 1986.
Haym, Cynthia, and David Morris. *Office hours*. Madison, Conn.: Market Power Institute, 1996.
Imai, Masaaki. *Kaizen: The key to Japan's competitive success*. New York: McGraw-Hill, 1986.

Kearns, Robert L. *Zaibatsu America*. New York: Free Press, 1992.

Kimball, David. An examination of the distinction between a company mission and a written mission statement within the strategic management process: A survey of the Planning Forum executives in the New York City area. Unpublished dissertation. West Haven, Conn.: University of New Haven, 1992.

Kingston, Wm. *The political economy of innovation*. The Hague: Martinus Nijhoff, 1984.

———.ed. *The protection of innovation*. Dordrecht, The Netherlands: Kluwer, 1987.

———. *Innovation, creativity and law*. Dordrecht, The Netherlands: Kluwer, 1990.

Levitt, Theodore. Marketing myopia. *Harvard Business Review* (July-August) (1960): 45- 56.

Lorriman, John, and Kenjo Takashi. *Japan's winning margins*. London: Oxford University Press, 1994.

MacMillan, Ian C., and Patricia E. Jones. *Strategic formulation: Power and politics*. 2d. ed. St. Paul, Minn.: West, 1986.

Maslow, Abraham, *Motivation and personality*. New York: Harper, 1954.

Miyashita, Kenichi, and David Russell. *Keiretsu: Inside the hidden Japanese company*. New York: McGraw-Hill, 1994.

Morris, David J., Jr. Strategic marketing: Customer-oriented mission, no—market power, yes. *Review of Business* 9(1) (1987): 3-8.

———. The railroad and film industry: Were they myopic? *Journal of the Academy of Marketing Science* 18(4) (1990): 279–283.

Pearce, John A., and Fred David. Corporate mission statements: The bottom line. *Academy of Management Executive*. (May 1987): 109-115.

Posch, Robert J., Jr. *Marketing and the law*. Englewood Cliffs, N.J.: Prentice-Hall, 1988.

Prestowitz, Clyde V. *Trading places*. New York: Basic Books, 1988.

Schnaars, Steven P. *Marketing strategy: A customer driven approach*. New York: Free Press, 1991.

Stein, Guenther. *Made in Japan*. 2d ed. London: Methuen, 1935.

Sullivan, Jeremiah J. *Invasion of the salarymen: The Japanese business presence in America*. Westport, Conn.: Praeger, 1992.

Tatsuno, Sheridan M. *Created in Japan*. Grand Rapids, Mich.: Harper & Row, 1990.

Tyndall, Bruce, and David Morris. Dynamic quantitative measures of the unitary theory of corporate process. *American Business Review* XII (1) (1994): 1-5.

Womack, James P., Daniel T. Jones, and Daniel Roos. *The machine that changed the world*. New York: Rawson, 1990.

# Direction (Means and Ends)

The setting of the direction that the firm will take is based on the operating system of its members. The ancient Greeks developed the concept of "teleology," the study and pursuit of purpose or final intent. This philosophy has been applied in pluralistic societies as a foundation to explain the behavior of God, humans, and nature. Sir Isaac Newton's discoveries created another form of direction. In my view, Newton was searching for a theological explanation or "First Cause" of the universe, but his work has somehow been misrepresented as only a mechanistic or reductionist understanding of the universe. The mechanistic position postulates that all the processes of life are mechanically determined. Thus, the laws of physics and chemistry will lead to a complete understanding of all circumstances.

Newton was attempting to provide an explanation for the First Cause, not to reject it. In this view, the universe has a purpose, and that purpose is the reflection of God's will and design for the universe. Until his death, Newton believed that an understanding of the universe could be a method to prove the existence of God. God and science were separated by Western scholars who used Newton's work as a justification. The quest for a First Cause was replaced with a quest to understand—without any religious foundation—man and nature.

## MEANS AND ENDS

The concept of "means and ends" outgrew teleology. "Means" include tools, techniques, processes, products, methods, objectives, enabling objectives, outputs, tactics, strategies, plans, and policies. Means are the focused and organized activities employed to achieve an end(s). "Ends" are goals, outcomes, terminal objectives, aims, purposes, or final intents. Because ends can turn into means, it is often difficult to separate means from ends. When individuals and organizations confuse or lose sight of their end(s), means become mere tasks and subtasks that have purpose only unto themselves. The concept of what constitutes a means or an end is derived from the KSA (knowledge, skills, and attitudes) cognitive process that goes on in the minds of those going through the exercise. A means and an end are what one determines them to be at any one time.

## PLURALISTIC

The determination of organizational direction in the United States was originally derived from the field of economics. This economic worldview was dominant until the middle of the 1950s. According to classic economics, the direction or outcome of any organization is the single end of profit maximization. This advocacy of a single end for the organization came under attack when it was argued that organizations should have several concurrent directions (ends). Peter Drucker, a writer of books on management, was instrumental in arguing in 1954 that the field of management should break with the classical economic model of business and pursue business as a separate discipline.

Organizations were seen as complex formations that have many directions (ends) that must be pursued at the same time. This led to a separation of economics and management into distinct fields of study. In some U.S. colleges, economics departments are considered to be a part of the arts and sciences, whereas in other colleges, economics is in the school of business. Business disciplines such as marketing grew out of and developed their theories from the field of economics. These disciplines have now incorporated theories from a spectrum of fields, including psychology, biology, physics, sociology, and philosophy.

### Pluralistic Organizational Direction

In the United States, several methods have been applied to determine the direction (end) that an organization should take. Each has one or more components or attributes (means) that are appraised through some type of measurement model. All these models are driven by the concept of separating. They are applied at the corporate, business unit, and functional levels. Several pluralistic models have been applied to determine corporate direction. Some of these models are discussed.

*Portfolio Model*

When reviewing marketing textbooks, I have always argued that the portfolio model is an outdated means of setting corporate direction and that it should be omitted from the text. My personal appraisal notwithstanding, it is a well-recognized model and should be included in this discussion. Although the portfolio model has several variations, it assesses two corporate indicators: relative market share and growth. This model advises companies to divide their businesses into strategic business units (SBUs) organized on the following criteria. The SBUs must have a clearly defined market with their own mission. SBUs are often built around a product or product lines. Each SBU must be a separate profit center responsible for its own profits. This requires a separating of accounting and other activities between or among units. The competitors of each unit must be distinct and identifiable. Each unit develops a separate strategy based on its own potential for market share and growth.

There are four possible assessment outcomes: stars, dogs, cash cows, and question marks. The company's leadership is supposed to build the stars, starve or sell the dogs, take all the money it can from the cash cows, and experiment with the question marks. The direction of each of these SBU activities is considered separately. The units' resources are not integrated.

### Porter's Models

Michael Porter, an economist from the Harvard Business School, has managed to reintroduce an economics model of direction back into business and management. As discussed earlier, the economic model came under attack in the mid-1950s in the United States. Porter took the research developed in the 1940s in the economics structure of industry literature and moved it back into the separated field of management. He calls it "management" to create the impression that his work is new and innovative. His ideas have had a great impact on American business. If he had called his work "economics," the reaction of those in management might have been far different.

The same tactic enabled another Harvard professor to impress the medical community with his "relaxation response." If he had called it "yoga," would it have been as easy to market in the West? Americans, in particular, seem to have great difficulty in accepting ideas that are thought to be from the past or from outside their specialized areas. It is easier to give such ideas names that are familiar in the separate fields. This cultural behavior has resulted in the separation of the past from the present and the future. Americans accuse the Japanese of copying them, but what is it called when Americans rename what they copy from the Japanese? Americans call it "creativity."

Economists, interested in competition, have identified three types of companies: monopolies (bad), oligopolies (imperfect), and perfectly competitive (great). Monopolies are evil and exploitative because they have no competitors and because, given the chance, they will exploit the world, the nation, the workers, and the customers. They have no interest in improvement because they lack incentives. Oligopolies are somewhat tolerable, but they must be watched to ensure that they do not turn into monopolies. The American car companies have been held up in many economic textbooks as the best examples of an oligopolies. Although they had some competitors, they were all generally reading off the same sheet of music. The Big Three (General Motors, Ford, Chrysler) were not improving their products, enhancing car safety, or lowering their prices. They were supposedly in an endless spiral of national exploitation. The role of government thus became to right these inequities because market forces had little impact.

The best possible world to the U.S. economist is perfect competition. From this vantage point, products are not differentiated. All firms are locked in a permanent price war. This compels businesses to constantly reduce their prices to the customers. In this idealized world, knowledge is perfect. Every company has equal access to marketing, human, physical, intangible, and financial resources (the "5Rs"). In the idealized world created by the economists, there are no barriers to entry anywhere. All can sell in any market as long as they play by the same rules.

Porter's revelation, which has made him famous, is that firms that are either monopolies or oligopolies have competitive advantages. Porter advocates that a firm should search for opportunities in which it will have an advantage. However, five threats should be assessed: threats from outside firms, threats from firms within the industry, threats from substitutes, threats from customers, and threats from suppliers. These five factors are always present in varying degrees. It is the company's responsibility to monitor these factors and to take the best direction.

Porter has also developed what he terms a "three-generic idealized model" for a company striving to achieve a competitive advantage: the low-cost/low-price seller, differentiated products, and segmented markets. (Porter's concept of segmentation is what this book will later refer to as "targeting.") He advocates that a firm's direction should be grounded on only one of these strategies at a time. He believes that to try to combine them will decrease a firm's chances of success.

*Ohmae Model*

According to author Kenichi Ohmae, consumers should decide what to buy based on the principle of best value at lowest cost. Government should not interfere in this process. A company must not view its organization with a headquarters mentality. Each market should be considered as the local market. If this cannot be accomplished, a company should seek alliances with other companies in the targeted markets. Company ownership and control must not be an issue when alliances are formulated.

The historic reliance on natural resources (classic economics) must give way to adding value. Companies and nations must be directed to add value to resources to create wealth. The components comprising the addition of value will change as competition is able to add value. Direction requires a constant search for new products that add value at the lowest cost. Ohmae argues that there are many such gaps between what is invented and what is produced. Such gaps give the company unlimited opportunities for success. The organization is directed to add value at the lowest cost by finding and producing products and services in markets that others have not yet entered.

*Forecasting Models*

Those who advocate forecasting as a method of predicting the future have significantly influenced the setting of corporate direction. Their model shows the organization attempting to predict the future and, once this is accomplished, to move to organize the company to respond to that prediction. Forecasters have developed all kinds of mathematical and nonmathematical models to achieve success. The idea is simple: if one knows what is going to happen, one can prepare the organization to take advantage of the situation.

The more a prediction appears to be scientifically founded, the more value it is thought to have for the organization. A common method of prediction is to extend the past and present into the future. If, in the last few years, the area of inquiry has improved at a particular rate, then it will improve at the same rate in the future. The longer the time line from the past to the present, the more it is supposed to be predictive. Twenty years are better than ten in validating a prediction. Some forecasters measure past events in waves or cycles. Observing and calculating the ups and downs, they attempt to identify when the future shifts will occur. For example, a forecaster may indicate that after a certain number of months or years of prosperity, a downturn will follow. This downturn, which itself will last for a predictable amount of time, will then be followed by an upturn.

Another popular method applied to predict the future has been to average the experts' predictions. This system (the "delphi method") includes various mathematical models designed to justify the results of the experts' opinions. Western society responds to those who predict future events (but not to those on the fringes of society such as astrologers and fortune-tellers). Forecasting, to be palatable to the Western appetite, must appear to be scientifically based. The right mathematical model and a large enough computer are thought sufficient to reveal the future.

## CEO Model

Many strategy books discuss the role of the chief executive officer (CEO) in setting direction. The CEO is described as the person who is concerned with the future direction of the firm. CEOs spend their time acquiring the necessary insights and information to decide the direction of their organizations. A CEO is chosen for the job in the first place because he or she possesses the KSA required to know what should be done within the organization. The CEO has the capability to move the company in the direction that he or she has chosen. How this decision is actually made may not be understood by those who lack the years of experience or the access to the proper information. A chief executive officer can be groomed within the ranks of the company over several years or brought in from the outside because the firm has failed to produce a leader.

## Strategic Planning Model

Many companies have a group of professionals whose job it is to set the direction of the firm. These experts assemble information from both inside and outside the firm. Because of their specialized skills, they are deemed to be especially qualified to set organizational direction. Strategic planners may be assigned to a particular SBU, or they may be responsible for the entire organization. It is up to the CEO or a management group to take the information provided by the strategic planners and put it into action. The group of strategic planners then decides the specific action to be taken by line and staff management to achieve its plans. The orientation of strategic planners varies depending on their background and focus. Some may take a finance approach to the process while others take a marketing approach. They are generally perceived to be unbiased and to be functioning in the best interest of the company. Strategic planners are advisers, not implementers. They set and monitor the goals and objectives of the firm.

## Goals-and-Objectives Model

Because the terms "goals" and "objectives" have not been clearly defined, many corporations misunderstand them when setting direction. Each company may define these terms differently, and it is not uncommon to have each SBU within the same company define them differently. There is no requirement for consistency of definition even within the same organization because each SBU is understood to be unique and to stand alone.

### Quality Model

Those advocating a quality approach to direction believe that quality will improve the decision making of a firm. For them, American firms have a problem not because of making models and mechanisms but because of their lack of a quality product or service. They believe that the Japanese do not know any more than Americans about quality and that they have copied American ideas. One difference between Japan and the United States is that Japan has historically introduced quality into its business approach, whereas the United States has focused on short-term solutions and mass production.

Customers—indeed, American customers—have responded to the quality approach of the Japanese by purchasing their products and services. American workers are able to produce quality when management focuses on quality rather than on unit volume and short-term returns. The way American business sets direction does not need to change; what is needed is a quality approach to direction.

### Cycle Time Model

The Japanese can bring new products to the marketplace much faster than their competitors. In a matter of months, the Japanese can come out with what would take the Americans years to produce. Americans react to this situation by attempting to streamline the product development time required for their companies. Moreover, the Japanese can bring products to the market with the involvement of far fewer employees than can their American competitors.

The American organization must take a new direction not only to improve cycle time but also to do it with fewer employees. This will require massive layoffs and early retirements in over-staffed organizations. American business must become mean and lean to compete with the Japanese. It is a new high-tech era, and in order to compete, the United States must change its old ways of doing business. The corporation must use technology to reorganize work methods and thereby eliminate unnecessary steps and processes. Production and marketing techniques, along with new and existing products and services, must be designed to reduce both cycle time and the number of per-job employees.

### Cost Reduction Model

The cost of production must be reduced in order to reduce the cost to the consumer. This is one of Michael Porter's ideas discussed earlier. Costs can be reduced by standardization, a reduction in product lines, imitation, and a general reduction of overhead. According to Porter, when a firm takes the direction of reducing the cost of production and the cost to the consumer, it often makes it more difficult for the competition to enter its markets. This, of course, assumes that it has a market for its products. All else being equal, the firm then achieves a competitive advantage.

*Entrepreneurship Model*

The U.S. government has emphasized and promoted the idea that small business start-ups have increased while large businesses have declined. It identified a shift in the workforce: more individuals are employed by firms that have fewer than five-hundred employees than by those that have more than five-hundred employees. The type of person, characterized as successful in a small business is now considered the same type of person who can generate success within the large corporation. Large corporations, therefore, are directed to have a new emphasis on entrepreneurial self-determination.

This idea of entrepreneurship seems to have evolved into the organizations dividing into many small businesses, each competing in a particular market. These small enterprises are to be operated by an entrepreneur who has the responsibility for all aspects of the business. Many large corporations are now open to proposals for new small business ventures. Present U.S. business structures are dividing and subdividing business enterprises in a new quest to achieve an entrepreneurial direction.

*Best Practices Model*

When one looks across the landscape of business, certain companies are outstanding in one or more aspects of business. For example, few companies can top L. L. Bean or QVC home shopping network when it comes to customer service. If a company wishes to improve its customer service, it has only to model itself on a company that is exceptional in that area. In many cases, it may contact L. L. Bean or QVC and actually send its people to learn how to do the job. Armed with this knowledge, the fact finders return to their own companies and attempt to duplicate the type of customer service that L. L. Bean and QVC have achieved. What makes this benchmarking procedure unique is that the company that one benchmarks does not have to be within one's specific field. Based on the best practices of any company in a particular area of business, direction is set within the corresponding area of one's own business.

*Statistical Model*

After World War II, Edward Deming developed a statistical model for assessing organizational processes. This model has been generally applied to the area of production. His model aims to decrease the number of defects to zero by setting standards. Once these standards are achieved, the standard of acceptable defects constantly moves toward zero. Deming's work was generally ignored in the United States in the 1950s. He found a sympathetic audience in Japan and has been credited for the great success of the Japanese quality movement. Today, Deming's model can be applied to measure every aspect of the organization. The Japanese are now accusing the Americans of producing inferior quality. This, they argue, is why the United States is no longer competitive. In response, many U.S. corporations have focused on quality as a key factor in their organizational direction.

*World-Class Management Model*

The concept of "world-class management" states that the person who under-stands best the direction that should be taken on any job is the one who does the job. The advocates of world-class management believe that management's lack of trust is the cause of many problems in the decision-making capabilities of the people who perform the jobs. Management often makes decisions in areas where it lacks ownership and daily work experience. These decisions affect the quality of the final product produced by the entire workforce. To counter this weakness, management should push decision making down to the lowest organizational level where it can be accomplished. Those doing the particular job should set direction. The combined performance of all empowered employees leads to a competitive advantage. World-class managers take into consideration all organizations selling products or services anywhere in the world. Management at all levels then strives to be the best in the world at what it does.

*SWOT Model*

Assessing the companies strengths, weaknesses, opportunities, and threats (SWOT) can set direction. Planning within an organization begins with a SWOT analysis. Once this analysis is completed, the organization pursues the areas where it has the most strengths, the least weaknesses, the most opportunities, and the least threats. What constitutes a strength, weakness, opportunity, or a threat is determined by the researcher and the particular company.

*Reengineering Model*

Organizations have to rethink the entire way in which they carry out business. The Adam Smith model of division of labor no longer produces wealth. Fewer workers should now perform more tasks that had been previously accomplished by many workers. This should be established through the use of technology. The process must be constantly streamlined as technology changes. This requires a continual training and upgrading of all employees. Interdepartmental teams will perform the jobs of the future.

*Management by Objectives Model*

In the 1950s, the concept of management by objectives was introduced in the United States. In theory, this would clarify responsibility for actions. Many com-panies spent a great deal of time and money to organize jobs with clearly defined objectives. It was believed that directed and rewarded behavior would lead to greater productivity. All standards were to be set in order to achieve these objec-tives. The movement has been less than successful for several reasons. The lead-ership of the organization is clearly to blame for not setting a single well-defined end for all to follow. Often, the problem existed because the CEO wanted to ac-complish multiple ends at the same time—a situation in which the means invari-ably became confused.

Management objectives that actually reflected the job were not developed. Func-tional areas had competing objectives. Some stated objectives were beyond organizational intent; therefore, they had little value. Two worlds were created: one in which people stated what they were going to do and the other in which people actually acted, often in ways unrelated to their previous statements. The job requirements would change, but the objectives were not changed to reflect the new environment. Evaluations were not based on the stated accomplishments. Some would accomplish their objectives but not receive promotion or salary increases. Jobs were defined by their tasks and subtasks. Members of the organization were unable to depersonalize the tasks and subtasks in their jobs, despite being expected to do so. It is absurd to think that actions can or should be depersonalized. Unstated personal factors, such as trust and attitude, were important to the success of each individual, but for legal and political reasons, these factors were not stated in objectives and were, therefore, often misunderstood by a large number of employees.

These negative outcomes forced a gradual rejection of the concept of management by objectives. New ideas on how to ensure a common direction, such as the quality movement, became popular. In a pluralistic culture, older ideas become outdated and unwanted. From a unitary perspective, an idea or its components may continue to have value in a larger combined effort. The introduction of one clear end, defined in terms of a terminal objective, enables all to fix responsibility, starting at the top. The company, under this system, no longer receives conflicting messages from the CEO. The functional areas become means called resources. All jobs have a standard (terminal objective) by which to compare their actions. This standard can now unify and direct behavior toward a common end.

## Summary

In the pluralistic view of direction, several choices are available to the corporation and its employees. It is unclear whether these alternatives are applied as means, end(s), or both. It is also unclear, in many of the examples, when a company should or should not apply a particular component to direction. Is there, for example, any time when organizational direction should not attempt to work toward reducing cycle time, improving quality, or modeling on best practices and implementing world-class management? The advocates of each of the above would most likely view their particular interests as essential for all companies at all times. Companies adopting the pluralistic model of direction may incorporate any or all models at the same time, without actually making an attempt to combine any of the models.

## UNITARY

A unitary approach to organizational direction searches for a way (means) to combine all possible influences to achieve a common purpose (end). This approach does not suggest that there is only one correct way (means) to achieve a common purpose (end), but rather that the realization of a common purpose (end) is the foundation of the concept of direction. All actions within the organization are organized on a philosophical underpinning of unity of purpose. When any knowledge, skills, and attitudes enter the organization, proponents do not try to create a separate structure but rather search for methods of inclusion.

With this in mind, the Japanese have never copied the Americans. Whatever they have taken from the KSA of the United States, it has not been directly transferred. Rather, American KSA is included in their overall unitary framework. When considering a plan of action, a businessperson must ask himself or herself, "Will this action contribute to the accomplishment of a common purpose (end) or direction of the organization?" There are other combinations or possibilities that will evolve, but they, too, must fit within the conceptual confines of moving the organization toward a common purpose (end). Both Western and Eastern philosophies have incorporated the concept of direction, but their interpretations of the concept are different.

The Western philosophical view, which advocates a common purpose, is founded on the Greek teleological approach and the three major Western religions. The Eastern view of a common purpose is founded on Hindu and Buddhist beliefs. The common purpose (end) is achieving *mukti* (freedom from this world), merging with Brahman (the universal soul), or reaching *nirvana* (like *mukti*, freedom from this world and the cycle of reincarnation). All work to achieve the same ultimate reality, which is beyond understanding and explanation. The means to attain this reality are *dharma* (the righteous path), *artha* (material wealth), and *kama* (pleasure). Western religion has a much narrower spectrum of means to reach heaven. Each one of the Western faiths—Christianity, Islam, and Judaism—perceives heaven as a different reality.

### Unitary Organizational Direction

For any given period of time the Japanese apply one direction (end) to achieve not organizational but national direction. Business direction is a means to an end, not an end unto itself. All activities are directed toward this end under the philosophical concept of combining. Each business area is applied to all aspects of the national purpose. The country and all its companies do not assess the future with long-term forecasts and then react to that future as we do in the West.

All aspects of the society—government, business, education, religion, military, family, and the individual—plan together for the future that they want and then work toward that future. The means to accomplish that future is not considered until they have agreed on the common direction. The Western procedure involves arguing about means, such as cycle time, best practice, or quality, before the end is set or in spite of the end. The following outlines a model for setting a direction (end) for a corporation. The model is based on the philosophy in action of market power.

### MARKET POWER ANALYSIS AND ASSESSMENT

Before an end can be set, the organization must do a market power analysis and assessment. "Market power" is defined as the use/employment of organizational capacity to block existing and potential competitors from access to targeted markets. A market power analysis and assessment indicates where the organization stands in relation to its competition. The organization, like a nation or an individual, must know where it is now if it is going to determine where it plans to go. To know oneself and to know one's enemy are imperative before any action is taken.

## Market Power Analysis

A market power analysis is interorganizational. It compares the organization with its competition. Each subsidiary contrasts its market power with that of its competition. This is done on a yearly cycle unless circumstances warrant it being done more often. The work required for a market power analysis is a full-time activity for an organization. Competition is analyzed on a daily, and in some cases on an hourly, basis.

The concept of a subsidiary is not the same as that of a strategic business unit. Because a subsidiary has a loosely defined market, subsidiaries assist and merge with other subsidiaries. The purpose of each subsidiary is to work as a means to achieve a common organizational end. The products or services produced and sold by any part of the organization are considered a component of the total products and services produced and sold by the entire organization. This concept is illustrated below using a company called ABC.

ABC Company is still applying the SBU model as a part of a portfolio-directed organization. A portfolio-directed corporation acquires and manages a number of businesses as separate companies. These companies are SBUs and are responsible to the central organization. They have little if any obligation to other SBUs in the portfolio. The central organization holds, builds, or sells its portfolio. For example, the General Electric Company generally sells any part of its portfolio that is not or cannot be number one or two in its served market. Although this arrangement appears to have been successful, this thinking is typical of the portfolio model of doing business. Market power requires applying all internal resources, not just a particular business unit, against the competition.

ABC Company had several companies in its portfolio: abc 1, abc 2, abc 3, abc 4, abc 5, and abc 6. A market power analysis looks at each of these companies as a subsidiary of ABC Company and not as a separate business. Each subsidiary is analyzed to compare its market power with that of its competitors.

It is a wise strategy to analyze existing and potential competition. A limited amount of work on this aspect of the analysis may prevent future disaster. For example, IBM probably overlooked Apple until it was too late for IBM to regain market share in the educational market without major resource expenditures. After identifying the competition, each of the five resource areas is analyzed and compared. "Know yourself and know your enemy."

As a director of human resources for the Syracuse Supply Company, (a Caterpillar Dealer) in the mid-1980s, I was invited to Peoria, Illinois for training. There I accidentally met with the Caterpillar management training class. When I asked those present who Caterpillar's major competitor was and how much discussion was given to that competitor, they answered that it was John Deere and that Caterpillar had spent a great deal of time discussing it. In the meantime, Komatsu, a Japanese competitor, was taking market share away from Caterpillar and threatening its future. My only explanation for their answer is that John Deere had been Caterpillar's competition for years and that Caterpillar was finding it difficult to consider a threat from another company. The same oversight can happen at a national level. The United States has had a very difficult time giving up the former Soviet Union as a major threat and considering substituting other possibilities. A market power analysis that contains existing and potential competition may even be useful in identifying actual competitors that have been overlooked by top management.

## Market Power Analysis Charts

The market power analysis charts consist of five broad resource areas: marketing, human, physical, intangible, and financial. These categories are referred to as the "5Rs." (An in-depth explanation of the "5Rs" is found in the resources module). The amount of time and effort that should be given to a market power analysis is a company decision, but U.S. corporate leaders would be well advised to devote a great deal more time to a market power analysis and assessment. This activity is not to be confused with strategic planning (as discussed in the module on pluralistic organizational direction"). Analysis comes before design or planning (as covered in the "Direction" module). A company must know itself and its competition before it plans to do anything. It then determines what it wants to accomplish after comparing its market power with that of competitors in targeted markets. To design (plan) without first determining a direction is dangerous at best.

If two researchers fill out the same market power analysis, the results may be different. The better the ability of researcher(s) to do the analysis, the more accurate the results. Correctly interpreting data depends on the capacity of those doing the job. The knowledge, skills, and attitudes of those within the organization matter.

Researchers must be prepared to defend their analysis before top management, but they should not feel hindered or tempted to present a false analysis and assessment because of fear of reprisals from top management. If this is the company's situation, it would be better to save time and money and forget the market power analysis. Dr. Robert Baeder, professor of management at the University of New Haven, has stated, "There is a difference between public and private truth." The results of a market power analysis is in the "private truth" category. The assessment must not be misleading because of internal political considerations. The information would be as useless as if military intelligences gave false assessments to the generals.

Many Western companies, in an effort to adopt a scientific method, have moved in the direction of heavy quantification of the numbers applied to statistical formulas. The illusion has been that, using this method, the results would not depend on the researcher. These activities are rarely if ever independent of the researcher. The understanding gained by previous market power analysis does not indicate that researchers are unbiased observers of life but that they are biased, informed participants in the process of life. The pluralistic view of research supports the idea that an unbiased model is possible because of its assumption that actions can be separated from the individuals performing them. This separating is often unnecessary and unproductive from the unitary perspective. The best observers, not the best statisticians, provide the best insights on a market power analysis. Figure

# Figure 6
## Market Power Analysis

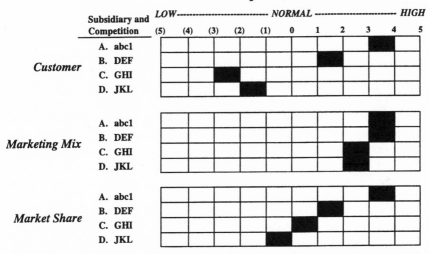

*Marketing Resources (Interorganizational)*
*Competitive Dominance*

Source: *Marketing Theory and Practice: A Unitary and Pluralistic Approach* (West Haven CT: University of New Haven Press).

6 represents the marketing, human, physical, intangible, and financial market power analyses.

### Marketing: Market Power Analysis Chart

The market power analysis compares the subsidiaries of a company with their competitors. In the following example, abc 1, a subsidiary of ABC Company, is analyzed. Abc 1's competitors are DEF, GHI, and JKL. They are compared on an interval scale. In an interval scale, successive numbers are evenly spaced. The researcher determines where the companies fall on the scale.

The marketing resource area is organized on an interval scale into three major categories: customer, marketing mix, and market share. Based on the researchers' KSA in these categories, numbers are selected that describe the position of the subsidiary and each of its competitors. The questions asked are how would one compare these four companies (abc 1, DEF, GHI, and JKL) and how would one rate them (best to worst) in terms of their service to customers. The degree to which the customers prefer to do business with one versus another or all others is given a number value between -5 and +5, with 0 as neutral. The -5 represents an extremely poor performance, and +5 represents an extremely good performance. This evaluation shows that abc 1 does the best job, but none of the companies has the highest possible score in the area of the customer. There is some room for improvement, so abc 1 is given a +4 and the square is filled in. DEF is not as good in the customer area, so it is given a +2. GHI gets a -2, and JKL a -1. There are differences in this category that could be capitalized on by abc 1 and the other subsidiaries of ABC Company.

The marketing mix is the next area to analyze. It includes four areas: price, product, promotion, and place ("4Ps"). These areas may be combined or separated. When combined, abc 1 and DEF are about even, with a +4 for each; GHI and JKL each get a +3. The differences in this category are not as obvious between abc 1 and its competition.

Market share is then analyzed. Abc 1 gets a +4, DEF a +2; GHI a +1, and JKL a -1. The differences are spread out within the market share category.

*Market Power Analysis Chart Summary*

The preceding market power analysis of ABC Company's abc 1 subsidiary and its competitors is intended to be an accurate description of the four companies. The same market power analysis charts used in the ABC Company example could be applied for the subsidiary of abc 2 and its competitors, abc 3 and its competition, abc 4 and its competitors, and abc 5, and abc 6 as subsidiaries of ABC Company.

It is not recommended that this analysis be done by outside firms. The knowledge gained by the employees participating in the market power analysis is invaluable. A creative way of doing a market power analysis is to include individuals from other subsidiaries of the company. Their participation contributes to the process of unification. If an outside firm participates, its analysis should be done independently of the company's internal analysis. The company can then compare its own analysis with that of the external team. Each team should then meet to compare findings and to develop the final document. Disagreements should be footnoted in the document. *Marketing as a Means to Achieve Organizational Ends*, 4th edition, 1992, offers an in-depth description of how to do a market power analysis.

**Market Power Assessment**

A market power assessment is intraorganizational. The assessment is performed to identify the competitive gaps among subsidiary resources. The market power analysis compared each subsidiary in terms of the five resources: marketing, human, physical, intangible, and financial. This information serves to compare the performance of the subsidiary against its competitors in terms of each resource category. It is important to note that the comparison is not between subsidiaries but between each subsidiary and its competition.

A market power assessment is normally prepared on a yearly cycle, but this timetable can change if the environment demands a more frequent assessment. The data for the assessment of market power should be collected at all times. The purpose of the assessment is not to place blame on any one person or subsidiary internally, but to assess accurately one's own organization. The enemy is always external. For example, if one subsidiary has been more effective against its competitors in a particular area, the entire company must decide how to apply that subsidiary KSA to outperform the competitors of other subsidiaries. The company stresses the following question: How can the organization as a unified whole apply all its resources against each subsidiary's competitors?

### Market Power Assessment Charts

Market power assessment charts are essentially the same as the market power analysis charts. The titles of the charts are different, but the categories and the order in which they are presented are identical. The essential difference between the charts is their function for the organization. A market power assessment compares each subsidiary with its competition. Using this consistent model contributes to internal unity. Pluralistic planners have different versions for short-term and long-term planning for each strategic business unit. This approach contributes to an internal separation because each type of plan is organized differently. A unitary approach has a different conceptional underpinning: all work from the same consistent model. In this approach, consistency is a critical component for the success of an organization.

In the ABC Company example, a market power assessment would include all subsidiaries. In this assessment, the examples include six subsidiaries: abc 1, abc 2, abc 3, abc 4, abc 5, and abc 6. If the organization had twenty-five subsidiaries, they would all be included in the company's assessment. The chart would simply be expanded in each category to include the number of subsidiaries in the organization. For convenience, the following example explores the categories that are displayed on the same page. This enables the leadership to view all categories at the same time. The market power assessment charts are the visual representations of the larger report. Figure 7 represents the marketing aspect of the market power assessments. A human, physical, intangible, and financial market power assessment should also be added.

### Marketing: Market Power Assessment Chart

The marketing resources market power assessment charts are divided into three categories: customer, marketing mix, and market share. The customer assessment of the subsidiaries of ABC Company shows that abc 1 received a +4 when compared with is competitors, abc 2 received a +2, abc 3 a +3, abc 4 a +3, abc 5 a +1, and abc 6 a -1. These figures are transferred from the market power analysis charts to the market power assessment charts. When the leadership looks at the market power assessment charts it should have all the market power analysis charts and backup materials for easy access. The assessment should raise many questions. How can the other subsidiaries improve their market power by learning from what abc 1 does in this area? How can the other subsidiaries combine their resources to gain more market power for each?

In the assessment of the marketing mix, abc 1 received a +4, abc 2 a +2, abc 3 a +4, abc 4 a +1, abc 5 a -1, and abc 6 a -1. What can abc 1, abc 2, do to assist abc 3, abc 4, abc 5, and abc 6 against its competition in this category? What can each do to help the others? The marketing mix category can be divided into price, product, promotion, and place. If the leadership desires such division, identifying

# Figure 7
# Market Power Assessment

### Marketing Resources (Intraorganizational)
### Competitive Dominance

| Company Subsidiaries | LOW (5) | (4) | (3) | (2) | (1) | NORMAL 0 | 1 | 2 | 3 | 4 | HIGH 5 |
|---|---|---|---|---|---|---|---|---|---|---|---|
| **Customer** | | | | | | | | | | | |
| A. abc1 | | | | | | | | | | ■ | |
| B. abc2 | | | | | | | | ■ | | | |
| C. abc3 | | | | | | | | | ■ | | |
| D. abc4 | | | | | | | | | ■ | | |
| E. abc5 | | | | | | | ■ | | | | |
| F. abc6 | | | | | ■ | | | | | | |
| **Marketing Mix** | | | | | | | | | | | |
| A. abc1 | | | | | | | | | | ■ | |
| B. abc2 | | | | | | | | | ■ | | |
| C. abc3 | | | | | | | | | ■ | | |
| D. abc4 | | | | | | | ■ | | | | |
| E. abc5 | | | | | ■ | | | | | | |
| F. abc6 | | | | | ■ | | | | | | |
| **Market Share** | | | | | | | | | | | |
| A. abc1 | | | | | | | | | | ■ | |
| B. abc2 | | | | | | | | ■ | | | |
| C. abc3 | | | | | | | | | ■ | | |
| D. abc4 | | | | | | | ■ | | | | |
| E. abc5 | | | | | | | ■ | | | | |
| F. abc6 | | | | ■ | | | | | | | |

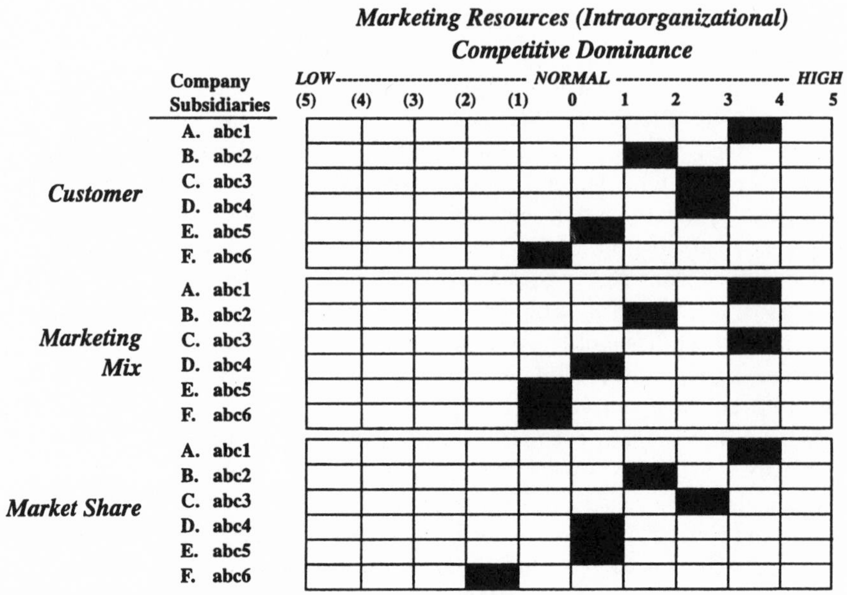

Ratings from Market Power Analysis
Source: *Marketing as a Means to Achieve Organizational Ends* (West Haven, CT: University of New Haven Press.

the same tasks would have to have been done at the market power analysis level for consistency. In the assessment of market share, abc 1 gets a +4, abc 2 a +2, abc 3 a +3, abc 4 a +1, abc 5 a +1, and abc 6 a -2. What KSA can abc 1 and abc 3 share in this category to help the others?

## Market Power Assessment Chart Summary

A market power assessment is the responsibility of the chief executive officer of the corporation and its board of directors. It is their job to coordinate the market power analysis and the market power assessment to benefit the organization. The analysis and assessment are founded on a principle of Oriental military strategy: know yourself and know your enemy. To know only oneself may allow one to win half of the time, but to know both oneself and one's enemy may allow one to win all of the time.

The analysis and assessment should not be exploited for political aims. The leader should select those who can and will do the job. Trust must be established between those who do the analysis and assessment and the organization's leadership. Without trust of the people who provide information the leader will not be willing to assume the risks required to make changes. All members of the company, however, should make their input available. The model resembles those adopted by the military. Those who are not selected to develop the strategy for a war are still expected to implement that strategy. If the strategy fails, all face death, metaphorically speaking, the same is true in business. A failed strategy may mean the destruction of the business.

The market power analysis and assessment should be carried out before direction is set. Those in the organization must not view this activity as the work of a specialized group but as a clearinghouse for information on their own company and its competition. As information is acquired, all employees have the responsibility to make their KSA available to their company. Three limits should be placed on the information gathering activity: it should not be illegal, immoral, or unhealthy. These suggested limits may be cultural and might be rejected by others who have a different worldview. A wealth of information can be gathered using honest methods. Once the analysis and assessment are completed, the leader must select an organizational end for all to follow.

## End

At the completion of the market power analysis and assessment, the CEO and the board of directors have the responsibility to set one organizational end. Only one end is selected at a time to prevent individuals from working at cross-purposes. When each person understands how his or her effort affects the achievement of the collective aim, this aim is more likely to be accomplished. The end must be absolutely clear to everyone in the organization.

Those who do not or cannot work toward that end must be convinced that their jobs depend on their accomplishing their tasks. The end as a target determines all decisions. Only the CEO, with the approval of the board of directors, can change the end. Once the end is selected, the CEO has the responsibility of ensuring that the entire organization follows that end. All others work toward the means to achieve that end. Although the CEO should not forgo the responsibility for selecting the means, others also need to contribute and take responsibility for actions to achieve the end. All actions then become a means to the end. The final arbiter in any dispute is the CEO, who is ultimately responsible for all actions within the organization.

### The Selection of an End

The end is initially selected from four alternatives: change or maintain market share, maximize profits, diversify risk, and return on shareholder equity. The CEO, however, may select from other possible ends that may evolve. Some have suggested that the organization should strive to achieve a monopoly as its end. At this point, this is conceptualized as an underlying philosophy in action (theory) and not as a particular end (such as maximizing profits).

Market share is achieved by blocking competitors from access to targeted markets. Maximization of profits is achieved by blocking competitors from targeted markets. Diversifying risk and return on shareholder equity are achieved by blocking competitors from access to targeted markets. When one end is selected over another, the means change. To block competitors from access to targeted markets, different means are employed to achieve different ends, as explained below.

*Market Share as an End*

When an organization selects market share as an end, it applies its means to change or maintain its percentage, unit, or dollar volume in comparison to the competition. Market share can be deceptive because many alternatives may be employed to measure it. The measure of market share also depends on the company's selection of its competition in particular geographic or product areas. Market share is also time-dependent; thus, it should be calculated in terms of a specific time frame. The concept of market share should be clarified before any numbers are acted on by anyone in the organization.

Market share may be a source of confusion because it may be an end or a means. The clarification of market share and the other possible ends is accomplished by establishing both a terminal and an enabling objective. (Terminal objectives are discussed in this module, whereas enabling objectives are discussed in the "Process" module). (A more in-depth analysis of market share is found in the marketing resources module.)

*Maximizing Profits as an End*

The organization selecting the end of profit maximization moves most of its available money to the bottom line within a particular time frame. Profit maximization is different from making a profit. Many companies do not have to make a profit to survive, and, indeed, thousands of large and small businesses continue to survive without making a profit. Profit is what is left after all the debts, including taxes, are paid. Companies making a profit can take several actions to reduce profits. Some of the obvious actions are hiring more people, increasing the salaries of present employees, purchasing new equipment, expanding into new areas, adding more money to research and development, spending more on advertising, and increasing dividends to shareholders. The list is endless. When the end is to maximize profits, a company does not allocate money to many of these areas so that it can move most of the available money to the bottom line.

Many American organizations (especially stock-held organizations) have destroyed their future and perhaps the future of the nation by seeking short-term profit. Profit maximization is not always the wrong course of action, but it should be undertaken with great caution. However, a company can and should attempt to break even when it has selected one of the other ends. It is a matter of how much profit is gained and at what cost to the future.

*Diversifying Risk as an End*

This end is to limit the firm's exposure in a particular targeted market or markets. Many companies find themselves in businesses that for various reasons may be too dependent on particular products or services. U.S. tobacco companies, for example, aim at risk diversification. Although these businesses have been profitable, management believed that the tobacco business would decline in the United States because of health-related issues.

Many companies in the defense industry may now have to switch their ends from profit maximization to risk diversification as the demand for defense goods and services lessens in the post–cold war era. Preliminary observation is that instead of making the shift, they have been laying off employees to cut costs. These companies still maintain the end of profit maximization because it requires an exceptional leader to articulate clearly a new direction for the company. A company may limit its risk by combining with firms in other sectors of the economy, or by exploring ventures built on the strengths of its present position. Present strengths include all organizational resources ("5Rs"), not just one product or service. In the past, companies have used a product or service prospective to diversify. This has limited the concept of risk diversification and its potential for use as an end.

### Return on Shareholder Equity as an End

Many corporate leaders are driven to increase the stock prices of their companies. When executive salaries are linked to increases in the stock's selling price, the companies' actions (means) reflect that direction. Many have exploited this end, and the future of many firms has been sacrificed for personal greed. Some of the more obvious effects of trying to gain short-term returns on shareholder equity are the destruction of research and development departments, massive layoffs, and the selling of profitable subsidiaries.

This whole area must be explored to create a system enabling a firm to acquire short-term capital in a less destructive way. The abuses now far outweigh the benefits. Return on shareholder equity continues to drive a short-term mentality, with little if any movement toward positive change, in spite of the nearly universal criticism. Often, CEOs, in order to increase their bonuses, have focused on raising the stock price. In the process, they have destroyed the lives of millions of U.S. workers. Return on shareholder equity as a measurement tool should not be generally emphasized as a corporate end; it should only be used in extreme circumstances. There are times when it is an appropriate end, but those times are rare.

### End and Terminal Objectives

After selecting one of the discussed four ends, the CEO has to offer some clarifications. For example, announcing that the company's end is market share is a step in the right direction, but this announcement requires clarification that is provided by a terminal objective. A terminal objective is a clearly articulated written statement describing the company's expectations concerning responsibilities and performance standards. CEOs and the board of directors, however, have traditionally preferred vague and noble statements, mainly because no one (least of all the CEO) wants to be measured.

Management consultants have convinced a generation of CEOs that they should not be concerned with the day-to-day operations of the company but should think about and plan for its future. This advice appealed to many CEOs and boards because it alleviated much of their operating responsibility. In the United States, football coaches are held to a higher standard than corporate leaders are because the measurement standards are clearer in football. A terminal objective enables others to assess the actions of the CEO and the board of directors against a clear standard that they have set for themselves. It is also a reminder to all within the company of the direction that should drive the daily behavior of each employee.

**Terminal Objective**

A terminal objective has four components: audience, behavior, condition, and degree (ABCD). The ABCD model was adapted from the National Special Media Institutes' instructional objectives model (see figure 8). The same four components are applied to assess each organizational end. The definition of each component remains the same although the end may change. Responsibility and performance standards are determined within a clear, formalized time frame. These criteria place the accountability for all actions and outcomes on the CEO and board of directors.

## Figure 8
## Terminal Objective

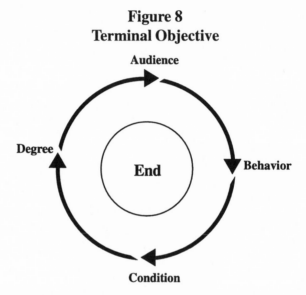

Adapted from: *National Media Institutes* (Syracuse, NY).

It is recommended that both privately and publicly held firms set direction through a market power analysis and market power assessment and select one end and a terminal objective. The process helps clarify and enhance thinking. When the underlying philosophical foundation of a company is to unify knowledge, skills, and attitudes, then this process has value for all participants. These activities represent a new clarification and commitment to a particular direction. Only the CEO and the board of directors can change the terminal objective because they continue to assume the final responsibility. The entire terminal objective should be stated in fewer than fifty words on a single page. It is simplified so that it can be easily understood.

*Terminal Objective: Audience*

The term "audience" implies an obligation being assumed by at least one person. The audience for a terminal objective is the CEO and the board of directors. The concept of management by objectives attempted to formalize work activities and expectations. The original idea was sound but the organization of the idea in practice became too complicated. The organizational end must be clearly defined, and responsibility for that end must rest on the CEO and the board of directors. Specific names are linked to the terminal objective so that there is no question that the leadership of the firm understands what it has determined to be the end for the entire organization.

*Terminal Objective: Behavior*

Behavior represents the actions to be carried out in the terminal objective. This concept must be absolutely clear to all participants. The terminal objective can be expressed in terms of tasks and subtasks. A task is a well-defined unit of work. A subtask is one component of a task. The behavior component of a terminal objective can have only four possible statements: change/maintain market share, maximize profits, diversify risks, or return on shareholder equity. These statements should be written in exactly this way, with the only deviation being in the selection of the word "change" or "maintain" to refer to the market share. If the CEO and board of directors select "maximize profits" as an end, then the behavior component would read "maximize profit" and nothing else. The same is true if they choose to "diversify risks" or "return on shareholder equity." These should be the only written statements under behavior and task. The company may also clarify the subtask. For example, if the terminal objective is stated as the task "to change market share," subtasks might include "to increase the number of customers," "to increase dollar volume," and or "to increase the units sold." There is no mention at this point of how much the company wants to increase the number of customers. This is a part of the fourth and final element, called "degree." The next element is "condition."

*Terminal Objective: Condition*

The "condition" element is comprised of the limitations and restrictions that will be placed on the evaluation of the terminal objective. Condition is the length of time that the CEO and board of directors have to achieve the behavior component. Limitations are influenced by the company's market power. By placing the constant of time on the terminal objective, the evaluator may compare behavior with the degree component (as discussed below). For example, the "condition" will be achieved by June 17, 1996, or by August 18, 1997. The time frame must be specific.

*Terminal Objective: Degree*

The "degree" component represents the performance level to be achieved by the CEO and the board of directors. The leadership of the firm sets the performance standards to be accomplished by the firm. The "degree" component returns to the behavior component and sets a specific performance for the task and subtasks. The tasks of changing market share, maximizing profits, diversifying risk, and creating a return on shareholder equity may be expressed in percentages (for example, a 20 percent increase). The "degree" component may also be expressed as a dollar figure, a unit volume, or a specific stock price.

**Conclusion**

The setting of the direction for the organization is one of the most important activities in which the CEO and board of directors will participate. All actions that occur in the organization follow from the direction that has been set. There must be one end and one terminal objective at a time. The CEO and board of directors are responsible for setting this direction and ensuring that all follow it until they (and only they) change that direction.

The first step is to do a market power analysis, which, applying the five resources (5Rs), compares the organization's subsidiaries with their competition. The company then does a market power assessment: it assesses the individual subsidiaries by comparing their results on the market power analysis. From the analysis and assessment, the leader (CEO) and the board of directors select one organizational end from the four possible choices: change/maintain market share, maximize profits, diversify risk, and return on shareholder equity. Once one of the four elements is selected, it is clarified through a terminal objective. The terminal objective is organized into four components: audience, behavior, condition, and degree (ABCD). The terminal objective is a brief statement of the intent of the CEO and board of directors. All activities then become a means to achieve this end.

**SELECTED READINGS**

Berry, Leonard, and A. Parasuraman. *Marketing services: Competing through quality.* New York: The Free Press, 1991.

Hughes, Charles L. *Goal setting: Key to individual and organizational effectiveness.* New York: American Management Association, 1965.

Kaufman, Roger. *Identifying and solving problems: A systems approach.* 3d ed. San Diego: University Associates, 1982.

Morris, David. *Marketing as a means to achieve organizational ends.* 4th ed. West Haven, Conn.: University of New Haven Press, 1994.

Ohmae, Kenichi. *The boarderless world. Power and strategy in the interlinked economy.* London: Harper Collins, 1994.

Porter, Michael E. *Competitive advantage.* New York: Free Press, 1985.

# Structure (Leadership)

Structure is defined as the working relationships between employees in an organization. The structure of a firm evolves from the underlying operating system of the members of the society. A structure evolving from a pluralistic philosophy is far different from that evolving from a unitary one.

## PLURALISTIC

American management theory and practice have created separate and specialized organizational structures, group structures, leadership structures, and individual structures. From a pluralistic position, an organizational structure represents the manner in which people are assembled to work within the firm. Group structure is the arrangement of people within work groups. Leadership structure is the power relationship with groups. Individual structure relates to the different categories defining how people are managed.

### Organizational Structure

The structure of an organization can be divided into four configurations: functional, divisional, strategic business unit, and matrix. Each configuration divides the organization into smaller and, therefore, supposedly more manageable elements.

#### Functional Organizational Structure

An organization configured on a functional basis combines the types of work that have similar or overlapping activities. The arrangement of early American railroads was based on a functional approach. This organizational structure has influenced, for 150 years, the configuration of large organizations within the United States. In this model, separate functional areas have evolved, such as marketing, finance, accounting, purchasing, operations, human resources, and information systems. These areas are often organized into departments, and the departments, in turn, are subdivided into smaller departments within the functional area. Specialists are trained not only in a particular functional job, but also in specialties within a function. The marketing function, for example, may have specialists such as marketing researchers and sales managers. Job loyalty and advancement is limited to the functional area. Many American corporations move managers interested in upper management between functions in order to expose them to all aspects of the business. Those who do not make it to the top return to a functional area.

### Divisional Organizational Structure

Divisional structure can be organized by product or geography. In the product divisional structure, the firm organizes itself in terms of a product or product lines. A firm selling tools, for example, could organize itself in terms of large power tools, small power tools, and hand tools. The functional areas within a divisional structure may be centralized or separated by product lines. This type of structure offers the advantage of enabling managers to identify specific profits and losses in a particular product category. Companies can expand this concept to include a multidivisional structure where several products are combined. The tool company could create a "tool" division that includes all types of tools and then divide the company into other divisional configurations.

When a divisional structure is organized on geographical terms, the same products are divided according to specific sales regions. The East Coast and West Coast, for example, may sell the same product, but the responsibility for those sales would be delegated to separate internal organizations. To justify this type of organizational structure, its advocates argue that different areas of the country (or the world) require a different approach to running the business. They suggest that, because laws, customs, and customers differ from one region to another, specialists must be employed to organize the sale of a product or products according to unique geographical, political, and demographical requirements.

### Strategic Business Unit Organizational Structure

An organization with a strategic business unit (SBU) structure arranges groups by divisions. Companies are then divided into autonomous business units functioning as separate entities, operated by the parent company with minimal interaction with each other. The SBUs are organized by markets, products, shared resources, and profit responsibilities. This separating, it is believed, is the optimal means to attain success. Although it is suggested that the SBUs should fit into the overall company strategy, resources are viewed as separate means to achieve that end. The SBU structure presumably ensures more individual accountability and creates an internal competitive environment.

### Matrix Organizational Structure

A matrix organization model attempts to decentralize power by assembling different groups to perform particular tasks. Once these tasks are completed, the groups are dismantled and reassembled to do another task. The matrix model has maintained the functional arrangement and, in essence, works by enabling employees from different functional areas to participate in a project. This has created a dual chain of command: employees work for one boss on the matrix project but still report to the boss in their functional area. The members of a matrix group are responsible for the successful completion of the project although their own functional area may often be hindering its success. At the end of the project, the employees will most likely return to their functional assignment. This position may impede the employees' ability to work within the matrix group.

The matrix structure was created because the larger organizational structure of the company was believed to be interfering with the rapid development of new products and services. The organization assembles representative employees from specialized functional areas to work specifically on a particular project. This group is then freed from the organizational bureaucracy and is able to cut through the red tape to bring out the new product or service in a more timely and efficient manner. The matrix model creates within the company mini companies to work on particular projects.

## Group Structure

Several modes of group structure are available to a corporation. In some companies, the organizational structure and group structure are coordinated. Many American corporations have adapted their group structure to the organizational structure. Recent developments, however, have begun to distinguish between and separate the two structures. This has led to a situation where the organizational structure and group structure are not matched. The following examples are representative of the available thinking in management. They reveal the pluralistic underpinning of group structure. Functional, divisional, SBU, and matrix organizational structures affect the makeup of group structure in the organization because the work groups that should be organized are the ones that support the organizational structures. These structures have become so pluralistic that a finance department may be organized on one structure and a marketing department on another.

### Scientific Management Group Structure

Scientific management was put forth by Frederic Taylor of Harvard at the turn of the twentieth century. Taylor proposed that all operations can be broken down into component parts. After measuring these components, management can find methods to improve all operations. Taylor proposed that management be conceptualized as a science. Thus, the field has to apply scientific principles to solve management problems, and workers should be trained in scientific methods as a part of the new scientifically based organization. The responsibility of management is to apply these new methods in order to optimize output. The manager establishes an optimal production environment by assessing areas such as time studies, physical positions of workers, and the amount of rest that workers require. Taylor's view of the organization is alive and well in business education and practice. The quality movement is founded on the same underlying principles.

## Quality Circles Group Structure

Quality circles are made up of small groups of employees who perform a particular job. These employees meet to discuss methods to improve quality, production, and working conditions. The members of the quality circle are often trained in the areas of statistical controls, problem solving, and group processes. The members work together to improve methods for getting their jobs done. Quality circles assume that those who do the job are best able to improve it. Because quality circles create more ownership of the changes identified by the group, the members are more likely to make the required changes. Group pressures may also contribute to employee implementation of any actions recommended by a quality circle.

## Statistical Process and Control Group Structure

Statistical process and control solves problems through a physical change in a process. Selecting the appropriate course of action requires accurate and relevant data. This is accomplished through a circular model comprised of five phases: analysis, design, development, implementation, and evaluation—known here by the acronym ADDIE. The ADDIE model provides a circular methodology to achieve process optimization. (The module "Process" explains this in great detail). The changes in a statistical process, as in all processes, are derived from the ADDIE model. Of course, employees may also use their intuition within a process. The ADDIE process is not limited to statistical control. Process is to force consistency of action. All employees are taught how to monitor their work in a continuous effort to improve the quality of their performance. The quality-control advocates have failed to conceptualize that process and statistics are different issues.

## Sociotechnical Systems Group Structure

Eric Trist in the 1950s proposed that a job has two components: technical and social. Both components must be emphasized within the organization. In this system, the total work system and work groups and teams are emphasized over individual effort. Jobs and work are designed to integrate people and technology.

## Leadership Structure

Several theories of leadership structure have evolved within pluralistic organizations. Many of these theories of leadership are in contrast to both organizational structure and group structure. Leadership theories in the United States have generally evolved from the fields of psychology and organizational behavior. From this pool of theories, corporate employees select one or more that they determine will help them accomplish their goals. Many employees believe that they need a distinct leadership style each time the circumstances change: under certain conditions, it is the leader's responsibility to adjust to the employees and, in others, it is the employees' responsibility to adjust to the leader. In many situations in business, it is now proposed that leadership is unnecessary. Proponents of such a theory believe that people can lead themselves. The following is a partial list of pluralistic leadership theories that may or may not be selected by any employee.

## Theory "X"

Theory "X" developed by Douglas McGregor in 1960 maintains that employees inherently dislike work and have little ambition. They try to avoid work at all cost. To get the job done, they must be coerced, controlled, and threatened with punishment. It is the role of the leader to monitor employee performance continually. Any employee who fails to perform adequately must be punished. Employees, it is assumed, are willing to do anything to avoid responsibility and work. They want only security and direction on their job. Communication is top down.

## Theory "Y"

McGregor also put forth Theory "Y," which considers work a natural activity like play. Humans want to work to achieve their potential. Thus, employees exercise self-control and self-direction in their jobs. They seek out responsibility and rewards for their efforts. The leader's role is to nurture and to direct the employees whenever they request assistance. The employees' true potential and ability is seldom utilized by the organization. Communication is both top down and bottom up.

## Theory "Z"

William Ouchi in 1982 proposed Theory "Z," which defines the work relationship that the Japanese supposedly have embraced. Employees are given great personal freedom to achieve well-defined objectives. Their potential is developed through formal education, training programs, and work experience. They are involved and participate in the company's decision-making process. Objectives of the team take precedence over individual objectives. The organization does not have clearly defined leadership roles. Although they can be temporarily configured to achieve specific objectives, work relationships are impermanent. Age and number of years of service determine the promotion within the organization. The requirement to build consensus slows the reaction time within this type of organization. There is a low level of functionalism where anyone may contribute to the group without fear of rejection.

## Situational Leadership

The Hersey and Blanchard model of leadership advocates a situational approach to leadership. In this model, leadership has two variables: the task-oriented behavior, or the amount of time a leader must spend in outlining roles to subordinates, and the relationship-oriented behavior, which deals with the personal relationship between a leader and followers. A leader adjusts to each employee according to these variables of task and the relationship. As the task and relationship skills of the employee improve, the amount of energy expended by the leader to accomplish the job requirements should decrease. Leaders should do their best in assisting those who require more task and relationship support.

## Leadership Traits

The trait theory of leadership identifies the characteristics or traits of successful leaders. It demonstrates the effects of factors such as educational level, intelligence and persistence in those who have already proven their leadership abilities. Once these traits are understood, an organization can identify them in younger employees and set up training programs to develop and improve these traits. Much of the work on leadership in the U.S. military seeks to identify and develop leadership traits.

## Maslow's Hierarchy of Needs

In 1954, Abraham Maslow developed a theory proposing that people possess a hierarchy of needs. This hierarchy is comprised of five categories which, in descending order, are self-actualization, esteem, socialization/affiliation, security, and physiology. Self-actualized individuals work at their full potential. Those who need esteem require respect and recognition from others. Those who have socialization/affiliation needs require belonging to and interacting with other people. Those who need security wish for freedom from pain and illness. The most basic needs, according to Maslow, are physiological—for example, sex, food, and water.

Maslow believes that the lowest level on the hierarchy must be satisfied before one can move to the next level; that is, if one lacks food, one is not concerned with security or affiliation. A leader who applies this hierarchy tries to move employees to the top of the hierarchy, to self-actualization regardless of their particular job.

## McClelland Achievement Motivation

David McClelland's theory of achievement motivation is divided into three categories of needs: achievement, power, and affiliation. Individuals who have a strong need for achievement are constantly searching for experiences that enhance personal responsibility. They tend to work very hard at a task, but once the task is completed, they forget about it and move on to the next task. This quality in leaders may interfere with their long-term approach to an organizational end. Because of their need for new achievements, they may not be able to sustain activities because of a search for new achievements. A leader with a high need for achievement may become easily bored, which can affect performance.

A person with a high need for power has a need to control people and situations. This need for power can be socially beneficial, but in some people, it can interfere with organizational means and ends. If this need controls the chief executive officer (CEO), the organization can become a tool of the leader's personal power drive. When the organizational requirements and the leader's drive are out of sync, the result can only be disastrous for the company. On the other hand, it can be a winning combination if they are coordinated.

Those who have a high need for affiliation strive to establish friendly and warm relations with people. In extreme cases, however, a leader's high need for affiliation may interfere with human-resource decisions that require layoffs or firings.

Such leaders may be unwilling or unable to make decisions because of their need for affiliation.

## Herzberg Two-Factor Theory

Frederick Herzberg's two-factor theory is composed of a "satisfiers/motivator" factor and a "dissatisfiers/hygiene" factor. Satisfiers include achievement, advancement, and a challenging job. Dissatisfiers include pay, work rules, and fringe benefits. The opposite of satisfaction, according to Herzberg, is not dissatisfaction but rather no satisfaction. Intrinsic and extrinsic factors lead to satisfaction or dissatisfaction. It is the leader's role to move employees away from dissatisfiers and toward satisfiers. Thus, the leader can motivate employees with this reward system.

## Path-Goal Theory

The path-goal theory of leadership links leadership behavior to follower satisfaction and the amount of effort expounded by a follower. This theory is founded on expectancy theory, which views individual motivation as a rational choice process. This choice is derived from the followers' perception that a particular behavior will determine the particular outcome. The leader modifies and manipulates these expectancies in the followers to attain the desired results. According to this theory, the leadership can adopt four sets of behavior: directive, supportive, participative, and achievement orientated. The directive leader informs followers as to their expectations. The supportive leader is helpful and considerate. The participative leader seeks out the aid of followers. The achievement-oriented leader sets goals for followers to accomplish. The underlying premise of the theory is that followers are capable of adjusting to these different leadership styles as long as they feel that the leader's style will help them accomplish their goals.

## Transformational Leadership

A transformational leader encourages and motivates people to perform better than they think they could. Such a leader, often described as charismatic or inspirational, generally emerges when the organization is in transition or under stress. This leader can rise from within the organization or be brought in from the outside. Because leadership is embedded in the culture of the organization and the society at large, a transformational leader may appeal to the underlying values of his or her employees.

## Individual Structure

Organizations that follow a pluralistic philosophy— separating organizational structure, group structure, and leadership structure—are divided into five individual group managing categories: top or senior management, middle management, first-line management, support staff, and labor.

Top managers are the CEOs and vice presidents. Middle managers are department managers and directors. First-line managers are supervisors and foremen. The support staff supports both the line and staff employees; for example, a secretary can work in many different line and staff positions. Labor is made up of the skilled and unskilled employees who work with machines to assemble and build products. Each group views its role as separate and distinct from those of others. Responsibility and control of each job category is unique to the particular location of the employee within any of these categories.

Each of these categories has been subdivided into line and staff. Line top management, middle management, first-line management and support staff employees have direct decision-making responsibilities over profit generation. For example, line employees are responsible either for the factory area where the product is actually made or for the sales area that calls on the customers. The staff division within top and middle management, first-line staff management, and support staff assist the line employees. For example, the human resource area assists in the hiring of employees but has no line responsibility. Line jobs are generally perceived as being better or more prestigious. Successful line experience is a road to top management, and few make it to top management without line experience.

Within each of the five categories, there are line and staff specialized groups. Large American corporations have developed many functional specialties, and in these companies, employees are valued for their functional specialization over all else. Salary and promotion are linked to specialization. This linkage reinforces the division into top management, middle management, first-line management, support staff, and labor.

*Top Management*

Top management is a group with distinct responsibility and accountability. The individual generally moves into the top management because of a successful career in middle management. Individuals can be selected for top management positions from within the firm or from the outside. When selected from within the organization, those in top management share many experiences with the other employees. Bringing in top management from the outside indicates to the employees that no one among them can do the job. The board of directors hires the CEO, but once hired, the CEO is responsible for selecting the other members of the top management team. Often, individuals with line experience are placed as heads of strategic business units. In some cases, a staff individual is selected to oversee the SBUs.

A company with an SBU structure may have a vice president at the corporate headquarters for each specific function, such as marketing, strategic planning, human resources, and quality. When these groups are located at the company's headquarters, the responsibility of reporting is not at the SBU level. When this occurs, the issue of to whom those in the functional areas (such as marketing or planning) are responsible is unanswered. Is it the functional group such as marketing at headquarters or the SBU?

In this type of organization, top management tends, to become isolated. It often interacts with only a small group of people; it interacts less often with middle management, support staff, and labor unless the company faces a particular problem. At these times of crisis, the role of top management is often considered destructive.

Many profess that the CEOs are supposed to keep their distance in order to be unemotional when they have to lay off or fire people. Thus, when the idea of management that "walks around" was introduced, it was a radical departure.

The CEO is generally concerned with the long-term direction rather than the day-to-day operations of the firm. The vice president of each SBU is responsible for all actions under his or her control. Headquarters finances these units, which are required to pay a part of their profits, called overhead, to support headquarters. Many in top management are paid bonuses for achieving particular goals. Utilizing the support functions at headquarters, the top managers of different SBUs compete with each other. The head of each SBU lobbies for a better allocation of company resources, generally financial, for his or her business unit. Resource allocation is often determined by the influence of the SBU top manager at headquarters. Many CEOs encourage and foster internal competition between SBUs. In this environment, the enemy is internal.

*Middle Management*

The work relationship between the middle managers in the SBUs and headquarters is derived from organizational structure. There is interaction with headquarters between functional vice presidents and members of a particular function, but if this does not exist, then middle management works entirely within its SBU. Middle managers, generally salaried employees, are organized by function. They view their power and value to the company in terms of their particular functions and SBUs. The job of the line middle manager has more prestige and advancement opportunities than those of the staff management within the SBU. Line middle managers are constantly devaluing staff middle managers and their employees. They argue that staff activities generate expense not revenue. Since the evaluation of line managers is based on the generation of revenue, line and staff management are in conflict at all levels of the organization. This conflict is further intensified when staff managers report at headquarters to a vice president who is not directly responsible to the line managers at a particular SBU.

The hostility, however, decreases when times are prosperous and increases when times are sparse. During difficult times of retrenchment, entire staff functions may be eliminated to save money. Since these interactions lead to a work environment full of strife, the top management may be unable to get middle management to accomplish its tasks.

*First-Line Management*

First-line managers are made up of supervisors and foremen. They are the link between middle management and labor. First-line managers, performing both line and staff functions because they exhibit an ability or interest in leading, are responsible for directing the labor force on a day-to-day basis. They are often, but not always, selected from the labor group. The labor force often has mixed feelings about these managers and frequently considers them the spies of management. Middle management often treats first-line managers as a necessary but untrustworthy group that has one duty: to implement their wishes. Consequently, the position of the first-line manager is one of the most difficult within the company.

First-line managers rarely interact with top management, and their relations with middle management and labor are often strained.

## Support Staff

The support staff may or may not support the particular functional area. The members of the support staff may be secretaries or clerks. They may work in reception, maintenance, postal department, health services, copy center, cafeteria, and security. They may or may not belong to a union. They are often, but not always, hourly employees and are paid for overtime. Salaried secretarial employees can easily move between functional areas. The top performers are respected within the organization and can make a good wage. Those in maintenance, security, and health services are often in a world of their own, and as long as their tasks are done, they are left alone. They have little opportunity and often little interest (assuming that they like their jobs) to move out of their area to middle management. If the employee wants to move into middle management, it can be easily accomplished. The quality of the work of the support staff, when protected by a union, may range from exceptional to poor at best.

To avoid unions and save money, many companies are now subcontracting these services to outside firms. The hired individuals, although working at the company, are really employees of another firm. Individuals who work for the contract firms have little if any loyalty and commitment to the hiring firm. People are shifted between firms as required. The trend is to move more and more organizational activities to contract firms. Little formal direction comes from any level of management for many of these groups within this category. This is especially true when the support staff works for an outside firm or vendor. In the case of the secretarial staff, they report to a specific person or are part of a pool. When part of a pool, the secretaries have a manager who generally comes from the ranks of first-line supervisors. This attempt to reduce the cost of the support staff through outside contracting separates this group from the other groups in the organization.

## Labor

Labor represents the group that works with machines in the factory to make the products. In the automotive industry, for example, they are the workers on the assembly line who build the cars or trucks. This category of employee is a product of mass-production techniques that have evolved from the Industrial Revolution. Such employees are generally paid hourly wages and may or may not belong to a union. This group has been in conflict with American top management for more than a century. Until recently, this skilled workforce has been protected by the U.S. government. The top management has been forced to increase wages and benefits for labor. In 1960, during the Kennedy administration, the federal government forced the steel industry to raise wages and not prices. The relationship between labor and top management has changed as companies were able to move operations offshore. This has enabled corporations to reduce the cost of labor and in some cases improve quality. To avoid the regulation issues related to pollution of the environment and lawsuits for unsafe labor practices, companies have moved offshore or to Mexico.

The top management has never felt an obligation to labor; thus, when it can, it will close plants with no intent to reopen them. Labor can no longer count on strikes as a means of securing top management concessions. The situations where a strike can bring top management to labor's position are now the exception rather than the rule. President Ronald Reagan's firing of the air traffic controllers sent a message to top management that the government would no longer support the unions. This has created a working environment where labor has been destroyed by top management in the industrial sector of the workforce. Middle management and many in first-line management, following the lead of top management, are antilabor.

Although now uncertain of their future, those in the labor movement seem unwilling to change and still identify with a particular job or skill even when it is no longer marketable. This is not true in the government sector where labor is made up of middle management, first-line managers, and support staff. In this environment, labor remains powerful. The government will keep giving in to their pressures for more money and benefits out of tax dollars.

## Summary

From the pluralistic viewpoint, organizational structure, group structure, leadership structure, and individual structure are separate and distinct. Each area may or may not overlap. The organizational structure represents the manner in which the entire company is organized; group structure, the configuration of work groups; leadership structure, the power relationships between human beings; and the individual structure, the division of employees into top management, middle management, first-line management, labor, and support staff. Each area has several compartmentalized possibilities. It is conceivable for one organization to have several structures in place at the same time. These alternative structures contribute to an individualized experience rather than a collective and unified one.

## UNITARY

From a unitary perspective, organizational structure, group structure, leadership structure, and the individual structure would at worse overlap and at best be the same. Organization, grouping, leadership, and individuals represent overlapping relationships between people within the same organization. For this association to be optimized, the same underpinning relationship must be reflected in all aspects that affect work and structure. However, all optimized structures and work relationships will not always strive toward good and just causes. This optimization within one company may cause pain to the employees of competitors and may even force them out of business. The Japanese have optimized their business structure to the detriment of the United States and its workforce. Should Japan consider suboptimization so that more American workers will keep their jobs? Of course not. It is the responsibility of Americans to act in their own best interest. A revision of the U.S. business agenda—philosophically and practically—would seem to be in order. The following is a theory of leadership that includes all aspects of structure.

## Theory "W"

Theory "W" was developed by David Morris in 1986. It hypothesizes that the same tribal model of organizational structure has been in place for 100,000 years and that it will still be in place 100,000 years from now. It also hypothesizes that if one understands the relationship among leader, trusted follower, and support staff, one has a better chance of gaining the trust of any group, anywhere and at any time.

A fundamental analogy that explains the alliance between the members of a group is the primitive hunt. Hunting was a very dangerous activity, and the hunting of lions was one of the more dangerous hunts. There is little wonder that a relationship of trust had to be developed among hunters to ensure survival. Each hunter was entrusted with the lives of the other hunters. This trust had to be proven through deeds, not talk. Those who have been in this position will understand the following analogy; and those who have not should accept it as a lesson they will inevitably need, especially to hold a job.

A lion is coming down a path. I stand in the path, and you stand to the side. When the lion jumps to kill me, you throw a spear and together we will kill the lion. When the lion jumps, I do not want to hear you say, "Excuse me, Dr. Morris, I forgot to tell you I am a member of the Lion Savers Association, and I do not kill lions." I also do not want to hear, "I have not had the course Lion Killing 534, and I am unprepared." I especially do not want you to throw your spear at me when the lion is in the air because I would then have both a spear and a lion trying to kill me.

Another analogy is used to explain the relationship between leader and trusted follower. When hunting elephants, you must select the correct person to carry your gun. Only a few gun bearers are trusted by hunters to carry the elephant gun on the hunt. As the elephant charges, the hunter's hand reaches back for the gun. If the gun is not there because the gun bearer has run in fear, the hunter is dead. This same primal hunt goes on in your company every day, and the hunters are your boss and his or her boss. Every young person should ask, "How do I get the opportunity to prove myself to the hunter or hunters so that someday I, too, can be a hunter?" If you prove yourself through deeds, the hunters will do all they can to teach you how to be successful, and if you do not, they will protect themselves by excluding you. They may tell you what they think you want to hear, but you will not be on the hunt.

This testing begins at birth and at every time you enter a new group. Others may recommend you to a group, but the members of the group have to determine the final assessment for themselves. If you become part of a group because of a recommendation and then fail to live up to that recommendation, the recommender is no longer trusted. An application for employment is a request for group entry: therefore, the testing begins before you enter the group. The first test will be as risk-free as possible to the group members and leaders. If you fail the first test, you may be excluded, and if failure occurs after you enter, you may not be given another chance as long as you live. This book does not advocate the killing of lions or elephants, but the analogy holds and will continue to hold.

## Theory "W" and History

The primary focus of Neanderthal humans—110,000 years ago—was daily survival. The Neanderthal organized their society into small closed units ("tribes"), which were on never-ending quests for food. Tribes had little interrelationship with outsiders, and most of the knowledge gained was passed on within the tribe. Games and rituals were used to teach the young the knowledge required to ensure survival. Hunting and protecting the tribe were the most dangerous activities in daily life. Hunting required several participants, made up of the older male members of the tribe. The dominant "alpha male," or hunter warrior, led the hunter scouts with the assistance of the support staff (women and children).

The decisions of the hunter warriors had life-and-death consequences for the entire group. The hunter warrior's word was law until he was replaced by another hunter warrior from the ranks of the hunter scouts. Any person who could not keep up with the group was left behind to die. Young males and females were looked on as a group asset and were trained almost totally by the support staff of women. Boys, after a ritual rite of passage, were accepted for training by the hunter scouts. Girls, after a different ritual rite of passage, were accepted into their roles as women. The woman's role, although different from that of the man, was respected because it held great power and was of special importance for the group.

About thirty-five thousand years ago, Cro-Magnon humans developed sophisticated tools and hunting weapons. This development might have occurred because their brains were larger than that of the Neanderthal and the game was less abundant. With the addition of more sophisticated tools, the Cro-Magnon no longer relied solely on physical power to ensure tribal survival. This brought on a change in group dynamics: members could specialize because the group could support more members. The Cro-Magnon, however, did not change the organizational structure of leader, trusted follower, and support staff.

Gradually, nomadic tribes settled into particular areas, which became city-states and then nations. About 5,000 years ago, civilization was born independently in Iraq, Egypt, India, China, and Central America. Food acquisition no longer required as much time, and large numbers could be fed from surrounding farms. Law ensured marriage and family property. The laws were guaranteed by force, both secular and nonsecular. City-states allowed people to obtain market power by continuing to specialize and develop trades and skills. The areas of specialization were agriculture, crafts, art, business, education, medicine, law, religion, military, and politics. From these beginnings, three groups dominated: the political, the religious, and the military. These groups continued to be organized on the tribal model of leader, trusted follower, and support staff. The hunter warriors became kings/ emperors, religious leaders, and generals; the hunter scouts became the nobility, priests, and officers; the support staffs became serfs, worshipers, and soldiers.

## Theory "W" and the Modern Corporation

As the city-states evolved, so did the merchant class. This class focused on business and trade and continued to pattern itself on the tribal model of hunter warrior (leader), hunter scout (trusted follower), and support staff. The business enterprise—the modern corporation—that evolved in both Europe and Asia, continued to follow the Theory "W" tribal model, which was handed down for 100,000 years. Corporations in the United States which have veered from Theory "W," have developed separate autonomous work relationships where the individual is self-actuated and has great difficulty working in groups. Even these corporations in times of stress attempt to reinstate the Theory "W" model because it satisfies the primal human response to danger. Once a threat is perceived, whether real or imagined, this primal tribal relationship returns. The question must be asked: "Why do American corporations persist in their presumed need to replace it as a structural model?"

In Europe, Asia, and Africa, the tribal model has never been replaced. To de-emphasize hierarchy, the United States repudiated the concept of the tribal model. The design of the U.S. government after the Civil War was aimed at destroying the tribal affiliations of the diverse populations and unifying them into single nation. America was to be the melting pot of the world. The political shift to pluralism in the United States began after World War II and has been accelerating ever since. By the 1980s, this concept of "melting pot" had evolved into "pluralism," in which everyone is now free to move in his or her own direction.

*Theory "W": Leader*

The composition of the group determines the roles of each member. Within the same organization, a member may change roles several times a day. At one moment, the member is called on to be a leader, then to be a trusted follower, and still later to be support staff. No one assumes the role of leader at all times in life because life is multifaceted. For example, as a college professor, I am the leader in my classroom. I must win if any student challenges this role; otherwise, my effectiveness is lost. When I am with the university president, the provost, the dean, or the department chair, I am a trusted follower. With other members of the university community, I am support staff. My students are my trusted followers, but they are support staff to the school. Outside of class, students may work as managers, whereby they are leaders. They are also trusted followers to their managers and support staff to all others.

Leaders have two roles in relation to their trusted followers: mentoring and protection. As a mentor, the leader must teach his or her trusted followers how to do their jobs to ensure the tribes survival. All the knowledge, skills, and attitudes of the trusted followers are within the domain of the leader's advice and counsel. The leader must assist the trusted followers and tell them both individually and as a group where they can improve and what specific actions are required to enhance performance. The hunt is too dangerous for any trusted-follower dissension.

The leader must foster a relationship that does not create animosity among trusted followers. If any friction is identified, the leader must stop it in absolute terms. The trusted followers who cannot accept this law must be severed from the group because they can no longer be trusted to implement their assigned tasks. Internal dissension among trusted followers is so destructive that it can lead to the eradication of the group.

The leader must also protect at all costs a trusted follower who is implementing the leader's enabling objectives. If the leader's or the trusted follower's survival is at stake, then both should go down together, because to betray a trusted follower who is carrying out the leader's wishes sends a message to all potential trusted followers that the leader will not protect them when things get tough. The leader must be able to select and reject those working for him or her so that a trusted-follower relationship can evolve.

Human resources should have absolutely no power to force any employee on any leader's trusted-follower group. Employees can move to where the work requires, but a group can reject an untrustworthy member. The new member is expected to become, through deeds, the trusted follower of the new leader. The trusted followers are expected to prove themselves through actions, simple to complex. Regardless of their past accomplishments, the trusted followers must continue to prove themselves each day. Unfortunately, some work hard for a few years and then coast for the rest of their work life. Such employees should not be allowed to remain in the group.

If some trusted followers willfully betray their leader, then they must be let go from the organization. When some members betray one leader, then they are able to betray another. This betrayal is unacceptable and should not be tolerated. Also leaders are obligated never to say anything bad about one of their trusted followers to anyone. To do so is unnecessary, and if it gets back to the trusted follower, the relationship may be harmed. If that occurs, it is difficult to rebuild, and the rebuilding takes time that should be dedicated to doing the job. The enemy is always external.

*Theory "W": Trusted Follower*

All members of an organization are the trusted followers of their leader. The role of trusted follower is to implement the *terminal objective* ("Direction" module) of the organization with the *enabling objective* ("Process" module) for their job(s). The trusted followers must be dedicated to achieving these objectives each day. They must constantly learn about and improve themselves in all aspects of the work and life.

When in the role of trusted follower they must put the objectives of their leader and the entire organization above their own. Under no circumstance should one in the role of trusted follower say or do anything to harm the leader, another trusted follower, or any of the support staff. Trusted followers must take advice from their leader even if they believe it is incorrect (most of us tend to disagree with any advice that does not reinforce our desires). The leader's advice should be taken seriously. A trusted follower should perform with enthusiasm the leader's requests. However, if the request is considered immoral, illegal, or unhealthy, it should be questioned and its dangers pointed out to the leader. If the leader refutes or ignores the concerns of the trusted follower, then the latter should consider leaving the organization or getting a transfer to another part of the business. This course of action should be taken only under extreme circumstances. One may be confronted with such a decision once or twice in a lifetime. Many people seem to think that these "dilemmas" occur a hundred times a day; thus, they spend a great part of their life in unnecessary conflict about almost everything.

After leaving the group, trusted followers should not speak against their former leader even though they were unhappy. Generally, they should not say anything because they may not be informed enough to make a valid judgment. If the situation is severe enough, it should be mentioned in an informal way to the leader's leader. If trusted followers take their "complaints" outside of the group, they must be prepared for the rejection of the group. The enemy is always external.

*Theory "W": Support Staff*

In the tribal context, those not involved in the hunt are support staff. During the hunt, they ensured day-to-day operations at home by keeping things in order. They ensured the continuation of the tribe into the next generation. They produced the future leaders, trusted followers, and other support staff. They assisted in the gathering of food and were involved in its preparation and production. Their numbers were directly related to the prosperity of the group. When times were difficult, measures were taken to decrease their numbers: the old and very young were the first to be rejected, followed by the females. In some situations, a hunter warrior and his trusted followers and support staff moved off to start their own tribe.

In the Theory "W" model, those who are leaders or trusted followers are support staff to all other members of the organization. If they can assist in any way in the performance of anyone's particular job and the enhancement of the entire organization (tribe), they should do it. As support staff, they can do thousands of things a year to help others. They should not do so to take any credit. If they believe that they deserve credit, their productiveness as support staff will be diminished. When all employees are willing to help each other without expecting reward, their organization will be much more effective. If a person rejects your help, then help others. By helping, I mean, for example, driving someone to the airport, sending someone a client, sharing some good idea, working on a company activity, letting someone use your telephone, picking up a bottle in the parking lot. The list is endless.

## Theory "W" and Organizational Structure

There are some obvious overlaps between the organizational and tribal structures. Several of these structures are transferable. The size of the organization is directly related to the success of the hunt. Growth can be sustained only when tribal members are able to apply sufficient resources to achieve a purpose.

The hunt or the application of these resources depend on the interchangeable relationship among leader, trusted follower, and support staff. When this relationship is suboptimized, energy is diverted from a common purpose. Large groups with individually directed members who are unable or unwilling to work together for a common purpose require more resources to sustain themselves than groups of the same size whose members work together in harmony. The size of the tribe impacts structural nuances. The group generally ranges in number from thirty, as in the college classroom, to hundreds of thousands, as in large companies, and even to millions if nations are considered as tribes. Organizations and nations still hunt to survive. The hunt is dangerous, and many starve (i.e., go out of business) when they are unsuccessful at maintaining their tribal integrity.

The members of tribes have historically distrusted anyone outside their affiliation. This is manifested in many practices and policy decisions that revolve around protection and exclusion. In a pluralistic environment, the separations are at the functional and subfunctional levels of the organizations, whereas, in a unitary environment, they are much broader at the organizational, interorganizational, and even national levels. For example, the pluralistic position maintains that those with functional specializations do not have enough transferable skills to perform in other functional areas. A marketing person cannot easily move to human resources because it is viewed as a separate and distinct area of expertise. This notion is even applied to salespersons moving between different SBUs: a trained salesperson from one SBU is often perceived to be unable to sell the products from other SBU. Differences in organizational structure act as cognitive boundaries: the memberships of the organization are separated from each other because of their philosophy of business not because of their capacity to do the job.

The unitary perspective emphasizes the need to move separations as far back as possible by eliminating the functional organizational structure, the divisional organizational structure, the SBU structure, and the matrix structure. In a drive toward individualism, western, especially American, organizational theorists steeped in the pluralistic tradition have attempted to separate organizational structure far sooner than is necessary.

The organizational structure evolving from the unitary philosophy has combined separate aims to the point where nations like Japan are unified in a common purpose; thus, corporate practices and policies reflect a larger national direction and purpose. At this level, it is unimportant if the employee works in marketing, in human resources, or in different sales forces, and it is unimportant if the company sells steel or radios. These differences are structural barriers to the larger unified purpose that has evolved from a worldview, not from a specific theory.

The structure of an organization is not based on SBUs, geography, product lines, or functions. According to "Theory "W," structure is derived from the relationships among leader, trusted follower, and support staff. The tasks and subtasks (jobs) are assumed by those who are prepared for the responsibility. Organizational structure is derived from the relationship between people. The company assembles its people to achieve an organizational end. It does not first select the business units, geography, product lines, and functions and then place people into those configurations no matter what the particular end. It selects the end and then assigns people, who prove themselves in deeds, tasks, and subtasks to accomplish that end. The structure (means) to accomplish the end are derived from the end. The trusted employees will be trained to do the needed tasks (jobs); they are not trained for a function before the end is determined. Training by function will cause the function to become more important than the achievement of an organizational end.

*Theory "W" and Group Structure*

All group membership is organized based on the leader, trusted follower, and support staff model. Trusted followers move into positions where the leader believes they can do the best job for the company and the leader. In the beginning of a person's working career, these positions are not threatening to the group because the person is being assessed. The new employee either will falter or will be considered a trusted follower and be given more experiences. If he or she falters because of a lack in ability but is still trusted, then in all probability, the employee will be kept in a position in which he or she can perform. For these trusted followers, job exposures are then curtailed, and more challenging jobs are given to other trusted followers, with greater capacity. All jobs are important, and nonperformance affects the entire organization. The leader must not move trusted followers into positions beyond their KSA (knowledge, skills, and attitudes).

A misguided CEO can destroy a company. A secretary who does not perform on the job may cause problems but, most likely, will not destroy the company. Any company or organization can survive only a certain amount of nonperformance. Thus, it is critical for employees not to be moved into jobs before they are ready. A trusted follower who cannot do a job should be replaced and moved elsewhere. When the leader and trusted followers hold positions far beyond their capacities, the tribe is threatened. Many factors determine when a tribe will fail to maintain itself. Knowledge, skills, and attitudes are key to continued adaptation to the environment. The group must relearn itself back to stability. This can be a painful process.

When assessing a functional organization, the leader's perception of the value of any particular function can be quickly revealed. If the most trusted follower is vice president of marketing, then marketing is the most important resource to the leader at that time. All arguments showing the value of a function mean nothing when a distrusted person heads up that area. In many cases, a distrusted person may become the head of a functional area for political or legal reasons. In these cases, the lack of trust compromises the efficiency of the organization.

The management of secondary functional activities may also be given to a trusted follower who is not yet ready for high-risk exposures. Movement up the corporate ladder is determined by the amount of risk that the tribe is willing to take: how much risk can it tolerate from those who have not yet proven themselves trustworthy? If all is going well, a great deal is tolerated, but very little is tolerated when things are not going well. Those who are separated from the tribe are perceived to be expendable. If this separation is not made in the interest of the survival of the tribe, it may cause the extinction of the remaining members. A tribe should always keep those who are important to its present and future survival.

Distrust of outsiders is manifested in the group structure when one organization takes over or merges with another. At times when this occurs, the leader and trusted followers of the subordinate firm are eliminated by the dominant firm. The leader of the dominant firm selects his or her trusted followers for new positions in the combined firm. Resources are moved into the dominant firm, and as many of the employees of the outside company (tribe) as possible are let go. Parts of the company that are no longer desired are sold off or just discontinued and written off as a loss.

The new organizational structure is assembled from the membership of the winning tribe. Occasionally, a leader and trusted followers from the losing firm are able to make the transition, but they are usually suspect and are often let go later. Many friendly mergers have failed because the members who were no longer necessary could not be eliminated and because the combined organization was incapable of sustaining the same number of members.

In a pluralistic model of the organization, individuals are selected for certain jobs because of their specialized skills. Systems are developed to enhance specialized output. The role of each specialization is to perform a particular job. The sociotechnical model described earlier applies to functional specialization but focuses on the relationship between people and technology.

The "quality circles" method brings together employees attempting to share in job performance to complete a task. At this time, they discuss improvements that can be made in getting the job done. The West has totally misinterpreted the concept of quality circles as representing an environment without hierarchy, as individualism gone to extremes. In the unitary philosophy, the quality-circle activity possesses the tribal structure of leader, trusted follower, and support staff. Western management's pluralistic belief that it does not need to participate and that employees do not require management's insights and understanding to accomplish their jobs flies in the face of groups working together to achieve a common purpose. Western quality circles also fail because employees find security in functional specialization. Such employees cannot give up their self-interest for the benefit of the tribe.

*Theory "W" and Structure*

Theory "W" proposes that only one theory of leadership has stood the test of time. All individuals will return to this tribal group structure in times of stress no matter what other theory they have adopted. People always have focused on trust and protection as key factors in relationships. These are primal requirements that any type of leadership configuration has to fulfill. People have been grouped in terms of geography, religion, language, race, sexual preference, family, common experiences, political ideology, and education. The list is endless, but the drive to combine is the same.

The specific reason for the existence of a group is secondary at best. Humans want to be part of a group where the members trust each other. Because this trust has to be built on merit, people keep rejecting some members and searching for new ones. Membership in a group is not always voluntary. Many become members of a group by birth or by force. A hostile takeover of a firm and the military draft illustrate membership by force. If there is no mechanism for acquiring new members, many groups may ultimately die off. When the members of a group are not trained to become future leaders and trusted followers, their group will be taken over by rival groups that view them as outsiders presenting a threat or an opportunity for plunder.

The concept of functional specialist in the group must give way to that of the multifaceted individual. The separating models such as the functional, divisional, SBU, and matrix models reflect an outdated philosophy unequipped to compete in a global arena. This separating philosophy now hampers America's ability to survive. The matrix model, thought by many to be the wave of the future, has failed to have any success because the group structure is still based on the functional or separating approach. It is now even more confusing to participants because the matrix structure requires dual reporting. In a Theory "W" organization, the leaders, trusted followers, and support staff are trained to work and think across resource areas. Functions become resources or tools to be applied to achieve a clearly defined organizational end. There is no need for a marketing specialist. Marketing activity still has requirements, but it is no longer the domain of a special interest group that must protect it at the expense of the company (tribe).

*Theory "W" and Individual Structure*

The most difficult spurning for any individual is rejection from the group (tribe). The individual structures of top management, middle management, first-line management, support staff, and labor have created another structural level for separating within the organization. Individuals who see themselves as members of one of these groups have separated themselves from all others in the organization. Theory "W" avoids this problem because the individual is aware that each person is a follower of a leader, a leader to his or her followers, and support staff to all others. The movement of employees between jobs becomes less threatening to those within the organization. The value of employees to the organization does not reside in their specific functions (these can be taught), but in the relationships built on trust and deeds. Such relationships create a unified structure on which the entire organization can be designed. Organizational survival is determined by the model of leader, trusted follower, and support staff.

If we are not achieving our own expectations within the tribe, then we must work harder at building trust through deeds. If this cannot be done, we should do our best or leave. If we wish to share time and loyalty with other groups such as family, part-time job, and leisure-time activities, we must consider accepting a minor role in the corporation. The hunt requires a life-and-death commitment from the high-risk takers.

Pluralistic organizations now possess many members who seek positions of power while providing a minimal input. They want more money for less time spent on the job. Another pluralistic challenge is those that insist on advancement only within their functional specialization. This is one reason that the United States has had such a rise in middle management. These functions must be specifically staffed without any overlap.

When a separating system is encouraged and taken to extremes, a government-granted monopoly is ultimately required to protect it. In an effort to stabilize the private-sector workforce, the U.S. government itself has become a monopoly. It continues to go to employment extremes because of its position as a monopoly. The private sector does not have this type of support. Organizations like the American automobile companies have been unable to change their structure and the government has refused to grant them a monopoly. If they fail to adjust to the threat posed by outside competition and if the government does not give them market power, they will be blaming their failures on different individual group structures within their firms, yet the problem may be external. These companies should be given market power through regulatory policy and a change in antitrust laws. Because virtually all Americans are involved in the American automobile industry, all Americans need to rethink the way America does business.

## Theory "W": Historical Research

When I first developed Theory "W," I knew little if anything about Asia and Asian thought. While browsing at the Syracuse University library, I found a book by Yukio Mishima, *The Way of the Samurai*. I was astonished to learn that the Japanese had thought through the way of the warrior in such detail. The concepts are rarely if ever mentioned in Western business schools or in corporations, even though the tribal model has worked for 100,000 years and is still applicable in present society. The similarity of the Japanese insights to those of Theory "W" led to the revelation that the warrior principles are the same all over the world, always have been, and always will be. I started to understand the Japanese because I understood the concept of tribe and the way of the warrior. The more I learned about the way of the *samurai*, the more my research took me through Japan, China, India, Korea, the Middle East, Europe, and to the United States.

### *Miyamoto Musashi*

Miyamoto Musashi (1584–1645) was one of the most famous Japanese warriors. His *The Book of the Five Rings* (*Gorin no sho*) is a classic known today by hundreds of millions of people. Musashi's major principle is to know yourself and know your enemy. Musashi, influenced by Zen Buddhist philosophy, adopted simplicity, humility, and hard work as virtues. He was never defeated in battle. He described the knowledge required to be a warrior in terms of five rings: ground, water, fire, wind, and void. Musashi advocated that the warrior should have an understanding of all things and the way of all professions. He was a farmer, an artist, a sculptor, a writer, a teacher, and a soldier. He maintained that a person should not do anything that is purposeless. A warrior pays attention to the most minute details and learns to perceive things unseen by others. As a warrior, one must maintain a combat stance at all times and be prepared to die at any moment. He gives the reader several specific actions that should be taken in battle, such as feinting an attack, assessing the enemy's reaction, and in a stalemate, changing strategy. Learning, assessment, deception of the enemy, and preparation are the cornerstones of purposeful actions.

Musashi is said to have been eating in an inn when some bandits came in to rob him. Although he knew their intentions, he kept eating as if nothing were about to happen. A fly began to circle Musashi. He grabbed it effortlessly with his chopsticks then let it go. Seeing this, the bandits decided it was best to leave. Such legendary accounts have made Musashi a most venerated character in Japanese history.

### *Yamamoto Tsunetomo*

Yamamoto Tsunetomo (1659–1720), another Japanese, is credited with the dictating of the *Hagakure*, the classic *samurai* manual on *bushido* ("way of the warrior"). On the death of his lord in 1700, he chose to become a Buddhist priest and devote his life to the compilation of the *Hagakure* (recorded by *samurai* Yamamoto Tsunetomo and completed in 1716). According to Yamamoto, a proper life is dedicated to four vows: never be outdone in the way of the *samurai*; be of good use to the master; be filial to your parents; manifest great compassion for the sake of mankind.

The way of the *samurai* is death, and a warrior should start each day by dying. If you fear death, this will hinder your judgment. Hardship causes rejoicing because it is through hardship that warriors can learn about themselves. Wisdom comes after the age of forty (in Japanese corporations, employees are assessed and perceived as novices until they reach the age of forty). A life is built on one resolution after another. Never miss an opportunity, and concentrate on the moment. Do not encourage weakness in times of disorder: life lasts but an instant. A *samurai* should take menial tasks most seriously. Many of these suggestions for daily action are founded on Buddhist principles of discipline and hard work. The *Hagakure* has had a profound effect on the thinking of the Japanese. It continues to be apparent in their lives and culture.

### Sun Tzu

The foundations of the Japanese way of the warrior can be traced to the influence of the Chinese Sun Tzu (400–320 B.C.). In his *The Art of War*, he wrote that war should be studied. Since it deals with life and death, it should be taken seriously. War is assessed in terms of five factors: moral influence, weather, terrain, command, and doctrine. These are similar to Miyamoto Musashi's five rings.

It is the generals' (warriors') job to assess these factors in relation to themselves and the enemy. Victory can be predicted when the general knows when to fight, how to use force, when the ranks are unified, when to wait, and when to avoid the interference of nonmilitary rulers. Sun Tzu advised the warrior to scrutinize the enemy's strategies to determine the enemy's patterns of thinking. David Morris applies ADDIE as part of an operating system to ascertain patterns (see the "Process" module). Probe to learn about the enemy. Determine the disposition (habits) of the enemy on the battlefield. Make sure that the enemy cannot determine *your* ADDIE. Your ADDIE must be kept secret so that the enemy will not be able to achieve victory. When the conditions of the battle change, then one must be able to adjust to these changes as they occur. This is why you should remain undefinable to the enemy. All warfare is based on deception. When you are strong, pretend you are weak; when you are weak, pretend you are strong. Lure your enemy with gain; feign disorder and then attack. Where the enemy is weak, attack. Where the enemy is strong, avoid him (or her).

Sun Tzu's story of a horse race illustrates one of many strategic lessons available to the warrior: A head of a kingdom had to race his three horses against three from another kingdom. He was advised that, to win, he should match his slowest horse against the other's fastest. His fastest against the other's second fastest and his second fastest against the other's slowest. This will ensure victory of two out of three of his horses. Victory comes from knowledge, skills, and attitudes and their creative applications.

### Romance of the Three Kingdoms

The Chinese anthology *Romance of the Three Kingdoms* was compiled during the Ming Dynasty (A.D. 1368–1644). The stories of the *Romance of the Three Kingdoms* take place after the fall of the Han Dynasty. The stories describe interpersonal relationships, both good and bad, during a turbulent time in Chinese history. The accounts of battles and their associations with the characters have been providing the Chinese with lessons in strategy for over a thousand years. Today, Chinese from both the People's Republic of China and Taiwan continue to study the *Romance of the Three Kingdoms* in school. An enduring classic, it demonstrates the importance of discipline and strategy in one's quest for personal success.

One example among its hundreds of stories is "K'ung-Ming Borrows Arrows." In this tale, Chou Yu wants to have K'ung-Ming, the great strategist, killed, so he makes K'ung-Ming agree to supply arrows for an upcoming battle. After accepting responsibility for the project K'ung-Ming is told that he has to deliver 100,000 arrows within ten days. Although he knows that if he fails, he will be put to death, K'ung-Ming insists that ten days was too long and the task should be completed in only three days. To ensure failure, Chou Yu orders the workmen to delay their production of arrows.

K'ung-Ming assembles twenty boats on the third day and fills them with straw. On the third night, he moved the boats out into the river and into the fog. He formed a line of boats in the water outside the enemy camp and began to beat drums and shout. From shore, the enemy, fearing an attack, shoot hundreds of thousands of arrows at the oncoming fleet. K'ung-Ming then moved his boats—laden with enemy arrows—safely downriver. Therein lies a fundamental principle of strategy: accomplish the task by using the enemy's resources.

## The Mahabharata

The *Mahabharata* is perhaps the longest epic poem ever written. It has more than 100,000 stanzas. The stories it relates were recorded in India as early as the fifth and sixth centuries B.C., but they likely originated centuries earlier and were passed down through oral tradition. In one section, the *"Bhagavad Gita"* ("The Song of the Lord") Arjuna, the commander-in-chief of one of the warring parties, has a dialogue in the form of questions and answers with his spiritual mentor, the Lord Krishna. Arjuna, refusing to fight his relatives and past friends has laid down his arms in despair. Finally, Lord Krishna, Arjuna's charioteer, is able to resolve Arjuna's doubts regarding righteous conduct, including waging a war, and goads him to action.

Essentially, Krishna's sermon describes the true self *(atman)* as immortal and the physical death as immaterial. The *Bhagavad Gita* imparts the discipline *(yoga)* of detachment, the detachment of action from its consequences, for these are beyond the control of the actor (human). Spiritual liberation involves freeing oneself from extraneous influences while performing actions. One should focus on the activity of work because it is possible to control one's activity. The consequences of success or failure should be of no importance because they cannot be controlled. The consequences are in the hands of God, and any outcome should be accepted as a gift from God. Human and God are one in essence. The relationship between human and God is achieved through the detachment of righteous acts that uphold social order.

### Theory "W" Communication Model

In a unitary organization, all verbal instructions, both formal and informal, should work from a standard model in order to give everyone a common underpinning and expectations. The Theory "W" communication model (figure 9) is based on the "ARCS" model developed for the U.S. Army by John M. Keller and Bernard J. Dodge in 1982. The ARCS model synthesizes the literature on motivation and places it into four broad categories: attention, relevance, confidence, and satisfaction (ARCS). The Theory "W" communications model applies these four components to a common communication process. ARCS then becomes the expected formal and informal working communications model among leaders, trusted followers, and support staff. It is applied when employees are discussing business activities. The ARCS model has a broad range of applications. It can be used in giving instructions, in making formal and informal oral presentations, and in advertising as a template or as an evaluation tool for any activity. The *Guidelines for Making Presentations* by Mary Rigali and David Morris (1994) applies the ARCS model and ADDIE to all communications. (ARCS is discussed further in the marketing resources module.)

**Figure 9**
**Theory "W" Communication Model**

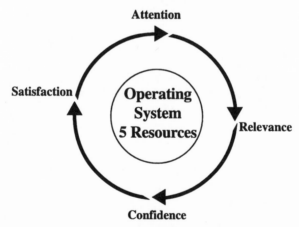

Adapted from: *The ARCS Model of Motivational Strategies for Course Designers and Developers* (Fort Monroe, VA: Training Development Institute).

### Theory "W" Writing Model

In a Theory "W" organization, all written communication should be formalized. Saad Ahmed and David Morris developed *Guidelines for Business Writing* (1991) for just this purpose. Written communications should be formal but not for the purpose of covering oneself against internal enemies. The enemy is always external.

Writing ideas and facts down serves several useful purposes. Among them, the activity of writing forces a clarity in thinking, encourages the creative process, and helps ensure agreement because written documents can be checked and studied. Michael Wood, in his public television program, *Legacy*, stated that writing is one of the main ingredients of civilization because it can send past and present knowledge into the future.

However, because of our highly litigious culture, negative findings or statements that may be used in court against the firm or any of its members should not be written. Certain findings or statements should be discussed before they are put into writing. As a trusted follower and especially as support staff, you should ask the leader if he or she wants your findings to be part of the written record or just the oral record. Written documents should have the following structure: title page, abstract (executive summary), introduction, body, conclusion, appendix, and references. However, the organization may have adopted other structures for writing other types of communications.

## Summary

The concept of tribe is founded on the assumption that being human is part of the unity of all things. By separating God, humans, and nature, the West destroyed and debunked the underpinning of the tribal way of life. The United States, as a nation, has moved back to this model in times of stress, whereas most of the rest of the world, particularly the East, never gave it up. I have known many Americans who are tribal warriors and who understand the way of the warrior. They reached their insights through informal education. This KSA is passed to others in spite of the rhetoric put out by business schools that support other models. All too often, the leaders of business and nonbusiness enterprises have now been replaced with managers and not with warriors. The selling of many companies by the top management in the 1980s is a graphic illustration of the loss of tribal values. These managers have destroyed the future of their tribe (company) for personal gain. This is a traitorous act that would never be accepted in a tribal culture. The leader has an obligation to ensure the future of the tribe.

## CONCLUSION

From the pluralistic point of view, structure has been separated into organizational structure, group structure, leadership structure, and individual structure. Each structure is understood as separate and distinct with little if any relationship with the others. In a pluralistic model, it is likely both within and between these structures that there are competing leadership positions. For example, every person within the marketing resource area may be assuming a different type of leadership style or theory. Each may be working hard at following his or her own leadership model. Unfortunately, such an environment does not unify but separates everyone.

In a unitary organization, organizational structure, group structure, leadership structure, and the individual structure are derived from the same model. Each member works from the same tribal model of leader, trusted follower, and support staff. All three roles may be assumed by everyone in the organization many different times a day. When it is time to be the leader, trusted follower, or support staff, each role should be performed with the same enthusiasm and commitment. This enables tasks to be accomplished because each member is willing to assume a particular role and is not constantly undermining and sabotaging the actions of others in a misguided power struggle. Each individual is given more responsibility as the tribe, with its own survival in mind, identifies through deeds which members can be trusted to do the job. Theory "W" makes use of the primal encoding that is a part of our collective subconscious history. It has been the basis of the formation of humans into groups for hundreds of thousands of years. Theory "W" helps to contribute to a unity of purpose by providing a structure known and followed by all.

## SUGGESTED READINGS

Ahmed, Saad N., and David J. Morris, Jr. *Guidelines for business writing*. West Haven, Conn.: University of New Haven Press, 1991.

Carriere, Jean-Claude. *The mahabharata*. Translated by Peter Brooks. New York: Harper & Row, 1985.

Chu, Chin-Ning. *Thick face: Black heart*. Mill Valley, Calif.: AMC, 1992.

Cleary, Thomas. *The Japanese art of war*. Boston: Shambhala, 1991.

Emry, Frederick E., and Eric L. Trist. *Towards a social ecology: Contextual appreciation of the future in the present*. Plenum Press, 1972.

Hart, B. H. Lindell. *Scipio Africanus: Greater than Napoleon*. New York: Da Capo Press, 1994.

Heidler, John. *The Tao of leadership*. New York: Bantam Books, 1986.

Hersey, Paul. *The situational leader*. New York: Warner Books, 1985.

Herzberg, Frederick. *Work and the nature of man*. Cleveland: World Publishing, 1966.

Keller, John M., and Bernard Dodge. *The ARCS model of motivational strategies for course designers and developers*. Fort Monroe, VA.: Training Development Institute, 1982.

Lussier, Robert, N. *Human relations in organizations*. 2d. ed. Homewood, Ill.: Irwin, 1993.

McClelland, David C. *The achievement motive*. 2d ed. New York: Irvington, 1976.

McGregor, Douglas. *The human side of enterprise*. New York: McGraw-Hill, 1960.

Machiavilli, Niccolo. *The prince*. New York: Bantam Books, 1966.

Mascaro, Juan. *The bhagavad gita*. Middlesex, England: Penguin Books, 1962.

Mishima, Yukio. *The way of the Samurai*. New York: Perigee Books, 1977.

Morris, David. Theory "W": The corporate warrior. *Performance and Instruction Journal* 25(8) (1986): 22-25.

———. Theory "W" leaders: Making presentations. *Performance and Instruction Journal* 25(10) (1986): 10–11.

———. Innovation: The changing perception of leadership. *Performance and Instruction Journal* 26(1) (1987): 20–24.

———. *The way of the warrior*. Madison, Conn.: Market Power Institute, 1994.

Musashi, Miyamoto. *The book of the five rings*. Translated by Victor Harris. Woodstock, N.Y.: Overlook Press, 1974.

Ouchi, William. *Theory Z: How American business can meet the Japanese challenge*. Reading, Mass.: Addison-Wesley, 1982.

Pin, Sun. *Military methods*. Translated by Ralph D. Sawyer. Boulder, Colo.: Westview Press, 1995.

Rigali, Mary, and David Morris. *Guidelines for making presentations*. Chicago: American Marketing Association, 1994.

Sadler, A. L. *The code of the Samurai*. Rutland, Vt.: Charles Tuttle, 1988.

Taylor, Frederic. *The principles of scientific management*. New York: Harper's, 1912.

Tsunetomo, Yamamoto. *Hagakure: The book of the samurai*. Translated by W. S. Wilton. New York: Kodansha International, 1979.

Tzu, Sun. *The art of war*. New York: Oxford University Press, 1963.

Wheatley, Margaret J. *Leadership and the new science*. San Francisco: Berrett-Koehler, 1994.

Yukl, Gary A. *Leadership in organizations*. 2d ed. Englewood Cliffs, N.J.: Prentice-Hall, 1989.

Zhong, Lou Guan. *The romance of the three kingdoms*. Translated by C.H. Brewitt-Taylor. 2 vols. Singapore: Graham Brash, 1988.

# Process (ADDIE)

Process refers to the methods, steps, or procedures used to accomplish tasks and subtasks (jobs). It is an overlooked and often misunderstood cognitive activity. It is the way in which we organize and apply specific and general information to accomplish means and end(s). It is heavily dependent on the culture's frame of reference. One may liken this framework to a computer's operating system, a set of preprogrammed instructions that are responsible for handling all future program tasks and subtasks. The Eastern unitary operating systems enable the user multipurpose approaches, whereas Western operating systems guide people into running linear programs. The function of process resembles that of an operating system in a computer. All human thinking follows a pattern like that of an operating system. This operating system can be designed for each activity or action (the linear approach) or it can be designed for all actions (the unitary approach).

Once people learn an operating system, they add different programs to the basic system. Humans, however, did not copy the computers, but the computers have had to copy the humans. The computer using an operating system may contain as many additional programs as the system will allow. If there is not enough memory, more may be added, but the operating system still remains intact. The same operating system can be used for playing games, telling time, doing math, writing, drawing, designing products, filing and storing information, and so forth. Several computer operating systems are available on the market. For example, although Apple and IBM both run programs, they do not use the same operating system and therefore cannot run the same programs without assembly language. Some day they may agree to use the same operating system. As for now, they have decided it is in their best interest to maintain their own operating systems.

One can argue that each culture has a unique operating system that underlies its actions. There have been few attempts to identify these operating systems within and between cultures because operating systems cannot be separated from actions. The operating system affects the programs. The program is visible, whereas the operating system is often hidden. Thus, studying the WordPerfect program does not lead to an understanding of such operating systems as DOS, OS/2, Unix, or OS/400.

The idea that WordPerfect can be observed and scrutinized appeals to the Western mind because what is not observable is considered unverifiable. The scientific revolution that began in the sixteenth century in the West was founded on predictable, repeatable observation. It rejected the concept that God exists or created an operating system within the universe. The issue was no longer God or what He did or did not do, but rather how the system works. Whether an operating system existed did not concern the West: it cared only about what was observable and repeatable. Western thinkers put forth the idea that all natural phenomena should be studied and categorized to achieve understanding.

Just as understanding operating systems is important in helping certain computer users manage their technological environment more effectively, the understanding of cultural operating systems is also important in order to manage the business environment. Comprehension of a cultural operating system fosters a deeper understanding that can lead to a more effective business relationship. If people do not perceive or even look for the operating system, then they will not be able to reach a deeper understanding of a culture. This is especially true in the case of businesspersons. To understand a culture merely by observing the behavior of its people is difficult at best. Westerners assume simply that others have copied them because the actions of others resembles Western ways on the surface. The other approach is that others function as independent individuals about whom no generalizations can be drawn. Both explanations have been popular. With little if any interest in or awareness of cultural differences (operating systems), real understanding may never occur. When an operating system separates the perception of life events, the structure of the family, the educational system, language development, and business are far different from a society that combines.

For the past five-hundred years, the West has undertaken to impose its operating system of separating on the entire world. This Western crusade promoting secular and scientific thought has been extremely successful. Some would argue that the momentum of this crusade is still building and that in time this worldview will dominate. Others, however, believe a different operating system or worldview has gained momentum, and that a world-power shift back to Asia has begun. Western business theory and practice have reflected the operating system of the United States.

## PLURALISTIC
### A Search for Process

From the sixteenth century, philosophers in the West have written about the value of method. Method, for them, unified all secular activities using mathematical reasoning. Many still claim that mathematics is the key to understanding. Through mathematics, nature can be comprehended and predicted. Mathematics was seen as the tool that enabled humans to progress from the dark into the light of understanding. It was to be the universal language of the new world system. Whatever could not be placed into a mathematical formula was not yet fully understood. Mathematics was divided into two areas: pure math and statistics. It was thought that the exact occurrence of an event could be predicted by pure math and its probable occurrence by statistics. Any field that rejected one of these mathematical tests was considered to belong to the realm of mysticism or wishful thinking. This total dependence on mathematics led to what became known in the West as the scientific method.

## Scientific Method

The scientific method is a process that the researcher can use to apply mathematical tools of explanation and prediction. The scientific method was originally intended to be applied to experiments. Western emphasis on separating quickly altered the concept of scientific method. Each scientific discipline had its own unique interpretation of the scientific method that it used to explain and predict within its particular area. As the scientific method became more popular, it was incorporated into the social sciences.

The idea of defining disciplines as "social sciences" shows the influence of the scientific approach on Western thinking. Each social science sought a unique scientific method by which to apply mathematics as a form of proof, based on its individual philosophy. Even subdisciplines developed their own methods or processes.

Process has also become an activity that can employ minimal mathematical explanations. The applications of process have different names such as a systematic approach or a problem-solving approach. Problem-solving approaches have become so ingrained in Western thinking, particularly within the social sciences, that they are almost invisible. Process has been taken for granted by generations of Western scholars and thinkers. The concept of a problem-solving approach as process has even been studied, but it has not really developed as a separate discipline. The quality movement of the last few years in business, particularly manufacturing, has renewed an interest in the concept of process.

The Western business approach has been to apply a different process for each functional area of the organization. This approach has been borrowed by the social sciences, where every action has been given its own unique problem-solving approach. These multiple approaches to process have been changed and modified within and among disciplines. In a 1993 study of textbooks in marketing, Andre P. Van Paris and Bob Lussier found that process changed as many as forty times in one textbook. Much of what is considered to be new and unique in business information represents a change in process rather than in substance.

The obsession with changing process in Western social sciences has been enforced by the pluralistic philosophy that demands separation at all levels. Westerners separate because this philosophy is ingrained in their cultural psyches and not because it is the only way to look at life. This separating at the process level has been seen (not always consciously) as a way to enhance and protect the careers of those researchers involved in the sciences and social sciences. The unitary portion of this module will show that this is unnecessary and counterproductive, especially in the field of business.

*Problem Solving*

Several problem-solving techniques exist, such as brainstorming, free association, persistence, and ideal attributes.

*Brainstorming*. During brainstorming, a group attempts to find answers by encouraging its members to say anything that comes into their minds. Even if an idea may sound absurd, it is written down for later assessment. Once the list of ideas for a preset time limit is exhausted, the group discusses each idea and the feasibility of implementing it. Although the idea may not be implemented, it is hoped that it will produce other ideas.

*Free Association*. Free association is used by psychologists to reveal hidden meanings. They apply tests, pictures (such as ink-blots), and other methods. The actual test or picture has no meaning in itself. The individual projects his or her own interpretation. From this interpretation insights are gained. Another free-association technique involves comparing unrelated tasks: for example, participants are asked to associate what goes on in marketing and masonry. This mind stretch, it is believed, will open up new ways of thinking and problem solving.

*Persistence*. Persistence assumes that problems are solved through long hours of hard work. Thomas Edison reportedly declared that "invention" is 1 percent inspiration and 99 percent perspiration. Asians believe that insights are gained through the repeated, exact duplication of the teachings and techniques passed down from antiquity. After years of duplication, the student breaks through to understanding. The last advice of the Buddha, in the context of attaining *nirvana*, was "Brethren, work diligently for your *nirvana*. There are no shortcuts to it." Persistence is an attribute that has not been encouraged in the West in recent years because of the Western interest in a quick fix and immediate satisfaction.

*Ideal Attributes*. A friend of mine, Dr. Abbas Nadim, uses an interesting technique to identify ideal attributes. A leader tells the group that an entire company has been lost and nothing is left. It is up to the group to rebuild the company in any way it thinks is optimal. The rebuilding, however, has to be done within the existing technological parameters. Nothing that was done before has to be done the same way in the new company. The way people worked together in the old company does not have to be the same way they will work together in the new company. Everything can be done differently.

*Creativity*

Because of what they see as their mandate from heaven, people in the West, particularly in the United States, seem to believe that they are the only creative people on the planet. Those who have not embraced the Western perception of creativity are considered less capable of coming up with new ideas and innovations. Westerners cite as examples of their creativity the great Occidental artists, musicians, scientists, and businesspersons. Americans especially believe that creativity can only be nurtured in an environment where the individual and individual freedom are allowed to flourish. Cultures that, for any reason, are believed to be more unified are deemed to be less creative. All successes within these combining cultures are believed to have occurred by accident or because they copied the West. Rote learning is an example illustrating the failure of a culture to be creative. The American educational system encourages creativity and has replaced rote learning and memorization with a more reflective approach to the acquisition of knowledge.

The East defines creativity differently. Rote learning and memorization are not considered monotonous actions but discipline-building activities. Repetition can assist the individual in gaining insights into life. Although these insights are supposed to be common to all who attain them, they are impossible to explain in words (Buddhism). Creativity is an internal rather than an external attribute, so that one who has attained this understanding, although it remains unspoken, is aware that the breakthrough has occurred in another person. The concept of creativity is determined by one's cultural perspective.

## UNITARY

From a unitary perspective, process combines knowledge, skills, and attitudes (KSA). One common, agreed-upon process supersedes all others. The terms selected to define a single process are not determined by any specific discipline or function. This process is then to be applied within and among all functions and disciplines that are conceptualized as resources. (See the resources module.) Likewise, a common scientific method is applied to all sciences. Although an experiment may be unique to its population, focus, and resources, the experimental method is the same. All experimenters use the same process in the same order. The meanings of the terms are universal. When one person discusses the process or any of its component steps, the terms are clear to all involved. The operating system is the same, although the programs can vary. All are aware of the operating systems and each action is built on that KSA.

### Advantages of a Common Process

Applying a common process within the corporation has the following advantages: the streamlining of work within a job, the streamlining of work between or among jobs, and the ability of individuals to do multiple jobs within and among cultures. Work in the West has been divided into separate activities, each carried out by individuals who have specialized in that particular activity. To optimize the results of these activities, it is believed, the individual should limit the number of unrelated activities that he or she carries out at any one time. Each job thus required new and generally unrelated training. Jobs perceived to be slightly different may require minimal retraining, whereas those thought to be very different may require a transition period of several years.

Of course the time frame that individuals need to master new jobs varies from one individual to another. The same job may take one person a few hours to perform but may take another several days. The time and cost it takes to learn a new job becomes a form of market power. A job becomes more secure for the one holding it if it is very costly to replace that person. The union movement has successfully countered the short time requirements to train a new person by banding together as a large group to protect jobs. Although it may be easy to train a new person for the job, unions have made it far more difficult for the employer because of the threat of strikes. This may also be true for nonunion jobs, such as those of doctors, college professors, and lawyers. The differences in strategies used to protect jobs are marginal.

The time required to train a person to master more than one task is more a matter of market power than of human capacity to perform multiple tasks and their subtasks. All jobs have two components: process and content. Process is the individual's method of solving problems within a job category; content is the unique and overlapping actions of the process to achieve a purpose. Although research data exist that identify how much of a job is likely to be content, my own intuition is that process accounts for as much as 95 percent of most jobs. Process accounts for about one out of seven, or 15 percent, of the module categories in this book. Thus, in the worst case, 15 percent of job A transfers to jobs E, F, G, and, in the best case, 95 percent of the differences between the jobs involves just process. The implications of this conclusion for the development and training of the workforce are enormous and could be a great source of global market power.

### Streamlining of Work within a Job

Process overlaps and transfers between jobs when process is kept constant. If, on the other hand, process is changed from one job to another, within each job, transfer is minimal. Companies can create, maintain, and enforce the use of a common process. This enables different individuals to enter the same process as they perform the multiple tasks and subtasks of a job. Assignments are deciphered and carried out with much more ease. All particular resource areas, now called functional areas, will decrease as the number of barriers between them declines. Daily activities and work assignments overlap.

For example, as a marketing professor, I have observed little overlap among courses within the marketing curriculum. Each course is viewed as a part of a linear sequence where what is learned in each successive course continues to increase. Each time a new area is given to the students, the content stays the same but the process is changed. This changing process takes time to learn and also takes more time as the individual compares processes that are part of other marketing tasks and subtasks. How much more could be taught in the same time frame if process were held constant? How much more could be covered in the testing of the students if process were held constant in testing? How much testing is just the unnecessary repeating of process?

From a company perspective, the idea of specialization within a function can and should be avoided. Specialization is universally unnecessary within functional or task areas. The separating of process has encouraged the separating of all aspects of jobs. Once process is combined, the functions dwindle in importance because it is easy to identify how much of their perceived differences was, in fact, no difference at all. Common process unifies all jobs and their tasks and subtasks.

### Streamlining of Work among Jobs

Process overlaps and transfers among jobs when process is kept constant. The working relationship among marketing, human, physical, intangible, and financial resources does not have to be unaccessible across these resource activities. Work relationships can be enhanced when all individuals can enter any resource area with confidence in their capacities to assist and contribute to the decision-making process. Concepts such as matrix organizations have failed because employees from each functional area come to the meetings with their contribution generally limited to their own functional area. They are unable to contribute to the development of resources outside of their function. One major stumbling block to this is process barriers among functions.

Functional areas have erected these process barriers to gain market power. When a person from human resources is discussing one concept or application of a process, he or she is likely to be discussing it using an entirely different set of definitions and meanings from the person in marketing. The combining of process among jobs is a major step in opening up the relationships so that all individuals may utilize outside information and resources within their own areas. It is like sending work that is written in American English to a place where the people speak Australian English. Much time and energy must be spent to ensure understanding. If a mistake is made, it may take years to rectify. When process is kept constant, understanding is more ensured and work relations among jobs are streamlined.

### The Ability of Individuals to Do Multiple Jobs

Resources are tools to be applied to achieve a common purpose. They are not the domain of any one person or group of people. The separating of resources is more a function of market power than a function of human learning capacity. There have been many times in history when people were encouraged to learn and perform in many areas. The Renaissance in the West was a time when one individual could combine being an artist, a lawyer, an inventor, an astronomer, a philosopher, and a skilled artisan. The job of farmer, which people have been doing for thousands of years, requires a multiskilled person. The concept of separating has also been with human beings for thousands of years, but the reliance on specialization that has occurred in the West, particularly in the United States in the second half of the twentieth century, has been without parallel.

The West still maintains individual unitary initiative in the area of small business. The small-business owner, through necessity, must do many different jobs each day. He or she must work with all the resources to keep the business viable. As the business grows, it is believed that the owner must give up control over all resource areas and turn them over to specialists. This transition is often unsuccessful for the company because this method is inherently inefficient. The new size of a business becomes a factor in the ability of the business to remain efficient. This has recently become a problem for large, inefficient businesses that once could afford these inefficiencies. At this time, however, unitary competition has turned these inefficiencies into destructive behaviors and the companies continue to decline to the point of extinction.

Perhaps companies that cannot turn themselves around should be treated as a large bank might be: when a bank is in trouble, an outside regulatory body (board of directors) enters without notice and assumes control in an attempt to save the organization. This has happened with many businesses in the United States during war efforts. Government and business worked together for a common purpose. Productivity was then unsurpassed in the history of mankind.

The East has had a long history of rejecting the concept of one person and one specialization. In the writings and teachings of the Japanese *samurai*, it is said that the person who specializes is a fool because that person has given up the understanding of all other things to focus on just one. The great Japanese warrior, Miyamoto Musashi (1584–1645) lived his life as a farmer, artisan, writer, and warrior (see the "Structure" module). When Americans send their specialists to compete against the Japanese generalists, the Japanese must see this as a sign of weakness. Musashi, and indeed Asian philosophy, in general, focus on the way (process), not on the specifics (content). When process is constant for all activities, an individual can enter and exit all tasks and subtasks with confidence because the person brings process with him or her to the new tasks and subtasks. New information (content) is easier to understand when it is held constant through process.

### Communication

Communication is constantly discussed as a key factor in the success of almost every human endeavor. A lack of communications has been blamed on the senders and the receivers. It is even said that wars have been fought because of a lack of communications. It is believed that if people could just understand what others are saying, the world would be a better place. To think that understanding breeds tolerance is wishful thinking. One important strategic concept is to know your enemy. A common process assists in communication when those involved are working to attain it as a means to an end. The implementing of a common process for all resource areas will have no impact when individuals do not want to communicate. The selection and rewarding of those individuals within an organization that can and do think across resources is an imperative for success. When discussing communications and process, the type of persons that should be selected to work in a unitary company are those who are comfortable with multiple resource experiences. These people are available and they can be encouraged to develop the required KSA once they have been identified.

The U.S. Navy utilizes this type of person in the submarine service. Members of the crew must be able at a moment's notice to do any job on the ship. If some specialist were to get sick or die when the submarine was, for example, under the polar ice cap, all could perish. Because of necessity, the navy spends a great deal of time and money in the submarine service finding and training the people who are capable of doing many jobs. A great deal of research and time has been spent within the U.S. military to accomplish this cross-training. Scholars and businesspersons can take advantage of this research when they begin to look at combining within corporations or universities. Separating is at its worst or best in the universities, depending on one's underlying philosophy. Universities will have the most difficult time of any organization adjusting to a more unified approach. Universities are not and have never been the leaders of society. They have subdivided to extremes and will continue to do so until education is seen to be necessary for the survival of the society. When that happens, universities will have to change or other alternatives for education will be found.

When the leadership of an organization knows that all individuals are going to have to do all jobs to a specific standard, then the way people are trained to work together will change. The present system encourages separation and a lack of communication. This does not mean there will be no room for the specialist in corporate society, but rather that there will be no long-term commitment to this type of person. Instead of the company playing musical chairs with its workforce they can select a more flexible workforce and then bring in the specialists (as required) to train that flexible, multiskilled workforce. The application of a common process allows for a much easier transfer of knowledge, skills, and attitudes in the organization. When that occurs, individuals are capable of communication with each other about resource tasks and subtasks. Remember that process is not the only unifying factor, philosophy, philosophy (KSA), philosophy in action, direction, structure, and resource areas are also components that unify.

## Communications among Cultures

The concept that cultures have different operating systems from which the daily actions of life evolve makes communications difficult at best. It is also likely that without real effort, little if any understanding will occur among groups. Companies that have people from diverse backgrounds and cultures may go a long way toward improving communication by applying a common process from which all actions will be understood and derived. This constant underlying problem-solving model enables all to move through a set of common steps. Each individual must incorporate the new process model and forgo his or her cultural model(s) to work with others in a unified manner. Those cultures that already have a common process model can accomplish this with more ease. This, then, contributes to an underlying system that all can embrace. All materials, written communications, oral instructions, and training programs apply the same process as a form of a common operating system. Everyone in every location adjusts and embraces a common process model.

## Creativity

It has been suggested that if everyone is forced to follow a common process, this will stifle creativity. As discussed earlier in this module, creativity is a cultural concept. If creativity means letting everyone do his or her own thing, then the concept of a common process may not be the ideal model. If people should be able to do what they want and how they want, there should be little interest in the coordination and synchronization of one task with another. The artist paints, but he or she paints to express himself or herself in his or her own unique way, not to copy or find insight by following someone else's way. To do that would be the equivalent of painting by the numbers.

Creativity may be viewed from a more positive and different perspective through a unitary approach to process. "Creativity" is an elusive term, and in the United States, it has been interpreted as "doing our own thing." I prefer to think of creativity as the disassembling and reassembling of tasks and subtasks into new and different assemblies. Process is not a major issue in creativity, but rather a template to assist in the movement through actions to achieve a purpose.

The maintenance of a common process model does not affect an individual's ability to be creative. Repetition of process, on the other hand, may open a person up to new and creative insights because he or she has been freed from the illusion that differences in process are somehow a creative activity. Process issues can account for 15 to 95 percent of understanding of tasks and subtasks (jobs). This translates into a significant reduction in time when moving in and out of jobs, if process is kept constant. This also can open up creative solutions because the person brings more to any job when he or she is able to transfer content between tasks and subtasks. Transfer occurs when barriers are broken down. Job barriers have been created by cultures. The ability to do several jobs is not a question of human capacity, but a market power issue.

*Creativity: Assembly Model*

The assembly model (figure 10) created by the author in 1985 views all activities as an assembly. These activities are conceptualized as coming apart (analysis) and going back together again (design). The description of the coming apart is reported through language. Each time something is taken apart and put back together, tools are used to assist in the activity. When the activity comes apart it may not go back together the same way it came apart. Different language and tools may be required to put back the disassembled activity. For example, the activity of building a house is an assembly. It is made up of subassemblies such as electrical, plumbing, masonry, and so forth. To construct the house, the builder must first visualize the disassembly of the house into parts and then reassemble the house, applying the language and tools required to put the house together. The built house then becomes the assembly. If something needs to be replaced, it is taken apart and replaced. This disassembling and reassembling uses specific language and tools to describe the activity.

The creation of assemblies is arbitrary. Each society determines where the assemblies begin and end. The language and tools to describe the assembly and disassembly activities are also cultural. In one culture, a person may specialize in medicine, whereas in another, the person may view specialization as learning to care only for the eyes. In another culture, medicine and spiritual study may be combined. Yet another culture may have no distinctions. The conceptualization of the assembly is culturally driven, as is that of the disassembly. Each culture determines what the disassembly will look like, the language used to describe the disassembly, and the tools required to take it apart and put it back together. Pluralistic cultures have developed smaller and smaller assemblies with more and more precise (specialized) language and tools to describe the activity.

Creativity is the ability to combine assemblies. The language and tools used in one assembly are transferred to another. For example, the filling of a hole in a tooth and the filling of a hole in a sidewalk are essentially the same assembly and disassembly. Both the dentist and the mason do primarily the same thing. The cavity or the hole in the sidewalk is chiseled and drilled out. The dentist and the mason take out as much as necessary until they return to solid material. Once they reach solid material, the holes are both grooved into a \ / shape. This shape allows the material to be held in the tooth or the sidewalk. Wire supports may be added when the hole is too large. A difference in materials requires that the dentist dry

## Figure 10
## Assembly Model

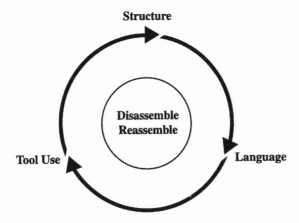

Adapted from: "Developing a Multi-Skilled Workforce Through an Assembly Model,"
*Performance & Instruction Journal*

the hole, while the mason must wet the hole. The material is then tamped in with specialized tools and polished off. In the case of the sidewalk, it is usually brushed with a broom, so it will have a rough surface and people will not slip. The idea of the assembly model would be for the dentist to look at masonry with its separate language and tools and find something that could transfer to the dentist's job. The same is true for the mason. These two assemblies and disassembles are more obvious than others. The less obvious the similarities, the more creative the ability to transfer among assemblies.

All actions are assemblies that come apart and go back together. The new configuration may appear different but it still remains an assembly. Assemblies are described through language and tool use. The taking apart is called analysis and the putting back is called design.

The ideas in this book were conceived using the assembly model. The idea that business is an extension of philosophy is the combining of the business and philosophy assemblies. This was reinforced by looking at other assemblies, such as the activities entailed by education, family, and religion. The notion of theory as the application of philosophy is the combining of theory and philosophy. The application of market power as a positive force was taken from the field of economics. Economists have viewed market power as a negative, whereas I conceive of it as something positive. One direction was also taken from the field of economics (profit maximization), whereas the thought of multiple directions were taken from the field of business. The concept of combining ideas into a new assembly was to maintain the idea of one direction, but those within the organization are able to change that direction. This frees the organization from the singular end of profit maximization. My Theory "W" joined anthropology and business leadership theory. Process was taken from the U.S. Army, which demands that all training material apply a common process. Resources as separate from functions was the combining of what I have experienced in my own life from having learned many different skills. I realized that barriers were cultural, rather than stemming from a lack of human capacity. There are many more examples of combining that have gone into the development of the ideas in this book. These examples demonstrate that the combining of assemblies is an endless activity. Cultures that combine find these activities less creative than cultures that separate do.

The assembly model needs more research, but the preliminary findings indicate that creativity is the combining of assemblies. Language and tools are often barriers to a broad understanding. Models such as the assembly model and the application of a common process are cognitive attempts to combine knowledge, skills, and attitudes. Humans are just as capable of combining as they are of separating.

## ADDIE

The acronym ADDIE stands for analysis, design, development, implementation, and evaluation (figure 11). These are the five circular steps that make up the universal process. This process is applied to all tasks and subtasks to achieve a purpose. The purpose can be either a means or an end, but the process remains constant. Process may be entered and exited at any of the five steps, but it is recommended that the steps follow in order and move in a constant circle of ADDIE, ADDIE, ADDIE. The advantages of a common process have been outlined. It is not important what one calls the steps, but rather that a set of steps are followed. As I tell my students, learn ADDIE; if you want to change the terms, do so after the class ends. Many students have returned years later and have told me that they still apply ADDIE in their work and indeed in all their activities. They have found it a successful tool.

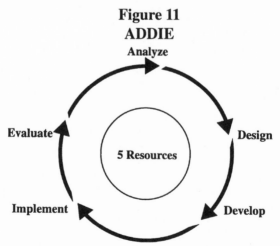

**Figure 11**
**ADDIE**

Adapted from: *Marketing as a Means to Achieve Organizational Ends* (West Haven, CT: University of New Haven Press).

If your organization has settled on its own constant process, then use that one. If not, apply ADDIE. Most Western organizations do not yet understand the concept of process and the value of holding this circular process constant. I have had a few corporations tell me that this is what they do, but further exploration shows it is applied selectively. Perhaps only one area does it. If any group is advanced in this area, it is the U.S. military. The statistical control advocates have alerted corporations to the value of a continuous process, but they have yet to make the connection that this can be applied to all means and ends. They have, following their pluralistic model, equated process with the concept of quality.

When process is freed from any one particular functional area, then that area is reduced in importance and the importance of any task or subtask (means) to achieve a purpose (end) is diminished. The Asians follow a common process to solve problems, but I believe it is intuitive rather than being based on a formal model. Because of this Asians are able to communicate more easily within and among all areas of the organization. Indeed, this is also a contributing factor in all areas of Eastern society working together toward a common purpose. People in Eastern cultures are, in essence, all working off the same operating system. When they deal with the West, they must translate the KSA that they acquire into their operating system. This takes a great deal of time, but once it is accomplished, they can move in unison toward their common purpose. To accomplish this goal of translating outside KSA into their operating system, they continue to send their best and brightest to learn Western ways, and then these students return to assist in placing the KSA into the Eastern process. The Japanese began this learning and returning in the mid-1890s. They sent thousands of their people all over the world to bring back the KSA of others and translate it into the Japanese cultural operating system. The Japanese had been doing this with the KSA of the Chinese for thousands of years.

*ADDIE as a Circle*

ADDIE can be applied in a pluralistic model as a straight line or from a unitary perspective as a circle. When it takes the form of a circle, ADDIE has several advantages. Process is seen as continuous. Many in the West talk about continuous improvement that is embedded in a linear culture that has delineated beginnings and endings for all aspects of life. When a culture sees no beginnings and no ends, the concept of continuous improvement moves beyond the short term to the infinite. New products and services do not come and go, but, instead, they are ever-changing and ever-improving through a common circular process. The following are the five steps of ADDIE.

**Analysis (Know Yourself and Know Your Competition)**

Analysis is the first step in the five-part ADDIE circular process. Many U.S. corporations have been accused of being paralyzed by analysis, which leads one to infer that they spend their time in analysis and never move to other steps in the process. Although this may be true for some corporations, it is generally an incorrect assumption. U.S. corporations do very little actual analysis from which to make a decision. Everyone on the staff may have an opinion, but that opinion is often founded on feelings and political considerations. Can you envision someone in a marketing function coming up with any information or data that would diminish the position of marketing within the corporation?

What happens in many corporations is that the staff does a very superficial analysis and then rushes to implementation. The author worked for a subsidiary of a Fortune-100 company that received competitive assessments every week or two. These were supposed to be important documents. Based on these assessments, we were to design our attack against the company's competitors. I believed these assessments were superficial at best, so I convinced the vice president of marketing that we should do our own assessment. We hired a friend of mine, Brian McLaughlin, from Syracuse University, and for the relatively small sum of $600 he did a far superior job of assessing our competition. All the top executives in the company were shocked to think that for such a small amount of money they could receive a far superior assessment.

Few actions of U.S. corporations (and even less so those of universities) are derived from an in-depth analysis. Decisions are often made on feelings and, at best, a limited assessment. Although there has been much talk about Japanese consensus management, it has been misinterpreted by the West as a struggle within Japanese corporations to gain acceptance of a particular position. The Japanese supposedly spend hours deciding on a course of action. This is true, but what has also occurred during that time period has been an in-depth, objective analysis. The Japanese have valued analysis for centuries. This is grounded on the Chinese military strategy put forth in the writings of Sun Tzu that the Japanese adapted into their operation system. According to Sun Tzu, those who know themselves and know their enemies will not be in peril. Those who just know themselves or the enemy will win only half the time. Those who know neither themselves nor their enemy will not win.

Analysis is an extremely important part of process. Although it may seem to take more effort than will be justified by the return, keep in mind that Western feelings may be culturally based rather than an assessment of what is required to make decisions. A great deal of information should be covered when the mandate is "to know yourself and to know your enemies." Western business must improve in this area.

The three broad areas for analysis are the company, the competition, and the industry. These three areas may all be analyzed on local, regional, national, and international bases. Each of these may be analyzed by looking at past, present, and future trends. For example, one could analyze one's own company within a region to determine what occurred in the past. What is then analyzed are the resources applying this model (see the next module for a discussion of the resources). All resources (marketing, human, physical, intangible, and financial) the "5Rs" can be analyzed by applying the local, regional, national, international, past, present, and future trends for the company, competition, and industry format. As many or as few of these may be selected for analysis as is deemed necessary. The list may be enlarged—for example, the areas of county, state, or trading block may be appropriate for inclusion. Terms such as "past" may be divided into more specific time frames. The system is flexible. What is inflexible is ADDIE. The process is continuous.

Market power analysis and market power assessment charts can also be derived from this analysis when it encompasses enough to make the decision (see the "Direction" module for a more in-depth discussion). Market power analyses and assessments are made to determine the organizational end and means. The ADDIE process is applied to all actions, from those that are all-encompassing to the most simple tasks and subtasks. Analysis is still the same concept whether it is used to determine an end or a means.

### Company

The same resources ("5Rs") that are assessed for the company are also assessed for the competition and the industry. One of the areas that is most often analyzed inaccurately is the organization that is doing the analysis. It is extremely difficult to assess one's own organization because of personalities. The leadership may have a "kill the messenger who brings bad news" mind-set. Any negative findings may be construed as an attack on those who are members of a functional area and may result in a ruined career. The leader of the organization may want to use information as a means of getting rid of old enemies. The potential for misuse has resulted in little positive application of this valuable part of analysis. My advice is to do the best one can within the real constraints of a company's tolerance for assessment and analyze the marketing, human, physical, intangible, and financial resources.

### Competition

When analyzing competition, the organization applies the exact same resources ("5Rs") that it uses to assess itself and the industry. The marketing, human, physical, intangible, and financial resources are analyzed for local, regional, national, international, past, present, and future trends. The decision as to who or what group constitutes competition is open to individual corporate interpretation. A model from military strategy discussed under the area of market power involves evaluating both existing and potential competitors. Terms and concepts are not changed because a different aspect is being discussed. Consistency is the appropriate course of action.

### Industry

Analysis of the industry is important because it gives the organization an indication of possible trends that may not become apparent in an analysis of one's own company and its competition. There have been many trends that have occurred in the marketing, human, physical, intangible, and financial resource ("5Rs") area outside a particular company and its competitors that later an impact on the company. These are better identified sooner rather than later. On the positive side, the industry may be ahead of a company and its competitors. Identified areas may give a firm the potential to gain market power over immediate competition.

A prominent Irish businessman Fergal Quinn owns a number of supermarkets in Ireland. He and his wife travel around the world visiting supermarkets. When he sees a good idea, he brings it back to one of his stores to develop (test). His competition thinks he is just a creative, innovative person; but in fact he is very good at analyzing the industry. The competition has not figured this out even though he has discussed the concept many times at Trinity College in Dublin. Industry analysis can take a form as creative and interesting as the one developed by Fergal Quinn, or it can be accomplished through other tasks and subtasks.

## Local

When the analysis is made of the company, its competition, and industry by applying the "5Rs," it can be done at the local level. "Local" covers an area defined by the company. It can encompass any area that the company wishes to consider for this term. The definition of "local" must be consistent and known to all the people involved in the analysis. "Local" can be as small as a neighborhood or as large as a state.

## Regional

Regional analysis of a company, its competition, and the industry may also be required to make a decision. For example, New England can be considered as a region. New York State could also be included in the region. Data are available on this region through many sources (sources for acquiring data will be included later in this module). "Regional" includes the same resources ("5Rs") as local. This does not mean that the company cannot modify the geographic areas, but this should be done as a conscious decision.

## National

National analysis includes the same resources ("5Rs"). Information on one's company, its competition, and the industry may be gathered on a national basis. Of course, the researcher can broaden this area, perhaps by including a new term that covers larger areas such as trading blocks.

## International

An analysis of one's company, its competition, and industry may also be done at the international level by applying the same resources ("5Rs"). Information at this level will vary depending on the area of the world in which one is trying to make an assessment.

## Past

When you analyze a company, its competition, and its industry, by applying the 5Rs, a very informative category is the past. The past as a part of analysis has been overlooked and avoided by Western corporations that are involved in the analysis step of the process. It is possible to learn a great deal about the present and future actions of Japan and Germany by studying their pasts. A word of caution, however, do not read about the past in current books and documents. The present often has a distorted view of the past. Anyone who reads pre-1950 documents about Japan will get an understanding that offers the greatest insights.

When you read about Japan in books that were copyrighted before 1900, Japan is depicted as a kind of primitive paradise or lost society. After the defeat of the Russian navy in 1904, Japan is portrayed as a brave and valued nation. After World War I, Japan is considered to be a troublemaker and an upstart that needs to be controlled. From 1930 to 1940 Japan is viewed as a potential enemy. It is apparent from documents of the period that the U.S. government knew that sooner or later there would be a fight. The United States was by no means the unsuspecting innocent before World War II. During the war, the Japanese were seen as an evil, robot race. After the war, during the trouble with China, Japan was viewed as a group of people who were misled by a few wicked people. Incidently, Americans came to the same conclusion about Germany during the real or contrived problem with the Russians called the Cold War. The Korean War began, and Japan was transformed in American consciousness into a stronghold of democracy that must be rebuilt industrially. After the Korean War, Japan could not be permitted to revert to being a second-rate industrial power, so the U.S. markets were opened.

The 1996 version is that the Japanese were a bunch of junk dealers, and with the help of two American heroes, Edward Deming and Joseph M. Juran, they were convinced to implement a quality program. Because Japan did as Americans said and not as Americans did, they were successful. If one believes this, one will believe anything. When doctoral students hear the idea that the present view of history is false they tend to disagree strongly. When they are forced to go back and read the books copyrighted before the 1950s they are astonished, to say the least. Do not accept the present view of history without looking at past generations' views of other cultures. Another way to gain insight is to look at other nations' present and past history.

One's company, its competition, and the industry have a historic record. That history can give great insights into resource allocations in the present and the future. Americans have for political reasons chosen to ignore the past. If Americans do not like the way they behaved as a people in the past, then the present generation changes behavior to suit present requirements. This is by no means an American trait but rather a universal trait. That is why the original writings are so important. One word of caution: with the preceding Japanese example, past generations were just as adept at creating their histories to reflect their positions as current generations. More on this view of history can be learned by reading *What Is History*, written in 1961 by E. H. Carr. This does not mean that history has no lessons to teach. History has a great deal to teach when one looks at what different times and different people (in different cultures) have said about the same thing. From that type of analysis, new insights evolve that can give a company market power.

*Present*

An analysis of one's company, its competition, and the industry by applying the "5Rs" should be done to determine present actions. It is important to monitor one's competitors and one's industry at all times. Present statements of action and actual actions are often far apart. Many times, a competitor and even one's own company will make comments that they cannot deliver on, because they lack the resources or the market power. Companies that failed to deliver in the past will more than likely fail in the future. There are, of course, exceptions. A change of leadership may indicate a change in the company's present ability to compete against other companies.

Many companies give out deceptive figures. This is illegal in the United States for public stock-held firms. It is not illegal in other nations and for privately held U.S. firms to create a positive picture where one does not exist. It often seems with stock-held firms that much of what is said is public relations rather than accurate analyses of their situations. To read beyond this is what separates the true ADDIE'ers from the ones that claim to be. There are very few whose insights could be trusted in a life-and-death situation. Thousands claim to be strategists, but few of them really follow through.

*Future Trends*

Although it is impossible to predict the future with any accuracy, it is not impossible to identify future trends. New and different products and services are constantly coming into the marketplace. This gives the astute observer the opportunity to test these products and services without the risk of incurring excessive losses. For example, a future trend appears to be a decline in the demand for the master of business administration (M..B.A.) degree. Schools that are heavily dependent on drawing students for the M.B.A. degree should begin to identify new markets while the market is still viable. It is a far more difficult situation to have miscalculated the future of one's markets when the decline is already on one's firm. The resources have begun to dwindle and it is harder to divert resources into new ventures.

It did not take a rocket scientist to predict a decline the U.S. military spending. The large military suppliers have had at least three to five years to begin to make a transition into new ventures. Several military suppliers have reacted to the decline with surprise and have laid off thousands of workers. Another suggestion for them would have been to move to new markets while they still had market power. Now their alternatives are far fewer.

The savings-and-loan scandal and the government bailout was bound to have repercussions on taxation no matter what the politicians were saying. These examples demonstrate the value of identifying future trends that may impact one's company, its competition, and the industry. One reason for a lack of leadership's response to these trends is that it is difficult for a company to move in a direction that seems to be unnecessary during prosperity. Unfortunately, it is even harder for the leader once the decline has begun. Another more unfortunate reason for failure to move is that many of those in responsible positions are unprepared to lead in difficult times. They have gotten their positions more on social and political maneuvering than on a broad understanding of the KSA it takes to run a business. These executives may be good at a party or at destroying internal competitors, but poor at running a business.

*Summary*

An analysis is the appraisal of a company, its competition, and its industry. The most difficult analysis is that of self—one's own KSA or the KSA of one's company. Competition is defined as existing and potential. Analysis may be done at local, regional, national, and international levels. All resources are assessed by identifying their past, present, and future trends. Analysis is often overlooked or misinterpreted as people present what they believe to be going on, without any time spent in research.

## Types of Research in Analysis

There are five types of research involved in analysis. They are applied research, academic research, quasi-academic research, theoretical research, and intuition. Each has its appropriate place. To rely on one type alone is to put one's analysis at risk. This is why the Japanese corporations place staff in the American research universities—because of the chance that they will improve their KSA and get a jump on competition.

### Applied Research

Many American businesses have a love/hate affair with applied research. Applied research is research for a specific purpose. In the pluralistic organization, the applied research function has shown little integration with the rest of the organization. Unfortunately, what is taken for applied research often would be questionable if performed by a high-school student, because most of the applied research that is carried on is so simple and obvious that it is unjustifiable to anyone with a modicum of sense. When times become difficult, the corporate leaders eliminate their applied research activity, despite the cries of "we will fall behind the rest of the world." The problem with corporate applied research is that those involved have failed to justify their existence. The Japanese do applied research that is directly related to present and future productivity. The worst offenders in the United States in applied research are the so-called Fortune-100 companies. If they have done such a good job, where are the results? Sooner or later, they will not be believed when they claim that they invented something and the rest of the world stole it. Remember, this is applied research, not theoretical research.

### Academic Research

In a pluralistic society, the research that is carried out in academic settings has been separated into functions. Each function carries on its own research, with little integration of findings with other academic areas. The research in these academic functions, except for a few of those professors within the top business schools, remains invisible to the U.S. corporations. Once the corporate person receives his or her M.B.A., he or she fails to value the work done in the academic realm. It is seen as an ivory tower and so far away from reality that it would be a detriment to one's career to suggest anything that was learned in school transferring to the job. A few graduates from the top schools are hired by corporations each year for prestige and entertainment purposes, but these new employees have little impact on the means or ends of the corporation. The reason for this is that tribal outsiders (Theory "W") cannot implement change in any group until they become a member of the group.

## Quasi-Academic Research

From a pluralistic research position, the organization has attempted to gain KSA from outside research firms. These firms are managed by or hire Ph.D.s to sell a particular educational program to corporations. These programs are said to be customized for the specific firm and industry. This customization often consists of changing the name on the materials from one company to another with few other modifications. These quasi-academic firms have been very successful in corporate America. Unfortunately for their owners, these firms generally go in and out of vogue with the corporations. Some larger firms have appealed to corporate America for years. These firms have supposedly done the research and they will share that research (at a price) with corporations. Most of what comes from the quasi-research area is not at a standard that is worth the money that is charged. The question is, what impact did these interventions have on assisting the company in achieving its end?

The academic researchers generally follow the quasi-academic research firms. This causes the quasi-researchers problems, because the academics either bash their ideas or jump on them so quickly that the quasi-academic research firms loose their markets. Academic research has unfortunately done a poor job of identifying areas that are considered to be of help to corporations. This is because those areas are conceived of as separate areas of study. A classic example of this relationship is the research on quality. Although the academics happily point to the rejection of the quality movement by corporate America as another example of their ineptness, few academics were the least bit interested in quality until the corporations responded to the quasi-academic organizations and their emphasis on it.

Now, as with many other areas, the academic researchers are calling for quality, quality, quality. Courses, seminars, articles, and conferences are proliferating from the academic world. All these activities cut into the quasi-academic market. Soon, the quasi-academic researchers will have to identify a new area to sell to corporations. When they do, the academics will become disinterested in quality and will be dedicated to the new area. It is this boomtown mentality in research that makes it difficult to take a long, thought-out view of research. The quality movement has failed just as all others have because it is placed into a pluralistic worldview that attempts to separate it from all other tasks and subtasks.

## Theoretical Research

America has been the world leader in the area of theoretical research. This was in great part driven by the U.S. military and the Cold War. With the end of the Cold War, the proliferation of theoretical research will decline. Theoretical research is research for research's sake. Theoretical research has now moved to Japan for several reasons. The Japanese have the money to support theoretical research in specific areas. They are interested in the domination of world markets in information systems, and they are investing in that area at a far greater rate than the nations of the rest of the world combined. The Japanese also resent the American viewpoint that the Japanese are not creative and innovative. They want to show Americans that they are and always have been superior in this area. Because of these psychological and political reasons the Japanese are going to invest heavily in theoretical research. As Western businesses and military factions cut back, the Japanese will continue to expand their efforts. When the competition cuts back in an area and a company or country continues to support and build in that area, it can lead to a position of long-term market power.

Theoretical research in the United States has also been supported by the U.S. government in grants to a select few U.S. universities. Many prominent schools have been accused of abusing these funds. This will have an impact on the government's decision to cut back on expenditures. As the government tries to identify areas of reasonable cost-cutting, this is a likely target. Much theoretical research has been directed toward the so called hard sciences. Although the social sciences have benefited from this government funding, the impact of anything they have done has been minimal because of the lack of unification of ideas and concepts. Everyone does his or her own thing for his or her own particular purposes.

*Intuition*

The concept of intuition plays an important role in analysis. Intuition has performed a dominant role in many organizations. Intuition should be no substitute for data and, in some cases data, are no substitute for intuition. Although the West relies heavily on data as evidence, other peoples of the world often rely on intuition to guide their decisions. After all is said and done, intuition plays an important role because nothing is certain.

**Unitary Approach to Research**

The concept of research from a unitary approach is different from that of research from a pluralistic philosophical foundation. The boundaries between applied, academic, quasi-academic, theoretical research, and intuition are not clearly delineated. All research is made available and combined so that duplication of effort is avoided. *Guidelines for Writing a Research Report*, David Morris and Satish Chandra (1993), and *Guidelines for Writing a Qualitative Research Report*, David Morris (1993), hold process the same by applying ADDIE. The Japanese combine research in several ways. Many companies can work on the same research together. This allows for a broader application of results. The U.S. car companies spend hundreds of millions of dollars just to duplicate the research of their competitors. This money could be better utilized by all to move the entire industry forward.

The Japanese government, through JETRO (Japan External Trade Organization) and MITI (Ministry of International Trade and Industry), combine all available research to assist in its decision-making process as a nation. These are national clearinghouses where data are stored and catalogued. The difference between the Japanese model and the Western model is that these data are then applied to the decision making process. Westerners assemble data, but the data are often not included in decision-making. It is up to each individual researcher to apply the data in his or her own unique way.

The federal government has no clear or even muddy understanding of where it expects to take the United States fifteen years or fifteen minutes from now. Because of this, it has little interest in any specific type of research. All funding has become a political issue. The Endowment for the Arts, for example, is getting much more attention than it deserves while the nation continues to decline as a business power in the world. The government has a mentality that encourages a wide division of funds so as many of its constituents as possible are happy. The other government decision-making strategy is to hurt everyone equally so no one can accuse it of favoring one group over another. At least when the military drove the research agenda of the nation, the United States had a unified purpose. Who will step into this power vacuum?

Corporations are going to have to become much more involved in the determination of the research agenda of all the research constituents. A business "joint chiefs of staff" must be formed to ensure that the United States is utilizing this national resource in the most effective way to attain and sustain market power. The question is not whether research is helpful, but how will research be used to help the nation and will the world be a better place in which to live? No person or company in one area of research can make that decision alone. It must be a unified effort derived from a common direction.

*Depth of Analysis*

The question of how much analysis is enough is one that cannot be answered easily. The answer for most companies is, probably more than they think right now. Analysis does not mean that everyone gets together in a room and discusses their views on the company, its competition, and the industry. Although this may have value, what is advocated is to look at what actually can be derived from the data. Spend the time to find and read the data. This will be time well spent. The work can be divided among the members of the company. This does not mean endless quantification. Give everyone a chance to participate in the analysis step. Some will do a better job than others. A way to take advantage of this fact is by assigning two people to a task. This does not mean that they work together, but rather that they work on the same task. They may present their findings together so that they may have the opportunity to coordinate their presentations. There are cost/benefit constraints on any task and subtask. When enough has been done, the group will probably know it. The depth is up to the people involved in the process.

## Data

Data gathering is much easier today with the advent of computers. There is a great deal of information that is available to companies on themselves, their competition, and their industry. Companies should monitor what is said about them that others can easily access. This information should be as vague as possible. Competitors should not be given accurate information. Federal law requires that companies report specific information when they are on the stock exchange. The way that it is presented should make it as difficult as possible for competition to assess the firm accurately. If competition comes to a false conclusion after researching a company, this will give that company market power. Data can be categorized as both primary and secondary.

## Primary Data

Primary data are collected firsthand by a researcher. Such data may be collected internally by the firm or may be paid for by the firm but collected by an outside research organization. These data are collected through surveys, experiments, questionnaires, observations, interviews, focus groups, telephone surveys, and mail surveys. Any good research book will outline how this is done.

## Secondary Data

Secondary data are collected secondhand by the researcher. Someone else has done the research and has reported his or her findings. Much can be learned from secondary data if they are collected from multiple sources. Multiple sources give the researcher a broader view from which to make decisions. Secondary data may be collected internally by the firm or through outside research firms. Secondary data are collected through government documents, books, journals, magazines, newspapers, television, company annual reports, 10K reports, and on-line database searches.

## On-Line Databases

Before computers, it was difficult and time-consuming to gather data. Researchers had to spend long hours in the library to do the same research that can now be accomplished in minutes with a computer and a modem. It is almost unbelievable how much is available through database searching. You can get information from industrial trade journals; local, regional, national, and international newspapers; business journals; news releases; annual reports; government publications; investment analysis reports; industrial studies; and magazines. Computers have made both primary and secondary data much easier to acquire. Marketing research was responsible for this task in the past, but today a good reference librarian with advanced search skills can be more effective. A researcher in any office or at home any place in the world where there is a telephone can access many libraries full of information.

Databases charge for their services. Cost is dependent on such things as volume, time of day of the search, the cost of the particular database, and the amount of time spent in the database. For a small fee, many databases will train you how to use them. Training programs are carried on all over the United States. Different databases dominate in different parts of the world. If a company requests it, a database representative will come to the company and train its employees, usually at no charge.

A word of caution about database searching: it can quickly become very expensive. This is one reason why it is wise to train employees how to search databases. Some companies actually buy all the data in a database and download them into their own computers. Employees can then search this down-loaded material as much as is required. Many databases offer as a service the ability for a client to receive through the mail, at specific time intervals, any requested analysis. For example, one can request that any time a competitor's name appears in the database where market share is discussed, one will automatically receive that information. This saves money in searching and ensures that the firm will not miss important secondary data. Automatic searches can be as large or as small as a company wishes.

## Summary

With the addition of the Internet the types of research analysis that are available to any individual today are greater than at any time in history. Unfortunately, this is not necessarily reflected in accomplishments. Data are only as powerful as the ability to apply them to achieve a purpose. Researchers have done a poor job in the West of combining what is done in research to accomplish a unity of purpose. Each is going in his or her own direction to accomplish his or her own separate purposes. Even in an ideal world where research is combined, analysis is still only one step in the ADDIE process.

## Design

The design step is the second element in the ADDIE circular process. After the analysis step, when one has gathered as much information as one thinks will be needed to make a decision, then one designs a plan of action. Many organizations begin with the design step in the ADDIE process. This is an unwise decision because the design step will be enhanced if one analyzes before one begins even to consider design. Remember, know yourself and know your enemy.

## Selection of the Means

Work tasks and subtasks are outlined in the design step by applying the same 5Rs: marketing, human, physical, intangible, and financial resources. The design step outlines what each resource will do, when it will be done, and how well it will be done. This is accomplished through what is known as an "enabling objective." Terminal objectives describe the end, whereas enabling objectives describe the means. Many organizations confuse ends and means. Both the ends and the means are described by applying the same four components (ABCD). As you recall, a terminal objective describes one of four possible ends. They are to increase market share, to maximize profits, to diversify risk, and to increase return on shareholder equity. One of these four terminal objectives is selected at a time and then it is described, applying the ABCD components for more about terminal objectives (see the "Direction" module). Although the components remain the same, the descriptions are vastly different. The advantage of describing the ends and the means with the same components is that it connects, simplifies, and unifies ends and means with a common ABCD process.

## Enabling Objectives

Enabling objectives (figure 12) are clear statements that describe the means of an organization to achieve an end. Enabling objectives determine responsibility and time frames for tasks and subtasks to be carried out. Enabling objectives are meant as a guide to enhance performance, not as a method for catching people in nonperformance. Enabling objectives may be changed at any time by the leader and trusted follower. But, of course, they must always continue to be a means to achieve the organizational end. If an employee is for any reason not performing an enabling objective it is the obligation of the leader and follower to figure out the reason(s) and rectify the situation. The follower must continue to work toward the achievement of the enabling objective to the best of his or her ability. If the performance is not good enough, other tasks and subtasks should be found for the trusted follower to perform. If none are available, then the trusted follower should be retrained or let go. It is leadership's responsibility to identify and assist followers in the performance of enabling objectives. Enabling objectives apply the ABCD model.

## Figure 12
## Enabling Objectives

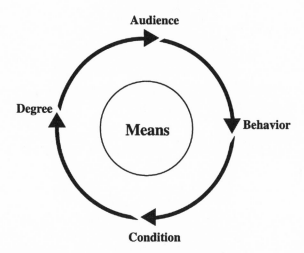

Adapted from: *National Special Media Institutes* (Syracuse, NY).

*Enabling Objective: Audience*

The audience for an enabling objective includes the individual employee, groups of employees, and the entire organization. This means that there will be some tasks and subtasks that one will do that are unique to one's assigned tasks and subtasks. There will be other tasks and subtasks that one will do that will be the same as those within the larger group within the organization. Tasks and subtasks overlap at the individual, group, and organizational levels.

A significant amount of what one will be expected to do, others will also be expected to do. All employees have significant job overlap. For example, all employees should have an in-depth understanding of all the products sold by their organization. They are all potential salespersons for their firm. This fact—that all employees are salespersons for the firm—is rarely emphasized or acknowledged. Another job overlap for all employees is that they are all expected, as part of their tasks and subtasks, to work for the benefit of the organization as a whole. They are all expected to treat each other and customers with respect. Although this seems obvious, many companies never recognize this as a part of all the employees' jobs. Customers are treated with respect by some, but not by all employees. This is not a question of management and labor, but rather the social interaction among employees. There are people at all levels in most companies that pride themselves on how much pain and extra work they cause others. These employees at all levels cause habitual problems, even though they may be perceived as capable, they should separate themselves from the group if they are unhappy with it, or the group should disengage them. This attitude is not condoned in war, and business is war.

*Enabling Objective: Behavior*

Behavior of individuals, groups, and the entire organization is represented through the KSA that are manifested indirectly and directly through assigned tasks and subtasks. A task is a well-defined unit of work, and a subtask is a component of the defined task.

The division of job activities (behavior) is accomplished by assessing the job and then finding or training the individual, group, and organization to perform to an acceptable standard. This is done through a task analysis. A task analysis is a written statement that outlines what is to be accomplished as a part of the ABCD components.

The number of tasks and subtasks that a person can handle at one time is far greater than Westerners envision in their pluralistic culture. Information-processing research has identified 7 (+ or -2). This number can be greatly enhanced if the organization uses job aids effectively. A job aid is a well-organized and clear training tool that enables the employee to do infrequent jobs by simply following the job aid. When you go up to a copy machine or a soda machine and it tells you on the front of the machine how to operate it, that is a job aid. Job aids are extremely valuable tools to help people perform infrequent and sometimes even frequent tasks and subtasks. With the proper training and the common process model of ADDIE for job aids, there is no limit to the extent of resource capability that employees are able to perform. The unique attributes of tasks and subtasks that prevent people from access to resources are eliminated. Most jobs require only a few typed paragraphs or less to outline required tasks and subtasks.

*Enabling Objective: Condition*

The condition element involves the limitations and restrictions that will be placed on the evaluation of the enabling objective. Condition is the length of time that the individual, the group, or the entire organization is expected to take to achieve the behavior that is outlined in the enabling objective. Limitations are influenced by the company's market power. By placing the constant of time on the enabling objective, the evaluator may compare behavior with the degree component. For example, a condition must be accomplished by April 27, 1998, or by March 9, 1999. The time frame must be specific.

### Enabling Objective: Degree

The degree element is the performance level that is to be achieved by the employee, group, or organization. The leader and the trusted follower set the performance standards to be accomplished by the trusted follower. The degree element returns to the behavior element and sets a specific performance for the tasks and subtasks. The tasks and subtasks apply to the "5Rs"—marketing, human, physical, intangible, and financial—and may be expressed in terms of percentage of increase, decrease in errors, dollar figures, and unit volume. Assessment should contribute to the desired outcome and should consider the costs in relation to the benefits.

### Summary

The design step determines who is going to do what, how well, and when. The design step of ADDIE applies the ABCD components to ensure organizational unity. All employees, as individuals, as part of a group, and as a part of the entire organization, are expected to do their best to accomplish their enabling objectives. The tasks and subtasks are given to trusted followers to carry out. Leadership's role is to assist trusted followers in this process.

## Development

The development step applies the "5Rs" to the circular ADDIE process. This is an overlooked but critical step. Development is defined as doing the design step on a limited basis for the purpose of testing. No one makes the correct decision in life every time. People are absolutely going to make mistakes. The illusion that somehow decision making will make one mistake-free is totally unfounded. Before one begins any process, one must understand that one will make mistakes, but it is necessary to work at learning from those mistakes and learning how to minimize the consequences of those mistakes. History is full of successful people and their running lists of mistakes, miscalculations, and failures. People can only try their best, make mistakes, and continue to try their best.

The Western interpretations of the quality movement have attempted to limit the number of mistakes by applying a statistical process. When machine operators discuss the calibration of their instruments to ensure that the gauges that they use to regulate the process are working properly, it is a test. When machine operators are doing this, they are testing and applying the development step in the ADDIE process. Suppose some instruments were not working correctly and every piece of product that came from a company was measured against that measurement? To test gauges at a fixed interval may save a company millions. This same principle applies to all thinking processes. (The concept of quality will be discussed in the evaluation section of the ADDIE process.)

Development as part of the ADDIE circular process is critical to the long-term success of the company. The development step tests everything ("5Rs") in the analysis and design steps. When an individual, group, or company determine a design to achieve a purpose, that design is always tested. The testing can be as simple as a few seconds to read over a letter that a secretary has typed or as involved as a three-year test to determine a market entry strategy. One thing about the development step that seems to always hold is that one has more time than one thinks to decide. In the Japanese *samurai* teachings, it is said that there are only one or two times in life where a decision has to be made at that moment. This means that countless millions of other decisions can wait for a test. This does not suggest that a test is a method to avoid decisions but instead it is part of decision-making process of ADDIE.

After a test, if results are found that indicate needed changes, those changes should be made and the test should be performed again. Companies such as McDonald's spend years testing. Each test area may have a different price, product variation, and promotional campaign. If, after the changes are made, the product is still not as successful as desired, a company may have to return to analysis. The reanalysis may show that the organizational end may have to be changed, or that the conditions that led to the decision have changed.

How does one know if a test is successful? The answer, like all others, is, will it achieve the desired end? If one has success and the results take one away from the end, then the end has to be rethought or the success has to be rethought. This may, in fact, require that the success is postponed or modified. ADDIE is directed toward a clearly defined purpose. That is its strength, so deviation from that purpose without a great deal of thinking is unwise. Many companies run from idea to idea with no sense of direction or purpose. This is dangerous at best.

### Different Testing Techniques

Testing can be as simple as testing a subtask, a task, a group of tasks and subtasks, or the entire direction of the organization. The advice is to test them all. One should get used to the inclusion of a test in all decision-making processes. Product testing is called test marketing. This is fine as long as it includes the "5Rs." If a test is limited to specific resources, the results will also be limited. This is the tyranny of the functional approach over the resource approach. The functional approach limits the capacity to combine, including the combining of testing. Testing helps decide if the who, what, when, where, and how of design should be modified, eliminated, or continued.

### Summary

The development step in the ADDIE circular process is important to the success of any means and end. This step allows for mistakes to be made that minimize the risk to the individual, the group, and the entire organization. Mistakes are always made and will always be made, but they can be controlled through the development step in ADDIE.

## Implementation

Implementation follows after the testing and modification that occurs during the development step of ADDIE. Implementation applies the "5Rs" in the circular ADDIE process. There are two different types of implementations: phased and total. Once the "5Rs" are implemented, there must be a mechanism to continue that implementation. If this does not occur, then the implementation may falter. The analysis of the company, competition, and industry affect implementation. The Japanese are far faster at bring new products to the market than are the Americans. This has forced many companies to rethink the way that they implement. For real improvement in this area, the entire ADDIE process is the issue, not just the implementation step. To implement without the other steps is folly.

*Phased Implementation*

Implementation of a means or an end can be phased into an organization. This entails the implementation being brought in over an extended period of time. This is done to limit risk and the expenditure of resources. If the individual, group, or entire organization is still uncertain about an outcome or has assessed that it will take a long period of time to accomplish, it may implement using a phased format. If the means or end develops a momentum that exceeds expectations, the timetable can be accelerated.

A phased implementation may be required because the organization does not and cannot do it any other way. For example, suppose that McDonald's develops (tests) and determines that pizza is a great potential product to sell. They still may have to implement a phased approach, because a company that makes special pizza ovens cannot produce them in the quantity required for the thousands of McDonald's stores. To have a phased implementation requires that McDonald's sell pizza state by state or area by area until it is able to sell throughout all its restaurants. This phased decision can be made in locations where the organization takes a low or high profile. If the company chooses a high-profile area, then the mistakes better have been overcome in the development step. If problems are evident, the whole program may collapse.

*Total Implementation*

In total implementation, the means or ends are implemented all at the same time. This is done if the organization has the necessary resources to do it all at once. A word of caution: even with all the resources available, a slower implementation may still be a wiser course of action. At times, a total implementation may be an indicator of deep problems within a company. This total change, depending on the severity, may indicate that past practices have collapsed. This is why the Japanese have instituted continuous improvement. It is less dangerous.

Americans as a cultural group like the bold move—the long touchdown pass in football or the Inchon landing in the Korean War. When these tasks and subtasks work out, they make history; when they do not work out, the losses are ensured. When the Japanese made the bold move at Pearl Harbor they were acting out of character. Perhaps that is why they did not occupy the islands, something that could have been easily accomplished. This is not to suggest that a sneak attack is not part of the *samurai* tradition. One is supposed to be ready, and there is no such thing as a sneak attack if one is always ready.

Some Harvard economists advocate shock therapy for nations that want to move to a free-market system. This is an attempt at total implementation and it is a highly risky move. One would expect this solution to be put forth by Americans. Of course, there are times when total implementation is the correct course of action, but it is just as likely that it could be a bad move. This decision should come from a market power analysis and assessment. The advocacy of total implementation for all circumstances lacks an understanding of life.

*Continuous Implementation*

Americans have been criticized for not thinking through the implementation process. Once something is implemented, it must be maintained. This is important because if something is successful and then it is not maintained, it can quickly deteriorate and all gains are lost. This is one of the advantages of a multiskilled workforce. Employees can quickly move into new tasks and subtasks. With a specialized workforce, new people must be trained for new and varied implementations.

*Summary*

The implementation step in the circular ADDIE process applies the same "5Rs" as the other steps. The form that the implementation takes depends on the available resources and the risks that the individual, group, and organization wish to incur. The speed of implementation of the Japanese is really a speed derived from process. Implementation is one of the steps.

**Evaluation**

All circular tasks and subtask components of the "5Rs" should be evaluated. Many organizations avoid evaluation because if the task or subtask is successful, then they do not feel it requires evaluation; if it was unsuccessful, they fear that evaluation may lead to finger pointing. The management of the organization fears that this may lead to a negative evaluation of its performance. The more people that are involved in any project, the less chance that there will be any retribution for failure to obtain a terminal or enabling objective. Many organizations have been accused of making decisions by consensus as a mechanism to avoid accountability. This position is the norm in many companies where those who falter are punished. Personal initiative can be a dangerous gamble. Unfortunately, this environment has led to a real fear of any type of evaluation.

Another unspoken problem with evaluation is that in our litigious society it has become almost impossible to fire a specific employee without the possibility of a lawsuit. An evaluation that is not absolutely capable of standing the scrutiny of a jury trial can cost the organization millions.

This is especially true in the public sector, but it has also become a large challenge in the private sector. To fire a police chief in Connecticut, for example, can cost a town up to a million dollars because of a state law that protects police chiefs from dismissal. This means that the elected officials of a town have to be willing to face a loss at reelection time because of increased taxes, even if the firing is proved justified in a court of law. The United States has, in the past, been a nation that has accepted the firing of employees. In many countries in the world, once an employee has been hired, it is almost impossible to terminate him or her for any reason. As a nation, Americans have moved more toward the model of not allowing a firm to let an employee go from the job. If this is going to be the norm, then Americans have to spend more time with selection.

At the opposite end of the spectrum, many good and loyal employees have been fired on a whim. Chief executives have betrayed their trust granted by the group, and through personal greed and ignorance have failed to lead their companies. These people are bankrupt at a tribal level because they have destroyed their tribe for personal gain. According to Theory "W," this is a betrayal of trust and in the primitive tribe would hold severe consequences.

Evaluation of all resources must consider the human consequences of actions for all members of the tribe. All employees are diminished by the firing of one person that through no fault of his or her own has failed to perform. Different people have different KSA. The issue may only be that the employee was not up to that particular challenge. This is why the leader/trusted follower model is so important. A trusted follower is assisted by the leader and not allowed to falter. The leader must step in and do the job if necessary. This is far more productive than waiting for the trusted follower to fail and then trying to assess who is to blame. The failure of a trusted follower is the leader's responsibility and the responsibility of that person's leader, right up to the chief executive officer (CEO) and the board of directors. Move the person or persons to a job that he, she, or they can perform. Retrain them if necessary. Many valued employees are broken for life because they were unable to perform in a new job and they were then fired. A move to another job may have saved a valued employee for years of productive work. Everyone cannot be CEO, nor would it benefit the company if it were otherwise.

### Formative and Summative Evaluation

There are two types of evaluation that can be applied to both the terminal and enabling objectives: formative and summative. Formative evaluation is constant, second by second, day by day, week by week, month by month, and year by year. Summative evaluation is at a fixed time. Both are important and necessary, because all people can learn by what they have already experienced. Evaluation should not be to figure out how to punish but rather how to improve.

### *Formative Terminal Objective Evaluation*

The terminal objective is a single organizational end identified from a market power analysis and assessment. It is selected from four possible alternatives—to change/maintain market share, to maximize profits, to diversify risk, and to increase the return on shareholder equity. This terminal objective is the responsibility of the CEO and the board of directors. They are responsible for the constant circular monitoring of the "5Rs" of the company, competition, and the industry. They should receive updates whenever they are available. The CEO and the board of directors should be as well informed as possible. This does not suggest that the organizational end should be changed on a second-by-second basis or, indeed, even yearly. What is advocated is an extremely well informed leadership.

### Summative Terminal Objective Evaluation

As the CEO of a company, one should monitor specific "5R" resources at definite time intervals. For example, every two months, the CEO should check to ensure that the correct employees are being hired to achieve the selected end. This would mean that a candidate for secretary, salesperson, personnel, loading dock, or any other position would be interviewed by the CEO to ensure that the means (hiring) are moving in the direction of the designated end. The CEO does not have to become involved in all hiring decisions, but should do so just enough to ensure that hiring tasks and subtasks are to the expected ABCD standard. All resources should be monitored by the CEO.

Another important role of a summative evaluation of the terminal objective is to determine if the organizational end should be changed or remain the same. This requires that a market power analysis and a market power assessment be performed at fixed time intervals. This is not to suggest that the CEO could not call for these two activities to be compiled at any time, but that the CEO should not change the end without the full analysis and assessment. This formal process forces the organization to consider all the "5Rs" before the important decision is made by the CEO and the board of directors on the direction of the firm.

### Formative Enabling Objective(s) Evaluation

All enabling objectives are evaluated on a second-by-second, minute-by-minute, week-by-week, month-by-month, and year-by-year basis. Each task and subtask is evaluated in relation to the defined enabling objective. Evaluation of performance is a constant part of process. The leader should step in to assist the trusted follower and support staff at any time to assure that the terminal and enabling objectives are met.

### Summative Enabling Objective(s) Evaluation

Enabling objectives that are described through the ABCD components should be evaluated at specific predetermined time intervals. Individuals, groups, and the entire company are responsible for different aspects of the "5Rs" being evaluated. The leader should have a specific time set aside to monitor the tasks and subtasks of his or her trusted followers. This monitoring is done in a mutually trusting relationship, so that the job gets done to the expected standards of performance.

### Evaluation and Quality

America has discovered quality and forgotten about—or has never understood—evaluation. Quality proponents advocate three things: process, continual improvement through fewer errors, and the improvement of the quality of the materials that go into a product. The example given is that if a car's dashboard is made of plastic and a new one made of oak is put in, the quality has been improved. Americans point to the Japanese experience and Edward Deming as an example of a person who tried to improve the quality of manufacturing in the United States and was rejected. He then was forced to go to Japan. The Japanese somehow saw the merits of Deming's statistical processes and embraced them, thereby turning their junk products into world-class manufactured goods.

This view has no historic evidence because the Japanese have embraced quality as part of their culture for a thousand years. Their products were junk in the export markets after World War II, but they have always kept quality at home because of the market power of the United States to block access at the high end. The Japanese used Deming as a decoy: if a nation is defeated, it tries to make the victor think subsequent actions were always that nations idea. In the story of *Brer Rabbit*, the rabbit pleads with the fox to do anything but throw him into the briar patch. Of course the fox proceeds to do just that and he is set free in his element. As Japan moves toward total independence, most Americans will be surprised and probably offended, that the Japanese will not give the United States credit for their quality emphasis.

Japanese quality is derived from Buddhism, not from Deming and Juran. Both Deming's and Juran's processes are flawed when compared to ADDIE. They both lack the number of steps to cover a process. They are both even more flawed because of their supposed insistence on a single activity called quality. They attempt to link quality and process, whereas ADDIE links all activities with process. To put the survival of the nation on a single (pluralistic) solution is an inherent weakness. The "Juran's Trilogy" of quality as a process contains quality planning, quality control, and quality improvement. The "Deming Cycle" includes plan-do-check and action. The quality movement has already peaked because it has failed to deliver to American industry.

All the quality in the world cannot overcome such obstacles as government barriers to entry. It is part of U.S. heritage to continue to search for the single solution. The solution can never be only one separate activity. It must be a unified and integrated approach. Is quality important? Yes. Is quality everything? No. Quality is a form of evaluation applying a simple mathematical technique. Is process evaluation? No. Process is analysis, design, development, implementation, and evaluation. Process is part of a philosophy, philosophy (KSA), philosophy in action (market power), direction, and structure. One component called quality (evaluation) is simply not enough.

*Summary*

Evaluation is a critical step in the ADDIE process because it gives both the leader and his or her trusted followers the opportunity to assess progress toward both the terminal and enabling objectives of the organization. It is the responsibility of the leader to ensure that the trusted follower is performing to expected standards on the ABCD components. It is also the responsibility of the leader to step in and assist the trusted follower in a mentoring capacity. Evaluation does not need to be a destructive activity that will be avoided for the self-protection of the individual, group, or company. Evaluation is the monitoring of tasks and subtasks to ensure a continual standard of performance.

## Conclusion

Process as an underlying operating system is applied as a common cognitive thinking process. This circular process moves in a never-ending sequence of ADDIE: analysis, design, development, implementation, and evaluation. The entire ADDIE model applies the "5Rs"—or the marketing, human, physical, intangible, and financial resources—to each step. Analysis is the gathering of data on one's company, its competition, and its industry. Design is the plan of actions proposed to achieve an end. The design is tested on a limited basis in the development step. This allows for the return to previous steps or the continuation to the implementation step. Implementation concerns the production of the product or service that was designed and tested. Evaluation is the continual monitoring of the accomplishment of individuals, groups, and the entire organization. The terminal and enabling objectives are compared with results in a formative evaluation and a summative evaluation. It is the role of the leader to ensure that these objectives are carried out to expected standards of performance. If the trusted follower is deemed to be unable to perform to these standards (ABCD), then he or she should be given tasks and subtasks that he or she is capable of performing; until that occurs, the leader and others must perform the tasks and subtasks.

## SELECTED READINGS

Benson, Herbert. *The relaxization response*. Avenal, N.J.: Outlet Books, 1993.

Carr, Edward, H. *What is history?* New York: Vantage Books, 1961.

Deming, Edward W. *Out of the crisis*. Cambridge: Massachusetts Institute of Technology, 1982.

Juran, Joseph M. *Managerial breakthrough*. New York: McGraw-Hill, 1964.

———. *Juran on leadership for quality: An executive handbook*. New York: Free Press, 1989.

———. *Juran on quality by design: The new steps for planning quality into goods and services*. New York: Free Press, 1992.

Morris, David. Developing a multi-skilled workforce through an assembly model. *Performance and Instruction Journal* 24(3) (1985): 15–17, 21.

———. *Guidelines for writing a qualitative research report*. Chicago: American Marketing Association, 1993.

Morris, David, and Satish Chandra. *Guidelines for case analysis*. Chicago: American Marketing Association, 1993.

———. *Guidelines for writing a research report*. Chicago, IL: American Marketing Association, 1993.

Gustafson, Kent, L. *Survey of instructional development models*. Syracuse, NY: ERIC Clearinghouse on Information Resources, 1981.

Onnis, Arturo. *The language of total quality*. Castellamonte, Italy: Topk, 1992.

Renteria, Luis, and David Morris, Jr. *A unitary approach to international mediation*. Madison, Conn.: Market Power Institute, 1996.

Van Paris, Andre P., and Robert Lussier. Marketing education should adopt a unified thought process. In *New perspectives on business: International conference Volume*. Ed. S. Lodha, K. Matsumoto, and D. Morris. New Haven, Conn.: New England Business Administration Association, 1993.

# 5Rs (Marketing, Human, Physical, Intangible, and Financial Resources)

## MARKETING RESOURCES

There are five resources that will be applied to the unitary operating system outlined in this module. These resources are generally termed marketing, human, physical, intangible, and financial (figure 13). Choosing these resource categories are arbitrary. It should be understood that in actuality there is no such thing as a marketing resource or a human resource. To identify them as such serves the purpose of continuing to separate within the organization. The concept of having a full-time employee who identifies with any one particular resource over another is limiting. The organization may occasionally hire a few people on a temporary basis who excel in a specific resource area. This should be the exception rather than the rule, and once their knowledge, skills, and attitudes (KSA) have been transferred, they should be let go. This does not mean that the organization should fire everyone and subcontract all activities, or only hire temporary employees. A unitary approach requires that the company move employees from task to subtask with ease.

Employees are selected, trained, and upgraded according to their capacity and interest to do multiple tasks and subtasks. The separation of resources into functions is cultural and has nothing to do with inherent human abilities. No company exists today that cannot achieve this transition to a multiskilled workforce. The market power of the West has allowed centuries of separating and protecting jobs, but this has now become a detriment to organizational survival in the international marketplace.

## Figure 13
## The "5Rs"

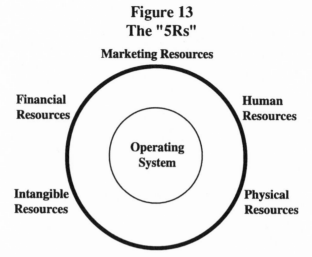

**Marketing Resources**

Adapted from: *Marketing as a Means to Achieve Organizational Ends* (West Haven, CT: University of New Haven Press.

The large organization of the future will be modeled on the lines of the small entrepreneurial firms of today. In these organizations, a small number of people have to work together and do it all. Resources are not the separate domain of any one specialized individual. Resources are variables that are applied by individual(s), group(s), and the entire company. These resources are manipulated by the organization's philosophy, philosophy (KSA), philosophy in action (market power), direction, structure, and Process. The relationships in organizations of the future may either be ones that separate or ones that unify. Those that unify will generally have the market power. The exception is a government-granted monopoly.

### Pluralistic

The marketing function is divided into three categories: customers, marketing mix, and reasoning tools. In a pluralistic organization, those within the marketing function develop their own philosophy in action, directions, structures, and processes. The marketing function identifies those attributes that separate it from all other functions. The marketing philosophy in action in the United States has traditionally focused on the needs and wants of customers. There is a small but growing movement that now focuses on relationships, but these relations are derived from needs and wants.

Marketing as a function responds to the multiple directions that the organization has identified. The structure of the marketing function is hierarchical. Promotion and advancement occur within each specialty. Marketing functional activities apply their own separate process to each and every action that is carried out. Those within the marketing function consider it the most important function within the organization. Members of other functions can only be tolerated at best.

## Unitary

Marketing is a resource that is divided into tasks and subtasks. These tasks and subtasks all share a common philosophy, philosophy (KSA), philosophy in action, direction, structure, and process. The selection of any one resource within the marketing resource area is for the purpose of achieving a unified end. Marketing as a resource is a means to that end, not an end in itself. The resource is divided into three general areas so that they may be applied as a checklist: customer, marketing mix, and reasoning tools. Consider these areas as if they were a pilot's preflight checklist. The order is not critical, but it is important to have an order. This avoids omissions because of human error and forces employees to think through the resource in the same sequence. It is possible to add to the list as needed, but once a step is added, it should not be omitted, because what is omitted today may become important tomorrow. This does not mean that a step cannot be omitted after it has been thought through at the individual, group, and organizational levels. The next time the sequence is repeated that term should appear again. This operating system is an endless circle.

## CUSTOMER

Many students misunderstand the concepts of "customer" and "needs" and "wants." Customers are a resource, whereas the construction of needs and wants is, at best, a philosophy in action. U.S. trained marketing executives have a difficult time separating the customer from the philosophy in action of needs and wants. Under the unitary philosophy, the customer is important, but the philosophy in action is market power, not needs and wants. This means that the company does not attempt to fill the needs and wants of customers as a philosophy in action, but rather the marketing resource of customer, as with all other resources, is directed toward blocking competitors from access to targeted markets.

This does not mean that the customer is unimportant, but the unitary concept of the customer is different than the Western concept. Customers do business with one company rather than another for many reasons besides needs and wants. Considering only customer needs and wants is so limiting that it is now inhibiting America's competitive position. Providing for the customers' needs and wants sounds good, but it is more of a wish based on separative American values than anything having to do with the reality of doing business. Needs and wants are derived from the philosophy of separating, in which a function called marketing has attempted to impose its limited view on the entire organization.

In a unitary philosophy, customers are not segmented into groups and then targeted because of their needs and wants. The company does not position an image in the customers' minds because of their needs and wants. Instead, the company applies all its resources to make customers buy from them and not from their competition. The company segments, targets, and positions in an effort to understand customers better than its competition. These are the customers that the company has determined that it has enough market power to extract wealth from in order to achieve its organizational purpose or end.

It is generally good business practice for a company to maintain its customers and continue to keep them away from its competition, but this may not always be the case. There are times when a company may want and encourage customers to go to the competition. The risk of maintaining them as customers may far outweigh the rewards and returns. Certain customers may not be able to pay their bills, although they may need and want to buy a company's product(s) or service(s). If they cannot pay, or if the risk of their not paying is high, then it may be to a company's advantage to have its competition have the problem with these customers. Customers are categorized in terms of segmentation, target marketing, consumer behavior (motivation), and positioning.

## CUSTOMER: SEGMENTATION
### Pluralistic

A pluralistic approach to market segmentation selects customers based on the customers, needs and wants. This separates the marketing function from other functions.

### Unitary

*Definition.* Dividing a market into one or more groups so that each group has similar characteristics, so that one's company can attain market power.

*Geographic Segmentation*

Customers can be divided by geographic location. The number of geographic variations that are available is only limited by the imagination of those within the organization. An organization that wants to maintain or gain market power should have a good understanding of geographic differences. The contrast from one city block to another or from one nation to another may be startling. A mountain range, a river, a road, a harbor, an airport, a town line, or a state line can be an important factor. The weather conditions within a particular geographic location may change a company's design. These factors should be assessed as if one were a general. One should get maps, go there and take the time to analyze as part of ADDIE (analysis, design, development, implementation, and evaluation). Many business decisions unwisely are made with very little knowledge. Americans have avoided the reality of earthquakes, volcanic eruptions, tornadoes, hurricanes, floods, and blizzards in decision making. Often, Americans feel that these things only affect insurance companies. However, hurricanes can mean unlimited losses or success for any who are unprepared or prepared.

*Demographic Segmentation*

An understanding of people can give a company market power. Who are these potential customers? How old are they? What is the size of the family? Are there changes in the age patterns of groups? Can one expect more people over age sixty-five, or fewer, within the next five years? What are the birthrates? What are the death rates and causes? What diseases are prevalent? Are they expected to change? How much money do people make? How much money do they spend? What are their holidays both religious and secular? What groups have power, and how do they apply that power? How do different groups get along, and how are they expected to get along in the future? Have they fought in the past? When did they fight, and how severely? Do they value education, the law, and their word? Do they do what they say they are going to do? What type of education do they value? Do they maintain what they have? The number of questions to be asked and answered is far more than one might think.

## Psychographic Segmentation

In the group of people being studied, are there specific life-style expectations? For example, is it considered a right or a privilege to own a car, obtain a college education, and own one's own home? What are the expectations of men and women of all age groups? Is an eleven-year-old crushed unless he or she has a $400 bike? Do belongings always have to be new? For example, the Japanese and those from many other nations do not sell their used clothing at garage sales. It would be considered a disgrace to wear someone else's clothes. Are there distinct social classes? Are these classes, religious, racial, political, intellectual, or philosophical in origin? Are there certain assumptions made about members? Are there assumptions for nonmembers? What are the stated and unstated issues? An open analysis of many of these issues is often avoided in American business because of a fear of being accused of some indiscretion that may lead to a lawsuit. This fear is not part of ADDIE process followed by other companies, those who compete against U.S. firms in the world marketplace.

## Behavioristic Segmentation

What are people's purchase patterns in various places or groups? Do they save and then purchase, or do they want to purchase on credit? What types of credit terms do they respond to for the purchase of particular items such as a car or house? How much debt will they incur for how long and on what types of items? What percentage of their income is put aside for retirement? What types of retirement instruments are available?

How often do they replace items, and what prompts the repurchase? What causes them not to repurchase? What type of status is associated with purchases? Is the status the same in all age groups, social classes, and geographic areas? Who makes the purchase decision? What is the order of importance for one purchase over another? For example, is it more important to own a large-screen television than a computer? How far will a person travel for various levels of savings for different types of products and services? For example, a person may think nothing of traveling three thousand miles for a college education, but may not want to travel twenty minutes away from his or her job to find a home.

## CUSTOMER: TARGET MARKETING
### Pluralistic

A pluralistic approach to targeting selects customers based on the customers' needs and wants. This separates marketing as a function from other functions.

**Unitary**

*Definition.* Focusing all the firm's efforts on a specific group or groups of prospective customers (defined by market segmentation) in which the firm has the market power to achieve its desired end.

**Targeting a Single Segment**

The entire organizational effort is directed toward blocking competition from one segment. This includes philosophy, philosophy (KSA), philosophy in action (market power), direction, structure, process, and the "5Rs." Many organizations target a single segment. Thousands of single segments are capable of sustaining one or more organizations. Associations such as the American Marketing Association are sustained by those who view themselves as being in the field of marketing. The same is true of such groups as the American Medical Association, the Boy Scouts of America, and the Episcopal Church. These groups focus on a specific group of identifiable people. All the resources of the group are directed at sustaining and building the group's defined single market. These groups find that by maintaining single-segment focus, they can achieve their ends. They may define multiple segments within their single targeted market, but their focus is really on a single segment. The day this changes, they will have to combine or go out of business.

The American Federation of Labor (AFL) and the Congress of Industrial Organizations (CIO) once separate organizations, now constitute the AFL-CIO. They did not combine because they wanted to, but because they had to. They had lost so much market power as two separate organizations that they had to combine in an attempt to regain their ability to appeal to a redefined single segment and block competitors from the new targeted market. In a society that has a fundamental philosophy of separating, combining is not viewed the same as in a society that is unitary. As an organization begins to lose market power with its single-segment approach, it begins to search for multiple segments.

This is not to suggest that a multiple-segment approach is always the result of a failed single-segment approach. The failure of the single-segment approach is obvious to anyone who looks at military suppliers of the Cold War. These firms are now attempting, with very little market power, to move into other targeted segments. A forced change from a single-target market segment to a multiple-target segment is very high risk. The move usually becomes a number of separate desperate acts rather than a unified, well-thought-out means to an end. However, those firms that use ADDIE are more prepared for the shifts in market conditions than those that do not. This requires leadership.

**Targeting Multiple Segments**

The entire organizational effort is directed toward blocking competition from two or more segments. This includes philosophy, philosophy (KSA), philosophy in action, direction, structure, process, and the 5Rs. Many organizations feel that they attain more market power by targeting multiple segments. Multiple segments open up the opportunity for a company to appeal to a larger market while still targeting a controllable number of segments. They also help diversify some of the risk that a company would have if targeting only one segment. One of the negative aspects of multiple targeting as it is generally considered in the United States is that these multiple segments require that the organization diffuse resource allocation. The organization separates its internal resources into groups that focus on one of the targeted segments.

When multiple segments are selected because they are part of a unified philosophy, targeting is a different concept. The American view has been that resources (conceived of as the "4Ps" rather than as the "5Rs") are allocated for each targeted segment. This means that the company has separate pricing, products, promotions, and places (distributions) for individual segments among the multiple segments. A unitary approach selects multiple segments where resources overlap. Instead of selecting segments and allocating resources to them, segments are selected that build the market power of one segment on another. If segments do not appear to overlap, then the challenge is to find ways in which they do. When this is done, resources are allocated from a unitary philosophy. Working toward combining resources for targeting multiple segments gives the organization the market power to achieve its ends.

An example of how a company functions under the American pluralistic view of marketing is Disney, Inc. Suppose it had decided to identify itself in the entertainment industry. It would then determine the segments that the company wished to target and with which products. Disney would then apply the "4Ps" to each of those targeted segments. Under a unitary philosophy, Disney's leader would determine, based on a market power analysis and assessment, what end the organization should achieve. An analysis of present market power would reveal areas in which Disney was able to block competition. Disney would assess those areas to determine how it could use its present market power to gain more market power. Thinking in this new way, Disney would no longer identify itself with the entertainment business because it would be too limiting, but would build its business on market power. Millions of people visit Disney's parks each year, and while they are there, they represent a captive market. Is the issue now what do these people need and what do they think they need? Specifically, Disney can feed, clothe, educate, entertain, transport, and protect these millions of people with impunity. The company could, if it desired, build and maintain its own hospital.

Since Disney currently has no competition in these locations it can raise the price of a hamburger with fries to almost $5 with ease. A pair of underwear with Mickey Mouse on it can sell for $18. The opportunities are endless. Disney has created its own society in which it can dictate what is sold and for how much. The customer, once he or she participates, must pay the prices charged at the park. Of course, the customer has the right to come and go at will and attempt to get a lower price outside of the park. This is difficult, however, because those businesses outside the park can also take advantage of the market power of their locations near Disney Parks to charge higher prices. When the family gets back to Madison, Connecticut, for example, a similar hamburger at Nick's costs $2.95 because the individual store cannot block competition as well as Disney. Nick's has to apply market power to block its competition. Nick's does this with great service, variety, and large portions. The Disney example is not meant as a negative example but rather as a positive one. People save for years to go there and enjoy themselves.

Another example is provided by a Canadian railroad that would each day take supplies and passengers up into the north and then return with trees for lumber. The trip up was empty and unprofitable whereas the trip back was loaded to capacity. Applying the concept of market power, the railroad realized that during the trip, up and back, the passengers were in essence, a captive market. The railroad had the opportunity to sell them whatever they would purchase during the long trip. The railroad could also determine where the train would stop and for how long. Because of this, the railroad was able to build hotels, restaurants, gift shops, grocery stores, outfitters, and any other business that gave them more market power along the route. The train then just stopped at those locations. Shannon Duty Free Shop at Shannon Airport in Ireland is a stopover for those coming from and going to Dublin, Ireland. One can remain on the airplane but few choose to do so. Few complain about the long time it takes before the plane takes off again. Anyone that thinks these are just random acts are not learning about market power.

**Targeting all Segments**

The entire organizational effort is directed toward blocking competition from all segments. This includes philosophy, philosophy (KSA), philosophy in action, direction, structure, process, and the "5Rs." There are few products or services that target all segments. In many cases, products that are considered commodities are targeted at a mass market. When a farmer sells corn, there is no differentiation between his or her corn crop and his or her neighbor's corn crop. The truck pulls up to a grain elevator and his or her grain is put in with all the rest. The price paid is the price being paid for that commodity at that time on the day that it is sold. When a company buys the grain and puts it into a box and calls it "Uncle Dave's Corn," the same item changes from one that the farmer sold by targeting all available segments to one that is sold by a company targeting one or many segments. In this case, the product itself is not the issue, but rather how the product is sold and to whom. The same product or service can be sold thousands of different ways to thousands of targeted segments.

There are few products or services in this society for which sellers do not differentiate between segments in their targeting. Vaseline and salt are essentially mass market items for which sellers have targeted all segments. However, there are even exceptions for each of these.

**CUSTOMER: CONSUMER BEHAVIOR (MOTIVATION)**
**Pluralistic**

The American pluralistic marketing philosophy has emphasized the field of psychology. In an attempt to make marketing appear more scientific, the behavior of customers is studied. There is absolutely no agreement that any particular school of psychology or technique may be applied to motivate the actions of consumers. What has occurred is the limited testing of specific motivational techniques on specific populations. The whole area of psychology as a scientific attempt to understand the behavior of humans is in itself a reflection of the Western drive to separate the mind, body, and the spirit from nature. This separation does not take in a culture that embraces a unitary philosophy.

Psychology at its best is cultural. Its value may exist only in those cultures that believe that it is valuable. This is not to suggest that people are not motivated or that they cannot be motivated to change short-term actions. Long-term changes in behavior take more resources than the knowledge provided in the West by psychology. Actions are driven by market power. An example from recent history is the collapse of the Soviet Union. The second that the threat of military reprisal no longer existed for the nations of Central Europe, they were back at their thousand-year-old conflicts. Decades of education and an entirely new generation of people did not or could not break the cycle. Some young and old Irish in the United States hate the English, often with little knowledge or understanding of their reasons, and all the education of a Ph.D. in psychology or years of therapy cannot overcome that stark reality. Individual behavior is rewarded or punished with great variations from culture to culture. Consumer behavior that we believe to be universal may be a cultural norm or a brief aberration.

Is there anything that has been learned in Western psychology that can be applied outside of a narrow cultural area? What has been and continues to be considered worthy of research and publication reflects the cultural norms of any given moment in time. Western marketing pluralists want, as discussed earlier, to divide marketing into an individualized single-targeted segment. These individualized segments are then tracked and manipulated to purchase products and services. It is constantly argued that everyone is an individual and that there are no cultural norms. This argument in itself is cultural.

## Unitary

*Definition.* The motivation of a targeted group to purchase and repurchase products and services to gain market power.

## ARCS

The ARCS model developed by Keller and Dodge discussed in the "Structure" module divides motivation into four broad categories: A, attention; R, relevance; C, confidence; and S, satisfaction. The ARCS model is only one of many resources that can be applied to motivate consumers to purchase and repurchase. It appeals to people from many different cultures and backgrounds.

## Attention

It seems reasonable that if you cannot or do not get the people's attention, it will be difficult to motivate them to any action. The question is not whether sellers require the attention of the customer, or group of customers but how they get and hold the customer's attention. This will have entirely different consequences in cultures that embrace a pluralistic or unitary philosophies. The focus on the individual in one culture may be disastrous in another. Asians are not sitting around dreaming of the day when each individual will be a market segment unto himself or

Market Power and Business Strategy

herself. It is not within their philosophical norms.

## Relevance

All cultures will respond to what they believe to be relevant to themselves. Historic events, religious rites, the education of the young, and indeed all actions are subsumed under the umbrella of philosophy (see the "Introduction"). For example, in the United States neither of the opposing sides in the abortion issue has suggested that the aborted fetus is fulfilling its *karma* and that it will be reborn to have another experience on its way to achieve *nirvana*. In certain areas of the world, to discuss the issue of abortion from either of the opposing American views would elicit much different responses.

When the West had the power of gunboats, they could impose their religious and cultural beliefs on others. When the gunboats were removed, the old values returned. Note that the positions of both Germany and Japan are changing and no longer reflect values of the Americans (the conquerors) as military force is removed.

## Confidence

For a consumer to move to action, he or she must have confidence that actions will bring predictable results. This is also cultural. In Hinduism, actions should be and are carried out without any interest in how others perceive the outcome. It is not up to humans to judge the outcome of actions; it is, rather, in the hands of the divine.

## Satisfaction

Rewards must be both intrinsic and extrinsic to motivate. The type of rewards that the individual strives to achieve are cultural. It is obvious that the United States has focused on the rewards to individuals, whereas other cultures have stayed with a system that emphasizes rewards to the family, group, and society, and so forth. To motivate those within different philosophical frameworks will require a far different emphasis.

## CUSTOMER: POSITIONING
### Pluralistic

There are two dominant views of positioning. One is put forth by Al Ries and Jack Trout, and the other is advocated by most American marketing professors. The Ries and Trout version is that an image should be placed in the mind of the customer. They put forth the idea that this is done through advertising. A company assumes a position in the market and then moves to support that position through their advertising. Ries and Trout are both in the advertising business. For example, if a company wants to position itself as having the best possible product at the highest possible price, it must perform in specific ways to create that image. Companies such as Rolls Royce and Tiffany's come to mind. Consumers do not expect Rolls Royce to advertise free hot dogs and balloons for the kids when customers come in for a test drive. A company may also want to position itself as offering the best product at the lowest price. Many Japanese firms have done a good job of creating this image.

The second group, the American marketing professors, put forth the idea that the company should attempt to create an image in the minds of the customers, but that this is accomplished through the "4Ps," or the marketing mix (the marketing mix is discussed in the next section). Both groups develop positioning maps that monitor the image of one company compared to another on several variables. These maps can be followed over time to monitor the results obtained by using either advertising or the "4Ps" for the creation and maintenance of a particular image.

### Unitary

*Definition.* Placing an image in the minds of consumer(s) and nonconsumer(s) in reference to the company, its competition, and the industry. This is achieved through philosophy, philosophy (KSA), philosophy in action, direction, structure, and resources of the firm.

The difference between the pluralistic view and the unitary view is that the unitary view proposes that the image of a company should be built on all actions. Reliance on advertising or on the "4Ps" is too limiting. A company is a representation of more than these separated resources. The issue of the created image versus the reality of what the company stands for is a much deeper problem. As a society, Westerners have begun to believe that reality is created not by the actions of individuals and groups of individuals but through manipulation of the marketing resource. In Syracuse, New York, the Carrier Air Conditioner Corporation announced a big layoff. Those in the town felt betrayed and reacted with hostility. Carrier's response was to hire a public relations firm to handle the negative image. The company showed no apparent sense that it had betrayed its former employees, but rather focused on how it could change the negative image of the company.

This is not to suggest that a company cannot lay off employees when necessary to survive and prosper. From a unitary view, however, the company has an obligation to the community, the state, and the nation in which it is a member. This also goes the other way: the community, the state, and the nation each has an obligation to the company and its employees. This commitment cannot consist of rhetoric and empty marketing campaigns, but rather, it must be backed by a philosophical foundation. Living the life that one advocates is far more difficult than creating a false image for personal, corporate, or national gain.

### MARKETING MIX: THE "4PS"

### Pluralistic

The marketing mix is considered in the academic community in United States to be the domain of the field of marketing. The general areas covered in these text books are the "4Ps": price, product, promotion, and place. Unfortunately, what has occurred in many corporations is that these areas are seldom, if ever, entirely under the marketing function. Pricing is often dominated by finance. Product development and implementation are dominated by engineering. Promotion is dominated by the sales force, and place by operations. If marketing is lucky, the company identifies sales with marketing. When the company refers to a marketing representative, it means a salesperson. Marketing from a pluralistic point of view has done a dismal job of carving out its turf and then protecting it from other functions. Finance has done the best job, to all our detriment. This is not to imply that marketing as a function has taken a unitary approach.

Those in marketing within the corporation have followed the academics' mantra and have now settled on the customer as their domain. They see themselves as the customer advocate of the group within the organization that bridges the gap between the company and its customers by monitoring the customers' feelings and desires. Marketing in many corporations attempts to involve the customer in its decision-making process through its particular functional area. This has had some success.

This inclusion of customers is a different view from the one put forth by the academics. The academics, especially the psychologists, want to do psychological profiles instead of listening to customers. The monitoring of customers to determine their feelings and desires has not had a direct or even indirect influence over the marketing mix. It is often a separate activity that has little influence or input into the whole. Unfortunately, competition and industry assessment of the marketing-mix components as a part of strategic planning has been lost. Strategic planning has either become a separate corporate function or a part of each disconnected strategic business unit.

### Unitary

*Definition.* Price, product, promotion, and place are resources that are applied as a means to achieve an organizational end. They are regulated by philosophy, philosophy (KSA), philosophy in action (market power), direction, structure, and process.

### Marketing Mix

The marketing mix is not a domain to be lost nor regained by any one group. The marketing mix consists of resources that are combined with all other resources within the organization. They are applied only to achieve an organizational purpose. Resources should not be applied just because the organization must have all functions represented. Functions that are not a means to achieving an end then become ends unto themselves. Resources must never be conceived of as an end, because there are too many of them. If a resource is a means, then the marketing mix and all its components are applied only as required. The following are the four areas of the marketing mix and several of their subdivisions. Each term is defined and then followed by an example of how an organization attempts to apply resources to block competition from access to targeted-market segments—sometimes successfully and sometimes unsuccessfully.

### MARKETING MIX: PRICE (INCREASES)

*Definition.* The market power to charge more for a product or service.

## Introduction

There are several reasons to increase the price of a product or service. The general rule is that a company raises prices because it can. This does not suggest that just because a company can raise the price of a product or service that is the accepted course of action. Prices are increased for a variety of reasons, as enumerated in the following.

## Supply Is Not As Great As Demand

Classic economics puts forth the false assumption that prices rise and fall based on supply and demand. This view of course, contains the caveat that the market must be free of unfair advantages. The decision as to what is fair and unfair varies greatly from nation to nation. What those in economics are really saying is that unfair advantages are those that have been defined as unfair.

## To Cut Down On Demand

There are times when a company may find it to its advantage to cut down on demand. One way to accomplish this is to raise the price. This is in the hope that customers will decrease their purchases. The marketing academics call this "demarketing." All of the "4Ps" are applied to the demarketing activity.

## To Appeal To A Different Targeted-Market Segment

There are times when the price is increased because a particular market segment expects to pay more for a product or service. It is expected that an education at Harvard University will cost more than one at the University of New Haven. The actual product that is delivered may not be better, but that targeted-market segment equates the price with the delivered product.

## Competition Is Destroyed

When your competitors are no longer able to block your company from access to your targeted-market segment, price may be increased. The price of Japanese cars has risen and will continue to rise because Japanese car makers have fewer competitors in targeted-market segments. Cadillac and Lincoln are now no competition for the Lexus. The price of a Lexus, as well as the price of a Camry, is moving up as competitors are unable to block access.

## A Regulated Monopoly Exists

Telephone and utility companies can raise prices by getting the regulatory agencies to allow them rate increases. This has nothing to do with supply and demand and everything to do with the type of case that is presented to the regulators. Every morning after workers for a local regulated utility company arrive at work, fifteen to twenty trucks with the utility company's workforce go to breakfast for between one half hour and to an hour and a half on company time. The company has had several people complain, but it does nothing about it. Why? Because the utility company cannot justify a rate increase to the regulators and still be able to do the job with fewer employees. If more workers are required to do the job, then more money is required to run the business. It is in the company's interest to have more employees rather than fewer, even if the job could be done with fewer. This is why so many employees are able to do less work and get paid more.

### To Influence the Sale of an Alternative Product or Service

It is not unusual for a company to raise the price of product A in order to convince the customer to buy product B, which costs more. Although product B may cost less to make, the company may wish to reduce inventory or it may make more profit from product B, even with its reduced price. Raising the price may also be a way of preserving some inventory for select clients when a product is being phased out.

### To Control a Market

Applying the Disneyland example discussed earlier, the company can charge more than four dollars for a hamburger because it can control the prices within its geographic area. As will be discussed later, price may also be raised through trademark and copyright protection. A pair of boxer shorts with Mickey Mouse on them can sell for eighteen dollars, whereas the same ones that say Syracuse University sells for about eight dollars. Syracuse University has less consumer interest in their boxers because there are many other competing companies with university logos on boxers. Syracuse also allows several different vendors to use its name on clothing. These factors tend to keep the price lower than that of the Disney shorts.

### MARKETING MIX: PRICE (DISCOUNTS)

*Definition.* Reducing the price of a product or service to gain market power.

### Introduction

The price of a product or service may be reduced for many reasons. The company can discount the cost of the product to the end user or offer a discount for a specific quantity of product or service consumed. When a customer buys more, he or she pays less per unit item. There are also discounts given to those within a trade or profession. When an auto supply store sells spark plugs to an individual, he or she has to pay more than the local garage would for the same product. The higher price is the supplier's attempt to offset the discounts given to companies, because it is an extremely competitive business. However, the do-it-yourselfer will still come out ahead because the job would cost much more if it were done at the garage. Prices are decreased for a variety of reasons, as enumerated in the following.

### Destroy Competitors

When a competitor is in financial difficulty, a company can reduce the price of its product or service. A classic example is the reduction of airfares at Christmas time by American Airlines and Delta Airlines. At that time, United Airlines was in Chapter Eleven and had counted on the holiday revenues. The holiday discount programs of American and Delta put United out of business within a matter of days. Of course, according to American or Delta neither had any idea, officially, that this would occur.

## Acquire Revenue

Many companies discount to increase their cash positions. This enables them to pay their bills and order new inventory. It is often a better course of action to sell inventory, even below cost, than it is to keep the product in inventory. This is especially true of dated or perishable items. To pay current bills may require short-term losses on selected inventory. Inventory is a means to an end, not an end in itself.

## Increase Market Share

Although it is not always true, a general rule of marketing is that when the cost to the customer is reduced, the percentage, unit, and dollar volume will increase. This enables the firm to incorporate economies of scale that can lead to a further reduction in price. Many products are sold below the company's costs to attempt to build a market. When this is done, these losses have to be offset.

## Keep Competitors from a Market Segment

When a competitor attempts to enter one of a company's segments, one way to counter this action is to discount. If the targeted-market segment is important, discounting should go as far as necessary to keep competition from a successful entry. It can often become a war of wills and of how deep are the company's pockets (financial resources). Can the company afford to take losses in the short run to protect future sales? Philosophically, Americans are bad at this game because of their emphasis on short-term results. If a company loses this fight, then it has a long-term competitor that may continue to erode its market share. A company should not give up market share unless it is a part of a well-thought-out ADDIE, or the company will have to regroup to survive.

In a company for which I once worked, a Japanese heavy equipment company was attempting to enter its market. The vice president of marketing moved quickly to reduce the price of our equipment in order to maintain our market share. At the end of the year, we had sold equipment, but the profits of the company were below expectations. The vice president was retired early by the chief executive officer (CEO) because of the vice president's failure to bring in expected profits. The new vice president was told to take fewer deals and only the ones in which the company could make the expected profits. All the talk about maintaining our markets by discounting vanished after one conversation with the CEO. Before that, he had seemed supportive of the concept. The moral of that story for me is to know one's CEO. What he or she says and what he or she means may be two different things.

## Attract Customers

Items are discounted as loss leaders in an attempt to bring customers to the company. Once the customer is at the company, it is expected that he or she will purchase a certain amount of goods and services in other areas. It is in these unexpected purchases that the profits are made. In the United States (and I am sure in many other nations), the loss leaders have never actually existed. Advertising these goods was just a trick to get customers into the store and sell them something else. Laws have been passed to stop this practice; if the company cannot produce the advertised items it is encouraged to give rain checks so the discounted price will be held when inventory is replaced. These laws do not apply everywhere, so customers should beware.

## MARKETING MIX: PRICE (ALLOWANCES)

*Definition.* A return of cash or its equivalent to the customer for the purchase of a particular product or service to attain market power.

### Introduction

Many companies are using allowances to obtain and sustain market power. They have found this much more productive than other applications of marketing resources. Allowances are tied to sales.

### Promotional Allowances

Many businesses offer promotional allowances to their customers. These allowances can be linked to such things as the quantity of the product ordered. For example, with the purchase of every ten cases of XYZ, the eleventh case is free. In another example, the product contains more for the same price. A certain brand of shampoo is always selling 25 percent more product for the same price. Other companies offer to share with suppliers or retailers the cost of advertising for a particular product. This arrangement may also vary with the amounts that are purchased. Some suppliers even offer to produce the advertising for their customers. Next time you see an ad for a major brand name and the beginning or end of the commercial features a local company down the street, this may be a promotional allowance. The quality of the advertisement changes when the location and store name where the item may be purchased changes.

The U.S. government prohibits a company from selective application of promotions. What is done for one firm must be done for all others that fulfill the specific criteria that has been outlined by the firm. However, there have been and still are preferences given to one firm over another. Laws vary from nation to nation. Allowances may make the difference between the selection or rejection of a product or service. Most allowances are tied to a specific time period. One danger of the use of allowances is that suppliers may wait for these times to make their purchases. Allowances may be used to counter competitive discounting or the development of a new product by competition.

Allowances tied to more product for less money depends on the margin of profit that a company can make with the additional product in its inventory. Extra products that are difficult to sell can be a burden and give your competition market power. For a supplier to buy more than is required in an attempt to save a few dollars is not wise. Inventory that does not sell may give a firm a loss of market power.

### Rebates

Cash is involved in a rebate, whereas promotional allowances generally do not involve cash. Rebates can take many forms such as those that are mailed in to the company by consumers after they have purchased the product. The idea behind rebates is that a temporary reduction in the price of a product allows the company to return, after the rebate period, to the original price without the customer feeling that he or she has been gouged. Automobile manufacturers have been using this for years to spur sales at different times of the year.

### MARKETING MIX: PRICE (TERMS)

*Definition.* Different forms of payment that the company agrees to with a customer for the purchase of a product or service, so that the company can gain market power.

### Introduction

The price of a product or service includes a determination of the seller's obligations and expectations of payment. Every action has the potential to gain or lose market power. Customers will pay more for a product if terms are available and necessary for them to achieve their ends. This does not suggest that terms always favor the buyer.

### Time

Terms generally have a time component. How long does the customer have to pay for the product or service? The time typically involved in the payment can change from nation to nation. In the United States, we expect a faster return on our money than, for example, the Japanese do on their money. The desire for faster returns drives the terms of the sale of all products in the society.

### Interest

Terms often have an interest component. Interest is usually charged on some type of a continuum from no interest at all, to interest after a specific date, to the maximum amount of interest allowed by law. There are legal limits to interest rates that can be charged in the United States. These limits do not apply universally. For example, the Islamic religion is against the concept of charging interest. There may have to be other means of payment that avoid the issue of interest on the purchase of products and services when dealing with countries or companies that follow Islamic practice.

### Other Costs

Terms can also include the cost of shipping. For years, L. L. Bean charged no shipping on its products. This has recently changed, but the company still charges less for shipping than most mail order companies do. I had planned to purchase a hat from another mail-order company. The hat cost $58, but the company wanted another $5.90 for shipping. This extra cost encouraged me to look in the New Haven Yellow Pages and go to Del Monico's, where I purchased a better hat for $49. I would have never looked elsewhere for the hat if the terms offered by the mail-order company had been fairer to me as a customer.

Other decisions that affect terms can include whether the product comes assembled or unassembled. How much extra effort must the buyer put in to bring the product to the level of acceptance? Bicycles are often sold either assembled or unassembled. Buying a bicycle already assembled, of course, adds to the cost of the purchase. Although I am using consumer examples with a limited number of single purchases, the same decision-making process holds for all levels of purchasing.

### MARKETING MIX: PRICE (GEOGRAPHIC DIFFERENTIATION)

*Definition.* The market power to charge more or less for a product or service in different geographic locations.

### Introduction

Prices for the same product or service can change on a local, regional, national, or international basis. Several factors contribute to variations in price from place to place. A company charges what it can charge and still achieve its end.

### Local

Prices may vary for a product or service at the local level. In my area, McDonald's charges more for meals at its restaurants on the highway than it does at its restaurants off the highway. McDonald's may, in fact, be incurring more cost for its highway operations. In terms of market power, it can charge more because there are fewer competitors on the highway for food than there are in town. Indeed, for the same reasons, McDonald's probably has to pay more for leasing the highway facilities because the owners of these facilities are also aware of the market power of a business that has a high flow of traffic with a lack of competitors. However, I would like to offer a word of praise for McDonald's. The prices are not much greater at the facility on the highway, and the quality is the same. In the past, food available on the highway was not satisfying and overpriced. McDonald's has done the traveler a favor.

The price of gasoline per gallon varies at the local level. From where I live, I can go to a town that is five miles in one direction, where I pay less for gas than if I go to another town five miles in the other direction. The reason for this is that the oil companies have decided that they can get more in one town than the other for gasoline. A friend of mine in the wealthy area of Fairfield, Connecticut, paid $12,000 for work on a septic system that would have cost me about $3,000. Fairfield is considered to be a wealthy area so they are charged more. It could have saved my friend thousands to hire someone from my area and have the person drive an hour to Fairfield. If all the people in Fairfield did this, the cost of having septic tanks installed by Fairfield companies would soon drop by thousands of dollars.

## Regional

Prices change for many companies' products or services from region to region. Some companies add to their shipping costs outside of a geographic area. Price is driven by market power where competition is a factor that allows for regional variations. Gasoline prices have great regional impact. Ships come to New Haven, only some thirty miles from home, with gasoline and fuel oil, I pay more here than I did in Syracuse, New York. To get the product to Syracuse, it has to be taken off the tankers, and on barges, and transported hundreds of miles up the Hudson River to the Erie Canal. Even with this additional cost, the price in upstate New York is less. The difference in tax rate between New York and Connecticut must be taken into account, but this is not the total picture. The reason gas costs less in Syracuse than in New Haven is that competitors are driving the price down in Syracuse; the oil companies have developed geographic pricing to boost the prices in certain areas where they can in order to offset the lower costs in other areas. Syracuse was considered by the oil companies to be less affluent than many areas of Connecticut.

## National

National pricing means that price is determined on a national basis. An organization charges the same within an entire nation to achieve market power.

## International

Prices are changed from nation to nation to gain market power. For example, the Japanese block access to their markets and therefore can charge more in their national market for their own products. This gives them added revenue, so that in other nations they can charge less than the competition.

American textbook publishers charge less than one third the price for the same textbook in Europe as they do in the United States. This is because students in Europe cannot afford to pay high prices for books. The American publishers change the pictures from color to black and white and take the hard covers off, replacing them with soft covers. They then reduce the price so that the books will sell in other markets. If they were applying the market power philosophy in action, they would employ the profits that they make in the United States to develop new targeted-market segments in other nations. With the insular view taken by American book publishers, I do not believe that this is the case. British book publishers are much better at the international book business.

This national application of market power to enter targeted-market segments is the model that is in place for most of the trading nations of the world. The same product may have huge variations in the price that can be charged from one nation to another. These prices are based partly on market power and the ability of the client to pay. This does not necessarily mean that a country is charged in accordance with its ability to pay. It is not always the ability to pay that determines the differences in price. Many other factors go into the pricing decision.

## MARKETING MIX: PRODUCT

*Definition.* What is sold or traded.

## MARKETING MIX: PRODUCT (BRAND NAME)

*Definition.* A unique name or identification given to a product or service to acquire market power.

### Introduction

Brand names may be protected by trademark law. This means that any money that goes into brand-name recognition is the unique property of the holder of that trademark. Brand-name protection is not internationally accepted. A company may have to apply from nation to nation for the right to use a particular brand name. There are companies that choose not to give their products or services brand names. These are loosely called generic products. The pharmaceutical business is an example; the customer can either order a brand-name drug or the generic equivalent. The generic is cheaper because the manufacturer does not have the added cost of maintaining a brand name. Another reason for this action is that the patent rights may have run out, and the cost of maintaining a brand name against competition is unwarranted. Generic drugs are often produced by the same companies that produce the brand-name products. This opens up another outlet for their drugs and prevents competition from entering that market.

The concept of store-brand names for products from soda to computers is another way to boost sales. The same product can be sold for less as a store brand to a different targeted-market segment. Coca-Cola Company may be producing the Stop and Shop supermarket's brand of soda. If so, the store contracts with different bottlers for its soda. The supermarket has not at this point considered having its own bottling company, so it purchases its store-brand soda from companies that make the brand-name sodas. Large grocery store chains could consider it as a means of gaining more market power to bottle their own brands of soda.

### Single-Product Brand Name

A company may choose to have a single product with a single brand name. Many companies start out with a single product and a single brand name and then move to multiple products under that brand name. Some laundry detergents such as Tide or Solo, are examples of a single product with a single brand name.

### Multiple-Products Brand Name

Ivory is an example of a brand name known for a single product that extended its brand to other, similar products. The company now has Ivory soap, Ivory shampoo, and Ivory dish liquid. If the company wanted to sell a toothpaste it would probably not create Ivory toothpaste because of the identification of the name with soap. Timex is another example of a company brand name with multiple similar products—that is, watches and clocks.

The Japanese turned this American idea of a product line and a brand name around. A Japanese company will give the same brand name to any and all products that it sells. For example, Yamaha sells organs, motorcycles, pianos, stereos, guitars, and many more unrelated products under the Yamaha brand name. American marketing advocates have put forth the idea for the past fifty years that this would never work, because customers needed specific product—brand recognition. Some still believe that it is not possible to sell all kinds of products under one brand name, even when faced with the stark reality of the success of companies such as Yamaha.

## Company Name and Product Name

The combining of brand name and company name gives a great deal of market power. The names of all products and services work together to help sell other products. McDonald's identifies many of its products by putting "Mc" in front of its products, such as the McChicken sandwich and the McDLT sandwiches. This is the company's way of giving its products a similar brand-name recognition. This is also done by DELL Marketing Corporation, which puts its initials in front of all its computer products. Company names and products can be effectively linked to the company market power.

## MARKETING MIX: PRODUCT (SIZE)

*Definition.* The amount and/or the physical size of a product or service that is sold as a unit or group of units to gain market power.

## Introduction

The size(s) of a product(s) can have a great impact on the organization's ability to block competition from access to a targeted-market segment. Size is a source of market power.

## Amount Per Unit

Distinctive targeted-market segments are responsive to products that are purchased in different quantities. As a general rule, the smaller the quantity, the more that can be charged for that product. Many organizations buy in large volume and divide the product into smaller amounts. It is this division into smaller units that generates the returns to achieve the company's ends. Much of what we know of as business consists simply of dividing large amounts of product into smaller quantities. The list is endless. I can buy fifty pounds of the best Indian rice for $40 (or about $0.80 a pound). In the same store, the same quality of rice, packaged into a smaller amount for the customer to purchase, costs more than a dollar a pound. A popular brand-name of white rice, which is not the same excellent quality as the Indian rice, retails for $1.49 a pound.

It takes a unified approach with many resources working together to create a company. Many companies simply take large amounts and sell small amounts. The organization has to be capable of storing and selling the divided products. When the products are dated because they are perishable, this creates an added barrier to entry for competition. Products may require refrigeration to store and preserve them, which could be a barrier to entry to those who cannot afford the cost of refrigerated storage.

### Physical Size

The actual size of a product can give an organization market power. One famous example is that when Lee Iacocca took over Chrysler, he made one of the cars a few inches shorter. This reduction allowed the company to put one more car in a railroad car for shipment to market. This reduced the cost of transportation for the company. The Japanese have been extremely successful in the electronics industry by making products smaller or larger than competitors. The size of a product is a factor in targeting market segments in which space is a factor in decision making.

## MARKETING MIX: PRODUCT (APPLICATIONS)

*Definition.* Different ways the same product or service may be utilized to gain market power.

### Introduction

The price may vary when the application changes. What is essentially the same product or service may command a different price when sold to a different targeted-market segment. These products and services are priced based on the market power of competition within the targeted segment. Cost is not a major factor in the price charged.

### Same Product, Different Application

There are many products and services that have different applications. Vaseline petroleum jelly, for example, is sold in sixteen-ounce jars for about $1.70. This product has been around for generations and has hundreds of applications. I used to use it on the speedometer cables in my cars to keep them lubricated. Vaseline now sells Vaseline Lip Therapy in a special $0.35 per ounce container for about $1.20. The Lip Therapy is successful because the company targeted a specific application. The success of the Vaseline product named "Lip Therapy" has been astounding when one considers that it contains the same ingredients as the much cheaper Vaseline products in the sixteen-ounce jar. To purchase sixteen ounces of Lip Therapy would cost around $55. This is a superb example of the same product being targeted at a different market segment.

I have seen textbooks with different titles and exactly the same contents, page for page, sold to different targeted segments. One is for the community-college market and the other is for the four-year programs. One may be a hard cover, the other a soft cover. The cost varies greatly between the two books. If a company can change the targeted-market segment, the new segment may pay much more to purchase the same product, one that consumers think has been produced for their particular application.

### Slightly Modified Product, Different Application

The field of marketing has taken essentially the same components and repackaged then in a number of ways. Hospital marketing, international marketing, industrial marketing, service marketing, and the others all say the same things. This book offers a different point of view. This will either give me market power or I will be blocked from access to the targeted-market segment and it will not be read by many.

Most companies that sell multiple-product lines sell essentially the same product with some added features. The management people are now pushing the idea of core competencies for companies. In most cases, that means that the company should maintain its core product and add other features and applications to those products. Different models of the Sony Walkman are far more similar than different. Automobile companies often sell the same cars with different names. These cars come off the same assembly line. For example, The Toyota Corolla is built in Fremont, California, by New United Motor Manufacturing, Inc., "NUMMI" and sold by GEO as the Prizm for General Motors with slight changes and variations. The Plymouth Voyager is the same as the Chrysler Caravan. These are typical examples of the concept of badge engineering, which has been in place in the automobile industry since the 1920s. These examples do not constitute an indictment, but rather provide an illustration of changing applications to block competition.

### Greatly Modified Product, Different Application

There is a great book, called *Connections*, that has as its thesis that the innovation of new products is the combination of two or more previously developed different products. For example, the Jacquard loom invented in 1801 is the same type of machine as the computer. The loom is a binary system of on and off. The basic difference in the computer is that it has the electrical application. Instead of colors of cloth, we have numbers and letters. If the makers of the looms had followed the concepts put forth in this book, they could have conceived of the computer and indeed many other applications of the principles put forth in the construction of the loom. *Connections* is filled with information tracing the interconnections between inventions. Innovation is to the author, James Burke, the combining of what is already with us. Burke takes a unitary approach to invention.

### MARKETING MIX: PRODUCT (QUALITY)

*Definition.* A measure of performance that is a part of the evaluation step of the ADDIE process.

### Introduction

The quality of a product or a reduction in the number of errors in production as part of the ADDIE process is now an important means to gain and sustain market power. This is not to suggest that "Quality is Job One" as the Ford Motor Company says in its slogan, a point of view shared by many others in Western management. Error reduction has a cost. That cost is embraced to achieve an organizational end and block competition from access to targeted-market segments. Perceived quality and actual quality may be far apart. I have been disappointed each time that my perceived perception of quality clashes with the reality of the quality of a product or service.

### Western Model of Quality

Western business now believes that the solution to all problems is to implement a quality program. I attended a seminar on quality in which an individual from a Fortune 50 company was discussing his company's implementation of a quality program. His CEO had come out in the national press with the statement that he wanted everyone in the company to have an obsession with quality. Speech after speech repeated this theme. This person was invited to meet with the CEO and several other top executives to discuss his quality programs. During the meeting the CEO asked the presenter, "What exactly is quality?" He told the presenter, "I haven't got a clue." Herein is the problem with the concept of quality in the West. It does not mean anything. It seems to be just talk. I am suggesting that rhetoric about quality is useless when the leader does not have a clear understanding of what he or she stands for. The leader must be able to communicate through deeds, not public relations events.

### Eastern Model of Quality

Is it possible that the Eastern CEO has a clearer understanding of quality? Yes, because it is a part of Eastern religious and philosophical belief systems. Quality means doing one's best in all activities. Quality is an outward manifestation of inward understanding. It is not something that is done to a person, rather it is what the person is. Can the Western CEO learn this in the course of an hour lecture by some professor, who learned it within the last six months? Although it is possible, it is highly unlikely. The organization in the West can improve the quality of work, but it comes down to all the individuals working to do their best at every daily action. It is supposed to be helpful for the employees to keep score of all their processes through math, but the real score is beyond math. The real score is how one lives every action of one's life.

### Quality and Market Power

There have always been quality products available to those who could pay. Museums are full of them. The American philosophy has been to mass-produce low-cost items for the vast majority of the population. The vast majority of American society has not considered, and still does not consider, that resources could be finite. Therefore, waste has not been and is not an issue. It is just part of the cost of doing business. Several cultures more directly confronted with finite resources and extended populations have incorporated the concept of quality into their philosophies of life as a form of resource allocation. A few quality items in one's life verses many that are of varying levels of quality.

The "Introduction" explores some of the reasons that science has not influenced these cultures to look to the external for explanation; rather, they have continued in their internal quest. The Japanese had quality mass production in place by 1900. After World War II, they were willing listeners to ideas that enabled them to develop added techniques to continue to accomplish those means. The United States encouraged the Japanese to sell into its markets so that Americans would have a fortress of capitalism in the East. This issue was more important to the American government and military than the success of any American industry.

If one company produces a better product than another at a greater cost or the same cost, then these companies can compete. If one produces a better product than the other and can then sell it below the second company's cost of production, the second company cannot compete. In this case, the second company is either an inefficient business (which sounds reasonable) or its competitors have some method that is effective in transferring costs to other sectors of the society (which is reality).

## MARKETING MIX: PRODUCT (FEATURES AND OPTIONS)

*Definition.* Distinctive characteristics added to a product or service to gain market power.

### Introduction

The same product can have several attributes added or subtracted to appeal to a different targeted-market segment. These attributes may or may not add costs to the manufacturer, but the attribute often adds costs to the consumer. For example, the color of a product may have an effect on a targeted market. A radio that is pink or blue may sell for less in a toy store than the same radio in brown or black in other stores, because the targeted consumer is not willing to pay as much for a child's radio as for an adult's. The company's version of the product in black could be sold in a discount outlet to teenagers for much more. A change to a camouflage pattern may open up a hunting and fishing market for the product, costing the consumer even more money.

### Features

A feature tends to be emphasized or added to a product or service as a selling point. The targeted customer is expected to respond to that particular feature. The same product—for example, a radio—may be sold emphasizing different features to different targeted markets. To one group, the company may emphasize a break-resistant case, whereas to another group, the company may emphasize the quality of the sound.

The Japanese have done a great job of improving products by adding features. Walkmans, for example, now come with auto-reverse. Americans produce a product and then try to keep that product in the marketplace for as long as possible without many improvements. Americans are constantly searching for a new product, whereas the Japanese are searching for ways to improve the features of their present products. They caught American industry completely off guard and gained a great deal of market power applying this as a means to an end.

### Options

An option tends to be sold as an extra to the customer. For years, automobile companies have been selling stripped-down versions of their cars. Customers would select and add options that they deemed necessary. These options were added to the car either at the assembly plant or at the automobile dealership. The time and cost of these changes added significantly to the price of the product. The Japanese made many of the most popular options, such as radial tires, air conditioning, power steering, and automatic transmission, part of the core product. Because these were installed at the factory, these options could be added at a significantly lower cost to the manufacturer. The savings could be and were passed on to the dealer and the customer. By the time the American manufacturers were willing to change to this system, the Japanese had acquired significant market share and market power.

## MARKETING MIX: PRODUCT (WARRANTY AND LIMITED WARRANTY)

*Definition.* A part of the common law system that states that a product or service is fit for the purpose for which it is sold. The extent of the coverage is explicitly outlined to obtain market power.

### Introduction

Warranty is a source of market power not because of the actual repairs that are done but because of the perception by the customer that the company is willing to perform needed repairs. Chrysler Corporation under Lee Iacocca was masterful in countering the perception that Chrysler was a poor-quality product by giving cars extended warranties. Most car companies at that time gave warranties covering twelve months or twelve thousand miles, whichever came first. Iacocca, in a desperate act, increased the limited warranty to five years or fifty thousand miles. However, the impression given and what is actually stated in the warranty may be far different. The impression is that everything is fully covered. The reality is that repairs are covered, but with decreasing commitments on the part of the company. For example, if the car is two years old, the company may pay only sixty percent of the repair cost; if the car is five years old, they may pay 20 percent of the repair costs.

### Reasonable

Computer companies such as DELL have, on the other hand, taken the concept of warranty seriously. As a customer, I had a problem with my computer screen. I called the company and told them about the problem; without question they told me they would replace it. The next day, I received another screen via Air Express. The following day, Air Express returned to my house and picked up the damaged screen. If, for some reason, I did not return the first screen, the company would have the right to bill me on my credit card for the second screen. The warranty transaction was a reasonable one.

### Unreasonable

My wife bought a major-brand-name video camera and purchased the extended warranty coverage. The camera did not work, and it was returned to the store and then to the service center. Two months later, the camera was sent back with a letter saying that nothing was wrong. The camera still did not work, and it was again sent back still under warranty. It then worked for a month or so before being sent back again for another two months. Now my wife is reconsidering the purchase of an updated video camera, at that time I will be surprised if it is the same brand. Warranty and repairs in this case created a negative image and did not give the company market power. Quality advocates suggest that if the company produces a product with fewer errors, that this will reduce the requirement for limited warranty claims. If this occurs, and the products hold up as expected, the extra cost of an extended warranty is a good source of added revenue for the company. My wife did purchase a new camcorder several months after I wrote the above and it was the same brand. So much for predictions of the actions of one's wife.

## MARKETING MIX: PRODUCT (SERVICING)

*Definition.* Repairing or maintaining a product to obtain market power.

### Introduction

Service can be an excellent means to obtain market power. American car companies were fearless when it came to the Japanese auto invasion, because they believed that their service networks would be a deciding factor in car purchases. The Japanese countered by producing cars that required less service to overcome the lack of service centers in America for Japanese cars. They also influenced dealers to take on their cars by giving them greater profit margins than would normally be considered appropriate for a sale at so low a retail selling price. The Japanese could afford the additional revenues to the dealer because they had not yet incurred the cost at the service end of the business that their American competition had.

### Producer-Owned Service

Producers sometimes own and operate the service and maintenance of the product or services that they sell. This adds a great deal of overhead cost to the company. Many companies have found that service is a difficult area in which to make money. In some cases, it is more effective actually to replace defective products with new ones rather than incur the cost of a repair operation. The product must have enough value to the customer that he or she will pay high enough costs for its service to make servicing profitable for the company.

When my washer motor stopped working, the cost of a repair person and a new motor was about $250, whereas the cost of a top-of-the-line used washer was $350, with an added cost of $50 to take out my old washer ($400 total). A new top-of-the-line washer delivered, with my old washer taken away was $650. Since the washer was a Sears product, I called the company and they could not provide anyone for several days to service the old washer. I decided to buy a different washer because the local dealer was available for service and installation the next day. Sears lost the service revenue plus the likely sale of a new washer. The cost of the service was too high and the job could not be done soon enough.

The problem with the service department in the proceeding example is pluralism. This service center is only interested in and rewarded for the repair of washers. Service personnel had only the slightest (if any) interest in turning me into a new-washer buyer. As a customer, I like Sears and like doing business with them. I have a Sears credit card, so I could have easily bought a new washer. Sears could have turned me into a new-washer customer with the slightest encouragement or incentive. Service could give Sears the market power to identify a large group of customers who are ready to buy a new washer. If a company has market power and does not use it, the company's future success is questionable.

### Nonproducer-Owner Service

I buy my heating oil from a local dealer. The company also maintains my furnace and hot water heater. This gives the company the opportunity to sell me a new furnace and hot water heater. If I am given an incentive to buy the furnace, I am a good prospect for the purchase of a furnace. For example, the furnace's cost could be added to the monthly oil plan (a plan in which the cost of oil is spread over the course of ten months). Why not let the customer pay half down and the other half over a ten-month period? The first half would probably cover the costs of materials and labor, and the second half would be the company's profits. This plan may be a good way to keep repair persons working in the off months. The question is, can service lead to market power? The answer is yes, but in reality, this usually does not occur.

Another type of service is factory-authorized service. In this case, the producer of the product gives specific dealers the right to repair its warranty products and services. This is difficult because the amount of control that the producer of the product may maintain is limited. In some cases, the cost of litigation to take away this authorization is prohibitive. A poor service center can cost a company a great deal of future business.

### MARKETING MIX: PRODUCT (STYLE/DESIGN)

*Definition.* The appearance of a product or service to gain market power.

### Introduction

The style or appearance of a product or service can affect the ability of the product to block other products from access to targeted market segments. There are entire industries that have depended on style as the dominant means to obtain market power. Unfortunately for many of them, style alone may not be enough to ensure continued success.

### Functional Style

The appearance of a product or a service can send a message of success or failure. My students are told that their papers have to look good. What they actually say and how the paper looks are linked in the reader's mind. In many cases, if work does not look as if it is well organized, the reader may not respond to the content. The problem with style is that there must also be substance. The

Jaguar automobile, for example, is beautiful and the designers have done a superb job, however I would not buy the Jaguar, because style is not the only factor in the decision. In this case, the car must function well in getting the driver from point A to point B.

A change in outward style may be necessary to appeal to different targeted-market segments. This awareness comes from an understanding of those targeted markets in which a company wishes to block competition. In some cases, a style that is different is the one that is appealing. For example, millions of people visiting Ireland make it a point to visit the Irish pubs, which have a particular style that appeals to tourists. Thousands of Irish in Ireland, however, go to a very success-ful bar that has modeled itself on an American style. Attempting to sell a product or service on the basis of style is a fickle pursuit.

### Nonfunctional Style

There is also an area in sales in which the function of the product is of minimal importance. For example, a customer may pay thousands for a wedding gown that she is well aware will be almost valueless after one day. There are people with a sense of style who can make a room (with the same furniture that another person owns) more beautiful in appearance. Style is probably a learned response that is derived from the cultural norms of a society. Style that is valued in one culture may not be valued in another. Some styles have had a universal appeal, such as certain gold jewelry. Gemstones, on the other hand, can have different values from culture to culture.

### MARKETING MIX: PRODUCT (PACKAGING)

*Definition.* Combining protection and merchandising of a product or service to achieve market power.

### Introduction

The packaging of the product or service is a critical component of market power. Packaging is a valuable means that can contribute to the success of a firm's efforts to achieve its clearly defined end. Packaging can make the difference between the success or failure of a product. Packaging has two related components: protection and merchandising.

### Protection

The package performs the function of preventing the product inside from being damaged or destroyed. A great product can be destroyed because of incorrect packaging. A book that I wrote in 1988, *Marketing as a Means to Achieve Orga-nizational Ends,* was very successful for the publisher, the University of New Haven Press. The book sold copies all over the world. In the beginning, the Press would get books returned that were damaged in shipment. This forced it to reas-sess its packaging and mailing. The Press upgraded its mailing envelope to a cardboard box and sent the books by United Parcel Service. If the Press had not done this, it might have been unable to make a profit because of the returns of damaged products. Packages may be treated with varying degrees of care in different parts of the world, so it is important to select packaging that will do the job. There is such a thing as more packaging than is necessary to do the job. A company should experiment with different packaging combinations to select the best for the money.

Soda and beer companies saved millions when they switched to aluminum cans. The reduction in the cost of materials and damage was astounding. There is a famous story in Ireland about a man who worked for a match company. He was supposed to have gone to the bosses stating that he knew a way to reduce the cost of each box of matches sold. If he could do this, he expected a percentage of the savings. The company, not wanting to pay the man, put their engineers to work trying to come up with a method to obtain the savings. They could not think of anything that could be done, so the company made the deal with the employee. Each of the matchboxes had a flint strip on either side; his suggestion was to leave the flint strip off one side. The company made this simple change and saved millions.

### Merchandising

Packaging may also be an excellent method to let the customer know about other purchases that he or she can make from a company. It is a simple and effective means to merely make customers aware. Many people do not know all the items that are available from a company. In fact, even people within a company may not know what the company sells. It is also effective to give a customer some type of incentive, such as a discount on subsequent purchases. L. L. Bean sends a catalog in the package with each order. It also includes in the package a flyer that has discounted items. These discounted items are available to those who have made a purchase. These discounted catalogs are changed on a regular basis, so it is an added incentive for the customer to order again to avail himself or herself of the special discounts.

Other companies will pay to have a company include their merchandise in its packaging. We have all received letters or bills that include an advertisement of another company's product. This is an effective way to offset the cost of packaging. A word of caution—a company's reputation will be greatly harmed if these other companies fail to meet the expectations of the purchasers.

Packaging can include instructions on how to assemble and operate the product. The quality of these instructions can affect future purchases. If the product is easy and relatively painless for the customer to use, he or she may be more likely to purchase future products. Some companies include a toll-free number for customers to call if they have any questions. Instructions for customers is an area that requires a great deal of improvement. Most computer software companies have technicians who will give over-the-phone help to any customer with a software problem. These technicians are generally knowledgeable and pleasant. I have dealt with WordPerfect Corporation, and I would buy anything from the company because I know I will have the help I need. The only reason that I know what else they sell is that a catalog was included in the shipping package.

## MARKETING MIX: PRODUCT (INNOVATION)

*Definition.* A change in the past/present means and end(s) of doing things to gain market power.

### Introduction

Product innovation has been emphasized, discussed, and put forth as the norm in the United States. Unfortunately, since World War II, product innovation has been less than spectacular. Thomas Edison, working with a small group, did more to come up with innovative products than have the thousands of engineers at AT&T, General Electric, all the electric utilities, and several other large corporations that owe their existence to Edison. This is not to suggest these companies have done nothing but build on the innovations of Edison. However, if one considers the number of years that have passed, and the amount of money spent on research, one wonders about their records. Edison's success is in direct contrast to the scientific methods that Americans have embraced since World War II. The values that he put forth are lost on those who think of themselves as the educated innovators of the present. This problem is not within the scope of this book but it should be explored. Americans have been living off the innovations of a single man and his small group of inventors too long.

### A Phase Innovation

This type of innovation is viewed as a major change or break with what has been previously embraced. Newton's mathematical analysis of planetary movements had a major impact on the change in thinking in the West. Einstein's theories hundreds of years later changed the theories that Newton had put forth. These are called "A Phase" innovations. The American military since World War II has funded and encouraged A Phase innovation. To underestimate the impact of A Phase innovation can bring a nation to its knees in three days. Ask those Japanese who are old enough to remember the end of World War II.

### B Phase Innovation

It is not enough to innovate with just A Phase. The products and services that are provided to a society and indeed mankind are termed "B Phase" innovation. For example, the discovery of atomic energy was an A Phase innovation, whereas the applications of atomic energy to medicine are B Phase innovation. The Germans and Japanese have outperformed the United States in B Phase innovation. Part of the problem is that the field of engineering in the United States has interpreted B Phase innovation in a narrow band of thinking. The engineers have divided themselves into electrical, mechanical, industrial, chemical, and many other categories. Each group identifies, as does each business, its separate territory. This territorialization of engineering has inhibited the application of knowledge, skills, and attitudes because of the limited understanding of, or interest in, the whole.

Engineering has also failed to become a part of the entire organization and indeed the entire society. Engineers have continually developed applications without determining if there is a market for them. A famous story about Edison is that he invented a voting machine and attempted to sell it to the government. The government refused to buy the machine, saying that it was unnecessary. Edison is said to have commented that from that time forth he would not invent anything without having a customer who was interested in paying for the invention.

American engineers have also misunderstood the possibilities of science in the process of taking their thinking from A Phase to B Phase. The Japanese have focused on B Phase, so they are especially interested in how to improve B Phase products that already exist, whereas American engineers pursued the more glamorous attempts to find new A Phase breakthroughs. New applications of B Phases were considered beneath their dignity. The Japanese, Koreans, Taiwanese, and Germans work on the improvement of B Phase products. Less glamour for the individual has meant more wealth for the nation.

## MARKETING MIX: PRODUCT (COST OF PRODUCTION)

*Definition:* How much it requires to produce a product or service to gain market power.

### Introduction

There are those who emphasize that the low-cost producer is in the best position to compete. Although the cost to produce a product or service is important, it is not as important as some would make it out to be. One of the problems with American business is the obsession to keep the cost of a product low. It is, rather, an issue of the interrelationship of cost and return. This is dependent on a company's market power. One could ask how much it cost the U.S. government to produce a military leader such as General Norman Schwarzkopf. Thirty years in the army, and the training of countless others who did not, or could not, make the grade as a general. The exposure to various experiences that he had, his education, and the time and effort of possibly thousands of people went into making Norman Schwarzkopf what he needed to be when the United States required him to lead in the Gulf War. The real costs could easily be a billion dollars.

Although this may seem an extreme case, think of how much it cost the society, your family, and your teachers to get you to the point where you could read and understand this book. Some estimate that it takes more than $200,000 to get a child from birth through college. The former dean of arts and sciences at the University of New Haven, Joseph Chepaitis came to talk to my undergraduate class about Russia and his successful trips to encourage Russian students to come to our school. My students enjoyed the talk, but they were unable to understand the conversation in the same way that he and I could. Not because we were more intelligent, but because of all that he and I had learned during the thirty years that we had lived and our students had not. Because in American society, the media talks down to the lowest common denominator, it was unusual—and refreshing— to hear a conversation that required an education and a broad understanding. Listening to Chepaitis, I became conscious of the staggering factor of cost and time (more than thirty years of continual education) that went into that hour of talk. I thought that some of my students would reach the same level of understanding within their lives. It astounded me that it could even be done.

## Obvious Costs

There are costs that go into a product or service that are easily calculated: cost of materials; cost of machinery; and the costs of labor, overhead, and taxes. It is a good exercise to try to get a handle on the cost of a product or service. It is then possible to compare savings and expenditures by applying some type of measurement. Accountants and financial specialists think that they understand cost. What they understand is what society wants to call costs, usually for tax purposes. These costs are interpreted from a worldview, not from any magical formula.

## Hidden Costs

Consultants make a living identifying costs to corporate executives that executives either overlooked or never imagined. I can remember my corporate days when a consultant revealed some hidden cost to the executive staff. The reaction most often was a cry to eliminate that cost, as long as it was not in the executive's functional area or in the overhead of the front office.

We spent hundreds of hours trying to determine how the costs of manufacturing and service should be divided to pay for the costs of human-resource development or marketing. At the time, I thought it was a good idea because it showed how valueless some of these areas were, and are, in a pluralistic organization. From a unitary perspective, these are resources, not functions. As resources, they may be necessary to achieve an organizational purpose. As functions, I question their value. It is important to remember, however, that they do not have to be performed by specialists. Many people can do many different jobs during the same day. It is done all the time in the small businesses of the world.

There are costs of inaction that affect the entire organization. These costs are never calculated. In a company for which I once worked, the CEO would veto any idea that came along. He was very good at it. He would take some projects right up to implementation and then cancel them. The only way things got done were if they were successful before he could make the decision to cancel them. This made it far more difficult for him to cancel a successful project. He still did it many times. It took years for the board of directors to figure this out and retire him with a huge salary. What were the costs to the company in lost opportunities during his leadership? One might ask why he would want to do this to the company. The answer is that he was unable to accept risk, and no one had enough power or interest to force him to do it.

## MARKETING MIX: PRODUCT (TECHNOLOGY)

*Definition.* The application of science to what is produced and sold to gain market power.

## Introduction

Technology is the application of theories that have been put forth by science.

These applications are the products and services that make up our daily lives. These come from both the A and B Phases of innovation.

## Product Selection

The issue of product selection is one that has not been explored. The myth is that if one builds a better mousetrap the world will beat a path to your door. Products, according to the author, are selected because the firm has some means to block competition from access to targeted markets. A friend of mine tells a story about a visit to Russia when he was a young man. Someone approached him and offered to trade a great deal of caviar for a pair of his old sneakers. My friend refused because he had no idea what caviar was or its value.

This story provides a lesson to the business attempting to sell a product or service. The customer must either see value or be forced to purchase. There are many purchases, such as automobile insurance, emissions controls on cars, school taxes, and sales tax that are forced on the consumer, who has no alternative. These are ideal business situations. The customer has no alternative but to pay. To do otherwise would result in a violation of law and the consequences of that action.

Insurance companies are interested in everyone being forced to purchase health insurance as long as the companies are the ones that will profit from the activity. Their resistance to national health insurance has nothing to do with health insurance and everything to do with their desire for assurances from the government that insurance companies will not have to pay for certain coverage that may bankrupt them. The government will have to assure them that these costs will not be their burden. When this happens, we should all have health insurance as far as the insurance companies are concerned.

Technology that does not have the force of law is much harder to sell. Providers of these products and services require much more KSA to make a living. If you do not believe this, watch the continued decline of the defense industry organizations as government support is withdrawn. If the government is smart, it will not let these companies go under because of their potential value in a future war.

### Product Nonselection

How are products selected out (kept from production)? There have been millions of products or services that have failed to make it to the marketplace. Millions have failed to move beyond the idea stage. This happens constantly. The process of nonselection is quite sophisticated. Products and services that do not fit into our worldview are selected out. It takes a great deal of time and market power to overcome these constraints. It is a difficult task for any application of a new product or service if a person, a company, or indeed a nation has to survive financially until the product or service is successful. Most products are not backed by sufficient resources.

### MARKETING MIX: (PROMOTION)
#### Pluralistic

The pluralistic view of promotion is that personal selling, sales promotion, public relations, point of purchase, and advertising are intricate parts of the marketing function. Each area is separate and distinct. They each have their particular specialists that are responsible for the success of that category.

**Unitary**

*Definition.* Communicating with the targeted-market segment(s) to achieve a purpose and gain market power.

## Introduction

Each organization develops its own unique means derived from its KSA to communicate with targeted-market segments. The promotion area consists of several areas that assist in the communication with targeted-market segments. The following definition is different from the ones generally embraced by marketing when it is perceived as a function. The concept of a purpose is not part of the promotion mix in Western thought. Many in marketing talk of the value of customer awareness. Unfortunately, awareness is often used as a means of avoiding the issue of achieving a clearly defined end. Awareness must lead to a purpose or it is an unnecessary and wasteful activity.

## Targeted-Market Segments

The following promotional areas of personal selling, sales promotion, public relations, point of purchase, and advertising may be targeted at a single, multiple, or mass-market segments. The order and the application of these promotional resources is derived from an organizational purpose or end. Each is applied as part of the philosophy, philosophy (KSA), philosophy in action, direction, structure, process, and other resources.

## Nontargeted Market Segments

There is no denying that the promotional activities of corporations are communicated to many individuals, groups, and organizations that are not intended to purchase from that organization. All the promotional activities in the world will not get me to purchase a new Harley-Davidson Heritage Soft Tail. I want it, but I cannot afford it. Any time and money that the company spends on targeting me is wasted.

There are products and services that I will never have the opportunity to make a buying decision about or influence the purchase of. Any costs incurred that expose these products or services to me are a waste of company resources. This may seem obvious, but millions are spent each day to expose me to products and services that I will never purchase. The pluralist wants to individualize the segmentation of targeted markets to avoid this cost. From a unitary view, resources are to be applied as a part of a combined effort to block competition from access to targeted markets to achieve a purpose.

## MARKETING MIX: PROMOTION (PERSONAL SELLING)

*Definition.* The person-to-person communication with a targeted-market segment to make a sale and gain market power.

### Introduction

The concept of personal selling has, in the pluralistic organization, been perceived as the salesperson or sales team that attempts to convince customers to buy the company's product or service. From a unitary view, everyone who works for the company is selling twenty-four hours a day, seven days a week. Everyone who purchases a product or service is also selling that product or service every time anyone sees him or her using it. Customers are especially selling if they discuss the product or service in a positive manner. The reason I might consider purchasing a Toyota Camry is that a friend of mine who is a car expert told me that it is one of the best cars for the money, and I see a lot of them on the road. My friend does not even own one. This means that there are people who sell a product who do not own the product and have nothing to gain materially from the transaction. When pluralists think of personal selling, they do not include other salespeople, they just think in terms of the individuals whom they have designated as salespersons. A change in the identification of who are the salespersons may gain any company a great deal of market power.

I have asked students at my college for years why they came to this particular university? The overwhelming majority, more than 50 percent, say they knew someone at the school and this influenced their decision. The marketing focus that the school has done and continues to do does nothing specifically to influence present and past students to encourage someone else to come to the school. You may ask why this is not done? The reason is that most companies have a narrow view of what constitutes selling and who should do that selling. Will they change that view? No. Why? Because the primary underlying philosophy is pluralistic. Selling is the domain of the specific people, not the domain of present and former customers.

### Dinosaur or Necessity

I have heard for years that the salesperson can and will be replaced by quality, better targeting, the computer, and just about anything else that seems remotely possible. This depends on how broadly the concept of personal selling is defined. Will there be fewer individuals on the road selling, as Howard Hill, a character in the musical *The Music Man*, sold? Probably. Is selling difficult? Yes. Is it going to get easier with the addition of technology? No, because to be a salesperson is to possess personal qualities, not external supports. Salespersons must become more a part of the entire organization. They must learn the jobs of others, just as others must learn their job.

### Academic Bias

The academic area of marketing has had a bias against sales for fifty years. This may be for many reasons, but I believe that the hidden agenda is that marketing academics have failed to guarantee the salesperson any KSA that is and can be reflected in increased productivity. This has left sales organizations with what I call "the entertainers." They usually call themselves the motivators. This means that they come before a sales force and tell their stories. They usually do a good job of entertaining. The salespeople are happy because they do not have to do anything but listen and enjoy themselves. The company is happy because it thinks it has contributed to the motivation of its sales force. No measurements of past and future productivity are taken. The good salespersons are still good and the bad ones are still bad.

Academics who attempt to enter this area and indicate that they can and will improve performance have failed to perform. The organization is unhappy, and the salespeople are unhappy. The sales process has changed little. There are still several proposed steps in the sales process, which includes prospecting, preapproach, approach, overcoming objections, close, and after-the-sale follow-up. This, of course, is a different process from all other processes in the pluralistic organization. In the unitary organization, all resources, including sales apply the ADDIE process.

## MARKETING MIX: PROMOTION (SALES PROMOTION)

*Definition.* Communicating with targeted market-segments with incentives to gain market power.

### Introduction

Sales-promotion items may be given away for free or sold to potential targeted-market segments. Items may be given or sold directly to the targeted segment or to someone who is perceived as having an influence on the targeted segment. Influencers may be a child whose parents purchase a toy oil truck sold for a low price at Christmas time. Every time the child plays with the truck, the parents are sent a sales-promotion message. When the real truck drives by, the child will be excited and will probably point it out to his or her parents. A sales-promotion item has the name or logo of a company or a product for all to see. These items may include toys, office supplies, coupons, contests, games, premiums, and samples. Such areas as point of purchase are emerging as major areas under promotion. The list is growing each day.

### Giveaways

When a company gives an item away as a sales promotion it is expecting that this act will give it market power. Giveaways can be targeted specifically at customers or influencers. Giveaways can also be given after the sale to thank a customer for his or her business. When my university's marketing department switched marketing texts, the sales representative gave each professor a coffee mug with the publisher's name on it. This by no means influenced the sale, but it was seen as a nice gesture by the recipients.

My radio show was given the money to purchase sweatshirts with the University of New Haven logo on them to promote the university. My idea was to get young people to be aware of the university at an early age. I gave them to eighth graders and younger children in my town. These people will be promoting the school every time they wear the sweatshirt.

## Sold

Promotional items may be sold to targeted-market segments. This can be a source of revenue for the company. In many cases, the cost of these promotional items is more than the cost of the item without the promotion on it. These promotional items may actually make the difference between the success or failure of a product or service. When you can get your present customers to buy more it is well worth the effort. These promotional items may give the customer and the employees a sense of tribal membership. According to Theory "W," these items are effective because members want to be identified with a tribal affiliation. It is a human longing to belong. Consider all the products that are sold in the United States to Americans that identify with a particular ethnic background. Because I am Irish and English, I would probably not wear a shirt that displays "Kiss Me, I'm Italian." This does not mean that I would not purchase other Italian promotional items.

## MARKETING MIX: PROMOTION (PUBLIC RELATIONS)

*Definition.* Communication with a mass-market segment to create and maintain a public image to gain market power.

## Introduction

Public relations generally provides the connection between the company and the wider society. It is concerned with the perception of the company and its products and services in the communities that the company serves. Public relations has several aspects and may be defined differently in various corporations. My own view is that it is the soft sell of the company (both internally and externally). Public relations attempts to present the organization in the best possible light. The organization generates its own public relations materials that it disseminates itself or gives to other outlets to disseminate. The most effective reporting is supposedly the unbiased observations of others. I hope by this point in the book readers realize that public relations is a source of market power and the organization has a great deal of incentive to direct its public relations effort.

## Generated and Disseminated within the Firm

The organization's public relations effort may be produced internally, externally, or by a combination of both. The organization can generate flyers, catalogs, press material such as news releases, product and service publicity, and corporate internal and external communications. Most of these activities are entirely controlled by the organization. The company produces and edits all material although most newspapers and magazines will also reserve the right to edit materials before publication. Very little that is in any way determined as negative or neutral comes from the company's effort.

## Generated and Disseminated Outside the Firm

Public relations materials may also be produced and disseminated by organizations outside the firm. Although the firm can influence these materials, the control may at times be minimal. A reporter does a story and for personal reasons or political reasons puts a positive or negative spin on what is said or written. Programs such as *60 Minutes* have put a negative spin on almost everything for years under the guise of being a news show. How many companies or persons interviewed have thought that they were going to have a positive piece done on them and suddenly they were under attack? These programs have now proliferated on television, and reporters make their careers by destroying reputations in the name of a free press. The good that may have been achieved in no way compensates for the destruction that has been done to the fabric of society. Companies and individuals are destroyed for ratings.

I used to enjoy the *Phil Donahue Show* and learned a great deal from watching. This no longer is the case. Other talk shows that have spun off are often worse. I have a radio talk show once a week on which I invite people from the community to have a pleasant intellectual conversation. It took more than fifty shows on the radio to convince many of my guests that I wanted to interview that I was not an attack dog.

## MARKETING MIX: PROMOTION (POINT OF PURCHASE)

*Definition.* Communication with the customers at a particular location to get them to purchase a product or service in order to gain market power.

## Introduction

Point of purchase as a means is applied more each year by organizations. The concept is to induce customers to purchase once they are already at a particular location. This inducement may take many forms. The general idea is to convince the customer to purchase a company's product or service at the place where the purchase occurs. This is different from trying to convince customers to purchase before they arrive at a location to purchase that item or items.

## Intended Purchase

The customer comes to the location to purchase an item (for example, a pen), and when there, he or she is induced to purchase one pen instead of another pen because a point-of-purchase incentive is offered. At that time the customer may also be persuaded to purchase more then he or she intended. For example, the customer can buy a pen and get a pad of paper for 20 percent off or buy three pens and get a free pen box. The pen company may find that it is more profitable to give away an extra pen or two than it is to advertise the pens to more of a mass-market segment. These inducements can and do take many forms—win a trip, get money back, get more for the same price. The store also benefits because it may get inducements to sell more. This can take the form of added discounts, trips for employees, or sales-promotion items.

### Unintended Purchase

An unintended purchase occurs when the customer is at a location and is given an inducement to purchase a particular product or service. When I went to the college today, I had no intention of purchasing a shirt from the fire-science students. I happened to walk by their table in the cafeteria and saw the shirt and bought it for a cost of five dollars. In this case, the inducements were a low price, the color, the size, and a fire-science insignia that included our college name. The ability of a business to induce customers to purchase a particular item or items at a location can give an organization market power.

### MARKETING MIX: PROMOTION (ADVERTISING)

*Definition.* One-way communication with the targeted-market segment(s), employing mass media to achieve market power.

### Introduction

Many have determined that marketing in a pluralistic functional organization means advertising. In a unitary organization, advertising is a resource to consider, but it should be viewed as one of thousands of options that are available. I have always felt that most of what is considered advertising is vastly overrated and not worth the price. Most if not all of the marketing books conceive of advertising as messages delivered through newspapers, radio, television, billboards, magazines, catalogs, and direct mail. There are two problems with all these means: the cost per reached customer and the difficulty in assessing the return on advertising expenditures.

### Cost Per Customer

It is difficult to assess the true cost per customer of advertising. Organizations inflate the number of potential exposures for an advertised message. For example, publishers do not count the number of magazines sold and give that number as a total population. They calculate the number of people who supposedly look at the same magazine over the life of the magazine. The argument is that the longer the publication is considered viable, the more likely it is that more people will be exposed to the message. This calculation for all advertising, no matter how impressive, errs on the side of more exposures rather than fewer. Newspapers have a short advertising life span, but they are supposedly better than radio and television because the same message can be viewed over and over again. On the other hand, television is supposedly better than newspapers because of the large numbers who view each televised advertisement at a time. If the ad is in the person's face for thirty to sixty seconds, it is supposed to be better than the same ad being seen by flipping through the pages of a magazine for about a millisecond.

### Assessing Impact of Expenditures

Advertising has also had a difficult time in assessing the relationship between sales with advertising messages. Some grocery stores are now experimenting with the use of bar codes and advertising messages received by participants. The experiment takes a television viewer of commercials and calculates how many times, if any, the person was exposed to a message. The bar codes representing the actual purchase are then compared to the advertising message that the person has viewed. Preliminary findings are inconclusive when trying to compare advertising message exposures with actual sales. That means no relationship has been proven.

There are many ways to determine the impact of advertising expenditures. One way is to have the customer ask for something specific that another customer who did not see the message would probably not know about. An example would be a newspaper ad that offers customers 30 percent off when they present the ad. Another, more simple means is to ask customers how they came to find one's business or product. This will give a company a pattern to determine what works and what does not. A company can count the numbers of customers who identify a specific advertising method or ad and then divide by how much it made on that effort. Most of the time, companies will be disappointed by the dismal results. An ad agency or the media will blame all failures on the company. The two reasons most often given are that the company did not spend enough or that it did not give the project a chance. If a company wants the advertising criticized that it just spent a great deal of money on, it can go to another media or ad agency and the reason given will be that the company did not come to them and let them handle its account. Advertising, for the most part, is a waste of time and money.

## MARKETING MIX: PLACE
### Pluralistic
From the pluralistic concept of place or distribution, each resource represents a separate activity unto itself. Channel, transport, inventory, and middlemen all function as parts of a divided organization.

### Unitary
*Definition.* The storage and movement of products, and services to achieve market power.

## MARKETING MIX: PLACE (CHANNEL)
*Definition.* The movement of materials, products, and services from their origin to the end user in order to gain market power.

### Introduction
The channel of distribution is conceptualized as the path that a product takes from its inception to the end user. An example of the inception of a product, taken to extremes, would be for a publishing company to consider as part of its channel the forest that provides the material for paper production. Other examples would be, for an automobile company, the coal mine that is required to make steel or the fast food restaurant that gets its supply of beef from a ranch. All channels can be owned by one company, or each step can be privately owned and operated by a

company unrelated to the others in the channel. In some cases, it is a combination of both.

The channel is generally conceived in the West as linear and also as just incorporating material items. This hinders thinking and allows for a limited number of possible actions for channel members. When an organization is unitary, business expansion may easily move outside predetermined channels. For example, Yamaha has expanded into guitars, motorcycles, pianos, electronics, and many other items that many have determined to be unrelated. Resources are related when they are freed from strict Western product categories. Relationships and nonrelationships exist in one's head.

## Control the Channel

The decision to own and control the entire channel is made based on available resources ("5Rs"). Many organizations can, without too much difficulty, purchase the business behind them (supplier) or in front of them (the business they supply). An example of incorporating the work of a supplier would be a restaurant's realizing that it could bake its own bread instead of purchasing it from the supplier. The restaurant can even purchase the bakeshop that supplies it and sell exclusively to the restaurant or sell to others as well.

The advantage of controlling all aspects of the channel is that the company can influence costs. This is also a form of expansion if it incorporates more aspects into a successful operation. If the restaurant is going to sell so much bread through the restaurant, it can ensure its new business—the bread business—a market. An example of owning the company in front of one's firm is the purchase by PepsiCo of Taco Bell and Pizza Hut fast-food restaurants. In this case, PepsiCo can ensure a specific amount of sales through that chain. If the sales are large enough, the entire cost of the operation may be offset through the assured sale of Pepsi-Cola soda.

## Do Not Control the Channel

The other extreme is for a company to control just its own step in the channel. This has been generally embraced by companies that cannot afford to own the entire channel. It is also for those who are in a boom-or-bust business. Oil companies that found themselves controlling their channels shifted their thinking to just controlling specific aspects. Everything else was turned over to others. When business takes a downturn, oil companies leave these companies and their employees to their own devices. The oil companies just pull out of contracts and others have to endure the losses and the pain. Many Western business decisions are now focused on this type of decision making. Manufacturing is sold to others. This supposedly unburdens the company of all the extra work and problems that were involved. The new right way is thought to be to search for others to manufacture products to the company's specifications and the company can then just sell them.

Like everything else, this has its dangers. These manufacturers can and do create their own outlets and a business may have little recourse to counter these moves. When manufacturers produce a product for a company, they can easily calculate sales and revenues. If the manufacturer does not give up on its research and development this allows it to continue to innovate while the firm for whom it has produced the products has long since lost its KSA in this area. These innovations can lead to loss of market power.

Western management has countered this reality with the misguided concept of core competencies. What this means is that a company gets others to do everything but the particular activity that makes it unique. This single-solution mentality discourages the possibility of minor or drastic changes that may lead to market power. The only core competency is the KSA of the employees and their philosophy, philosophy (KSA), philosophy in action, direction, structure, process, and resources. To focus on one thing and give the rest to others may sound easy, but it leads to a loss of flexibility for the company.

## MARKETING MIX: PLACE (TRANSPORT)

*Definition.* The movement of products and services to achieve market power.

### Introduction

The cost of transportation is often overlooked as a form of market power. Products and services that must be moved add additional charges to the costs of doing business. The transportation of all products and services is, of course, assisted by the development of the national infrastructure. Water, air, rail, and road infrastructures are essential components that the government can contribute. American railroads had to build and maintain their own tracks and bridges, whereas the highways were paid for by the federal government though taxation. This contributed to the destruction of American railroads. When the might of the government is put behind one form of transportation over another, the results are usually the same as what has happened to the railroads.

There are many times when the cost of transportation is a factor in the decision to purchase or not purchase a product or service. The sources of transportation can be owned and operated by the company that is selling the product or service, or transportation can be contracted to another firm. When one sends a letter through the U.S. Postal Service one is in essence, paying the U.S. government to assist in the conduct of one's business. The price and delivery time of a letter that is sent has an impact on the ability of a company to do business, collect bills, and communicate with its targeted-market segments. The postal system of a nation, like all other forms of transportation, assists the business of a nation.

### Owned by Organization

The decision to transport a product or service depends on the market power that a company may attain or lose if a competitor handles its own transportation. Does the transport of products and services contribute to the organizational end? For example, the cost of sending a letter may be too high through the U.S. mail, so the company may choose to add its own internal postal system. This post office may be able to move what is called interoffice mail at a cheaper rate than if each employee were to receive mail through the U.S. Post Office.

Transportation costs should be monitored through both formative and summative evaluation and more cost effective methods should be explored. Voice mail, fax machines, and computer mailboxes are other methods to offset and improve on the transportation cost of moving information. The same principles hold whether a company is thinking about the cost of mail or the cost of a fleet of oil tankers.

### Owned by Another Organization

Transportation of products and services may be owned and operated by independent companies that contract their services. When I was in the oil and liquid petroleum gas (LPG) business, all the LPG was piped and stored in salt mines in New York State. One trucking company delivered the LPG to all the different distributors. The dealers then sold the LPG to their customers. Many times, customers would tell me that they preferred our gas to the competition's. I never told them it was the same. There are many examples in which competitors use the same transport and the same products. The differences, then, are in other resource areas.

The reasons that a company may choose to use transportation through another firm rather than to do the job itself is that it believes that this will give it market power. The United States, at both the state and national levels, has attempted to regulate the transport of products and services. This has been done so that one firm or type of transport cannot gain an unfair advantage over another by significantly reducing its costs. This government regulation has attempted to restrict the transportation industries, but regulations have been selective at best. The government did this under the guise of stabilizing the industry. The government's role in transportation is far more intrusive than our fantasy illusions about the American free enterprise system.

I would not be against this intervention if it had a purpose that led to a clearly defined national end. Does anyone think it was a good idea to destroy mass transportation in the United States? The select few involved in the automobile business probably thought it was a good idea. This destruction happened because the government was unable to take a unitary approach to transportation by viewing its role as contributing to a balanced transportation industry. It is not the automobile industry's fault that it tried, but the government's fault that it encouraged the automobile industry's success without a purpose. Simple linear solutions have few long-term positive results.

### MARKETING MIX: PLACE (INVENTORY)

*Definition.* The accumulation and storage of materials, products, and services to achieve market power.

### Introduction

Inventory control is a critical means of attaining market power. Each hour that inventory is not sold, expense is incurred. This cost adds to the total price of doing business. Inventory has varying degrees of perishability. This influences business decisions and helps to determine the price(s) that may be charged. Perishability can be related to the weather, style changes, geography, and technological innovation. The list is endless.

## To Stockpile

The accumulation of inventory is done for many reasons. The cost of this as a means must be calculated into the short- and long-range costs of doing business. Without a continued supply of inventory, companies and indeed nations may go out of business. The U.S. military has stockpiles of many years' worth of inventory in case of a war. During a war, inventory becomes a matter of national survival. If you run out of bullets, and your opponents do not, the consequences are severe. Shock shows like *60 Minutes* try to embarrass the military for stockpiling. If the time comes that these materials are required, then those who inventoried will be sainted.

The latest fashion, supposedly from Japan, is called "just in time," which means that inventory arrives as close to the moment that it is actually required or sold as possible. The problem with just in time, is what happens if those the company relies on do not deliver? Does the company have a buffer to switch suppliers before the business is destroyed? How long can you go with no business? The entire American automobile industry shuts down in a matter of a few days if there is a strike at a plant that supplies parts for its cars. Strikes can be settled, and in an extreme case, the army can move in and do the job. If it is a more critical loss of production—for example, one based on a political decision by another nation to withhold computer chips—an entire nation may be crushed.

## Not to Stockpile

The danger of not stockpiling is that the company has no cushion. The disadvantage is that to stockpile costs money that adds to the cost of doing business. The Japanese force their vendors to assume the burden and cost of the inventory. In this case, they are assured that they have an inventory flow back one or two levels in the channel, and they can avoid the cost of keeping inventory themselves. This requires relationships with those who can be trusted to perform and maintain their own businesses.

One way to counter the risk is to have more than one supplier. This also has its difficulties. Maintaining uniform quality-control standards is one difficulty that comes to mind. The Japanese have been successful in driving American suppliers in the United States out of business because the suppliers are never able to perform to expectations. Inventory is rejected, and in a continued effort to be successful, the Americans keep the game going, rejection after rejection, until they are bankrupt. If these firms also supply a company's competitors, then this is an effective means of eliminating suppliers from one's competition. How many critical suppliers of the competition does one have to force out of business to affect one's competitors? What happens if these are also the company's own suppliers?

## MARKETING MIX: PLACE (MIDDLEMAN)

*Definition.* Those who sell the materials, products, and services within and between channels.

## Introduction

Personal selling entails having a salesperson sell a product or service for a firm or for a group of firms. Making a distinction between this type of business activity, which in essence sells to other business, is based on the pluralistic drive to separate and search for differences rather than similarities. Salespersons and organizations that sell through the entire channel may take ownership at any time or just bring together a buyer and a seller for a fee.

## Take Ownership

Those who take ownership assume higher risks. Once ownership is transferred, the new firm is responsible for the storage and resale of the product or service. The organization that takes ownership is not required to improve or alter the product or service to be successful. Distributors may just assemble a number of products and services to sell to the next organization in the channel. Many large organizations are dismantling their sales forces and turning over the sales responsibility to another channel member. They are themselves giving up the role of manufacturing and sales so that they can just manufacture products and let another group sell them. They are becoming more and more separated and specialized as they search for short-term returns.

## Not Take Ownership

The job of the middleman who does not take ownership can be very rewarding financially. His or her risk is limited because he or she does not have to purchase the product or service. This reduces the middleman's cost and the risk to his or her organization and to the salesperson. Middlemen take a fee for their services. This fee can be, among other things, a percentage of sales, a specific amount of money, or so much per unit sold. Jobs that fall into this category include some types of food brokers and stockbrokers. The stockbrokers do not own the stock, they just sell the stock to others for a percentage of sales or for a fee.

### The Japanese and the Middleman

Japanese business has a great many more middlemen in the channel than business does in the United States. A product or service may be bought and sold three or four times more than in the West. This is because of a national employment philosophy. The American model is to streamline the channel to give the consumer the lowest price. Individuals and companies are then taxed to pay for those who are not working. The government creates great bureaucracies to handle this redistribution of wealth.

The Japanese add these people to the channel, and they then pay taxes as productive citizens. The government does not require a huge bureaucracy to handle those who are out of work. Another advantage of the Japanese system of adding channel members is that it hinders the entrance into Japan of foreign products and services. When foreign firms move into this system, they cannot absorb the added costs, and their products are soon priced out of the reach or interest of Japanese consumers.

The Japanese have a different system for Japanese firms that compete in the international arena. Japan blocks access to its domestic markets for foreign products and services, and this enables Japanese businesses to charge more in the home markets. The added revenue is then used to sell Japanese products outside of Japan at costs lower than the cost of production. This drives foreign companies out of business in their own nations. When these firms counter with lower prices, the Japanese companies can simply raise the price at home and use the combined revenue to lower prices still further and conquer the more difficult markets.

## MARKETING REASONING TOOLS

### Pluralistic

Each functional area has developed its own unique measurement systems. These measurement techniques are developed generally to reinforce the functional area. Marketing has incorporated several measurement tools that are applied only to the marketing function.

### Unitary

When functions are considered to be resources, then the reasoning tools and their applications are altered. Marketing does not try to use math and statistics to justify itself to the detriment of other organizational resources. Reasoning tools are applied as a means to determine the progress toward an end. They are just measurements. Market share means nothing unless the measurements are effective in moving and adjusting the means to achieve an end. I would like to see the reasoning tools used by American firms changed to reflect a more unitary philosophy. Until this occurs, the reasoning tools that are in place can be applied with caution.

## MARKETING REASONING TOOLS (MARKET SHARE)

*Definition.* The measurement of percentage, unit, or dollar share of a specific market at a specific time against specific competitors to monitor means and ends.

### Introduction

Evaluating market share as a reasoning tool may have many applications. It can be used as an organizational end that is selected by the leader after a market power analysis and a market power assessment are completed. Market share can be applied as a means to describe the relationship of any product or service to a similar product or service that is sold by competition. The definition of market share as an end and as a means should be made clear to the entire organization. This is done by using terminal and enabling objectives. Market share has also been used as a means of misleading both inside and outside the organization. The term "market share" when described must be clarified exactly for all to understand.

### End

Market share can be an overall end that the entire organization is working to achieve. The Japanese, Germans, and people of many other nations have been successful in focusing on market share as an end. The entire nation works together to obtain market share in targeted industries. Although American firms, as a rule, do not have the market power that many competing firms have because of competitions' unified effort, American firms can still focus their ends on market share. In the case of Airbus, several European nations are working together to obtain market share in the airplane-building business. It seems fairly easy to predict that future dominant airplane builders will be the Europeans and the Japanese because Americans cannot unify and respond to their market power. Americans will lose this industry just as they have lost the automobile business. A friend of mine who is an automobile expert tells me the Japanese can now take market share from the Americans at will in the automobile business.

American companies cannot join together to gain market share in the world markets. This should not dissuade them from choosing market share as a possible end for their organization. They will have to apply their limited resources much more effectively and with much more guile than their international competitors, but they can still stay in the game longer than their competitors have calculated.

## Means

Market share can be used as a means for measuring relationships between product or service areas and competitors. For example, the University of New Haven has a doctoral program. This program currently has about fifty students. This figure could be compared with other competing schools in the state, the region, or the nation to determine the school's market share. The market share for the undergraduate programs may need to be calculated using a different list of competitors, and the school may have more or less market power in any particular program because of its market-share position. Market share considered as a means will change to reflect the calculations of the organization in its quest toward a unified end.

## Deception

All measurement tools may be described in such a way as to lead the recipient of the data to erroneous conclusions. Those who are responsible for getting the most accurate market share information must be constantly alert to possible misperceptions. Even if one wants the world to be misled, one should not delude the leader of the company. This may have to be a private conversation, and the risk to one's job is there, so one should tread lightly. The leader must know the time frame in which the figures have been taken, who the competitors are that have been compared, and what measurements were used. Market share can be measured using percentage, units, and dollars.

The classic deception using market share occurred in American automobile companies during the 1970s. The automobile market share was calculated in dollars. Because Americans sold larger cars that cost more and because prices were rising, the market share of the car market was calculated in dollars. All the money made in the automobile business was added up, and then U.S. share in dollars was determined. The untold story was that the number of units (of American cars) being sold was declining. U.S. companies were making more money on fewer cars sold. The issue was units sold. All was kept quiet. I often ask my students what they think would have happened to them if they had raised this issue as an employee of General Motors at that time? To avoid this trap, one should ask for market-share figures using all kinds of different competitors, time frames, and measurements. One should also look at how competitors have calculated their market share and compare it to one's company figures. Have two people, one from within the company and one from outside, independently come up with the figures, and have them justify their results. If the company does not know where it stands any direction that it heads in may be based on misinformation. One needs to know oneself, even if it hurts.

## MARKETING REASONING TOOLS (FOCUS GROUP)

*Definition.* A sample of present or future customers who discuss their reactions to different possible means that an organization can apply to gain market power and to achieve its end.

### Introduction

A focus group as a marketing reasoning tool is a fancy name for the selection of a group of current or future customers in order to ask them their views and opinions. Participants in these groups may be either paid or unpaid. In some cases, for example, if the focus group consists of medical doctors, they are paid quite well to give their opinions. The group sessions are almost always recorded, and most of the time, they are put on video. Scripts can be transcribed of everything that transpires. The group can be led by a professional or someone from the firm. Group numbers are generally small, fewer than ten people. The group can be informed or uninformed about the name of the firm that is interested in the information. A great deal of useful KSA can be acquired from focus groups.

### Advantages of Focus Groups

Focus groups are a great source of information. Especially if customers do not know what firm they are assessing, they will be brutally honest. This honesty may be unavailable from those who are connected with a product or project. Employees may be more concerned about their survival than the success of any project and, therefore, will tell the boss what he or she wants to hear. On the cautious side, one focus group may actually be nonrepresentative, and the actions taken as a result of information gained from them may not be appropriate. This is one reason that several focus groups with different group leaders may be helpful. It is most advisable to keep the focus groups on the ADDIE format so that information fits into the overall company process.

Focus groups can be monitored over a period of time to assess and compare the performance of a company with its competitors. There are companies whose business is to monitor customers continually in a particular industry. They then sell that information to anyone in the industry who wishes to have a comparison of his or her company and its competition. The competitors described in these focus groups can be either national or international.

## Disadvantages of Focus Groups

Focus groups are not the be-all and end-all of marketing measurement tools. A focus group is just one more measurement of sample opinions at a specific time. The answers are extremely dependent on the moderator or questioner. A bad questioner who thinks he or she is a genius can be devastating. What I continue to find at all levels is that some people think they are better than others at everything. The ones that talk the best talk may end up at Harvard, but I would not automatically trust them with fifty cents of my money. It is hard to find competent people who will work. Some focus-group leaders may inform competitors of your ADDIE and even give you erroneous information to lead you away from insights. This is one of the advantages of training several of your own people to do the job.

## CONCLUSION

Marketing is a resource that is applied as a means to achieve an organizational end. It is derived from philosophy, philosophy (KSA), philosophy in action, direction, structure, process, and resources. No one in the organization should believe that marketing is his or her long-term personal domain. When marketing is viewed from a pluralistic philosophical point of view, it becomes a separate activity carried on by experts. These experts often imply ever so subtly that their functions must take a dominant position in all decision making. The end determines the means that are applied and the makeup of those means. The marketing resource can apply three different actions to contribute to the unitary approach: customer, marketing mix, and marketing reasoning tools. These are contributing actions that are applied to common unifying models. Marketing is no more or less important than any other of the five resources. The following sections discuss human, physical, intangible, and financial resources.

## HUMAN RESOURCES

There are five resources that make up the general resource category for a unified organizational approach. They are marketing, human, physical, intangible, and financial. The organizations of the future will continue to de-emphasize the resource areas and the outdated concept of the functional specialist. This does not mean that the organization will not select, train, and upgrade personnel, but rather that these activities will be the combined responsibility of the entire organization (tribe). Someone may take a leadership position on a particular project at a specific time, but that person will not view that as an indication that this is his or her undisputed domain.

The importance of selection, training, and upgrading of employees cannot be overemphasized. Businesses are similar to athletics in that one must have the players to win the championship. In the United States, coaches are able to terminate people from athletic teams but it is much more difficult to terminate employees that either will not or cannot perform. Suppose, for example, that I was in Ireland wanting to play soccer for the Irish Cup team. The argument goes: Why should I be excluded from the team? I have just as much right to play on the team as anyone else. It should not matter what type of condition I am in, how old I am, how hard I expect to work, whether I attend practice, whether I am supportive of the team, and so on. The Irish would laugh, and no court in the land would support my efforts to get on the team. Why? Because they hate me? No. Because they want to win and winning requires that I do not play. I could possibly play in the school faculty/ student game. I may even find productive employment, but it will not be on the Irish Cup team.

There are games that are arranged so that all can play and have a chance, as in peewee-league baseball. But should this be true of international business? The Japanese and Germans put their best and brightest on their international business teams, but Americans tend to put in anyone who wants to play. The Japanese provide intensive education for their young, and those who perform are rewarded with the best jobs in the society. Is this fair? Yes and no. Unfortunately, if one wants to play and cannot make the rules, then one's team must be as good as or better than that of the competition to win. If one does not like it one can try to get the rules changed or not play. Some try to make their own rules for their own games. In the last ten years, America has tried to get the rules changed by accusing the Japanese of not playing by "the rules." The next step will be for Americans to say that they refuse to play. More and more markets are going to be turned over to the rest of the world. The reasons given will be elaborate, but the results will be simple and devastating. When one loses market power, one cannot make the rules.

The best and the brightest must be selected, trained, and upgraded. Of course, this does not mean that those who went to the supposedly top business schools should be hired. Corporate America has tried this with disastrous results. People deserve a chance, but if they cannot or will not perform, they must be removed from the businesses that compete in the international arena.

Too many employees in business have guarantees similar to those provided by tenure to college professors because of government, union, age, and many other forms of protection. This protection, although well intentioned has detracted from the issue of performance for a huge portion of the workforce. Anyone who suggests eliminating incapable employees in business is evil, but anyone who eliminates incapable players in sports is considered a great coach. This leads me to believe that to win in sports is much more important in the United States than to win against international competition. When one has no competition or one can control competition, then anything one does will be successful. One has market power.

## Pluralistic

Human resource development in a pluralistic organization is a separate functional area. Its role is to determine the staffing requirements of the firm and to ensure that these are met now and in the future. The human resource department is informed by line managers as to their specific requirements. Based on this information, human resource specialists advertise either within or outside the firm, or both, for the position. Applicants are screened, and after this screening process, a number are interviewed by the line manager and are then hired, rejected, or considered for another possible future position.

Once the employee is hired, the human resource function schedules the employee's training programs. These programs are both general and specific and depend on the level at which the employee enters the organization. When I was hired by a Fortune-500 organization, I was put into a one-year training program along with fifty other trainees from all areas of the company. Once the training program ended, I was given other training on the basis of the results of tests given by the assessment center. The human resource department, through an assessment center, would determine how my future in the corporation would unfold. Several employees at my stage of development in the organization, including myself, were assessed by more experienced employees from the company over a three-day session. At the end of this assessment, a plan was developed based on their having identified my strengths and weaknesses. Weaknesses were given training intervention, and strengths were to be encouraged by my supervisors.

Training was included that was very specific to my job, but general training (on, for example, public speaking) was also required. The human resource professionals, along with my immediate supervisor, were involved in this process. As new jobs became available, I was recommended to interview for those jobs. I could ask for an interview, or the human resource specialists could recommend the interview. To ask would be considered pushy or would indicate that I was unaware of my actual development. From these interviews, I could be rejected or accepted for the position for which I was applying. This process would continue until I quit, was laid off, was fired, or retired.

If the company no longer wanted me, it would abolish my job and give me three months to find another job in the corporation. At the end of three months, if I could not find a job or was blocked from finding the new job by the company, then I would be let go with tears in the human resource professionals' eyes but no tears in their hearts. Dr. Judi Neal of the University of New Haven has said that the human resource function in many companies has been reduced to keeping litigation to the minimum. They assist the company in firing unwanted employees and avoiding law suits. If a law suit is imminent they gather information to be used to enhance the company's position in a settlement or in court.

### Unitary

Human resource development is concerned with the selection, training, and upgrading of all employees. It is the responsibility of each employee to assist in whatever way possible in this process. All have a responsibility to help others to succeed and to develop their knowledge, skills, and attitudes. It is the responsibility of those who have gained experience to help others to develop within the company. This is not an alien concept in the history of mankind. The family, community, and nation each have taken varying degrees of responsibility for this activity for the past 100,000 years. The survival of all is related to the ability of an organization to change to new means and ends and to ensure that all its members are successful.

The CEO is not exempt from participation in the hiring of the vast majority of employees? This is not to suggest that CEOs become involved specifically in every hiring decision, but rather that they should select at random any applicant that enters the corporation and become active members in the process. The CEO, like all other employees, has an obligation to participate in the process. For example at the University of New Haven the president of the college has a meeting with all new people that are hired by the university. Because of this, he is well aware of what is going on with the college human resource activity.

The unitary approach links and connects the selection, training, and upgrading of all jobs so that each job builds overall KSA. The KSA is not job-specific, but rather each job contributes to an individual's development of KSA. For example, if a person chooses to get in shape, the particular activity he or she chooses may not be important, because all activities have the potential to get the person in good physical condition. Is racquetball better than baseball? Is dance better than soccer? Is it better to do one sport or play many sports? Can one be good in more than one sport or should one specialize?

## Summary

The selection, training, upgrading, and performance appraisal of all employees is the responsibility of everyone within the organization. It is a community decision that has been shared for 100,000 years. If the decision is made for the group by outsiders, then that group's performance is most likely diminished. The group has an obligation to work with all members to ensure present and future survival. This obligation is to be taken as an ancient trust given to them by past generations, which they then pass to future generations. People are aware of performance and nonperformance of those with whom they work each day. When a person is new to the group, the group will tolerate the indiscretions of the uninitiated. When a person moves to the status of one whose direct responsibility is to ensure the present and future survival of the organization, the group is less forgiving because the consequences of failure are so severe.

The same operating system is applied to selection, training, and upgrading. The areas to be improved by all are philosophy, philosophy (KSA), philosophy in action (market power), direction, structure, process, and resources. It is everyone's responsibility to work with all these attributes in a unified environment. The ability of all employees to shift to new means and ends is what ensures the future survival of the group.

## PHYSICAL RESOURCES

There are five resource areas that have been identified within the unitary approach. They are marketing, human, physical, intangible, and financial resources. Controlling physical resources is another form of market power that can be utilized by the organization to block competition from access to targeted market segments. Physical resources consist of any asset that is concrete and has a value. Land, buildings, furniture, machinery, and software are examples of physical resources. I went to visit another university a few years ago and thought it was beautiful. The location, the buildings, and the land put my college to shame. I received this impression before I met even one person or student who worked at the institution. The physical resources convinced me that I was in a great place. I was in awe when I found that each professor had his or her own office and each also had his or her own computer. I felt that I had somehow failed as a college professor to make it to a "real" school. Why did I feel this way?

The answer is that the physical resources indicated to me that this was a real place of learning with great teachers and students. The reality of my experience was that I was disappointed when I met the group, because the students and faculty did not live up to the expectations raised by my appraisal of the physical resources. I then realized that I was not as impressed as I had been and although the physical resources were still beautiful, they no longer gave me the same impression of the institution. Of course, potential students and a potential student's parent would not have the same experience or insights when they make a decision on what college the student should attend. They would continue to be as impressed as I was when I first saw the school's physical resources. This experience showed me the power of physical resources.

## Pluralistic

The acquisition of physical resources can be separated and applied to each particular functional area. Those with authority in each function make the decisions concerning the physical resources that are controlled by that function. In larger organizations, the acquisition of physical resources is performed by a separate department with its own specialists. There are other organizations that have further separated their physical resource specialization into subcategories. Staff in these subcategories do not necessarily even report to the same leaders in the organization. Acquisition of land may be done by one group of specialists, while the acquisition of office furniture and products is handled by another. Computers may be purchased by one group and computer software another. When physical resource acquisition is separated, the input on what to buy and how much to buy is coordinated by a physical resource functional specialist. Under these conditions the organization cannot work as a unified group to achieve a purpose. These specialists have all the same weaknesses and self-protective interests as those in any other functional area. Their decisions then reflect what they view as best for their functional area and not necessarily what is best to achieve an organizational purpose.

## Unitary

The acquisition and maintenance of all physical resources are for one purpose only: to achieve an organizational purpose. No physical resource has any value unless it is a means to an end. Having fancy offices for the top executives may not actually be a means to an end but rather an end unto itself. The question has to be asked is, how does taking the whole floor of a building and giving it to ten or fifteen executives benefit the organization? I once went to visit one of the top executives at a Fortune 50 company. I entered a large room through two large glass doors. The room was lavishly decorated around the corners but it was basically empty in the middle. At the far end was a lone secretary—about two-hundred feet away, it seemed to me. The secretary escorted me through a beautiful door to the top executive's office. That day, the company had just laid off thousands of workers. I described to the executive how the company could combine resources and improve efficiency. He listened to me and said in a perplexed tone, "I am an accountant." He repeated "I am an accountant. I am an accountant." We then had nothing more to say, and I left through the two-hundred foot room. Later, when I told the story to another executive who was visiting the company, we understood why all the employees had to be laid off. How many employees' yearly salaries did it take to build and maintain that office complex for a few executives? How isolated had they become? These physical resources were, in my view, not a means to an end.

## Summary

Physical resources can be a source of market power when they are a means to a clearly defined organizational end. The acquisition and application of all resources working together under a common philosophy, philosophy (KSA), philosophy in action (market power), direction, structure, process, and resources are required in today's global marketplace.

## INTANGIBLE RESOURCES

There are five resources that have been identified that make up the unitary approach: marketing, human, physical, intangible, and financial. Intangible resources are those that are granted through an identifiable authority. In most cases, this authority has its basis in law. This is similar to William Kingston's view of market power, in which he believes that all market power has its basis in law. Most marketing texts divide actions into "micro" and "macro"; it is postulated that there are activities over which the company has control and those over which it has no control. This idea could not be farther from the truth. The company can and should use intangible market power as a means of blocking competitors from access to markets. Intangible market power affects the decision to apply various means and ends. American business has done a poor job since World War II of using intangible market power. The idea of intangible market power in the United States is the assurance of a level playing field. This is a naive approach, because intangible market power should insure a steeply sloped playing field—one where the American company is on top looking down at international competitors.

Although this is rarely stated, it has been the model for millennia. As long as there are different nations and cultures, they will all continue to function in their own self-interest. To think otherwise is the dream of a few (very few) or just another method of gaining market power. If America or any other nation or corporation can convince any competitor to willingly give up its own self-interest and not try to gain market power for itself, I will believe that Elvis lives. The colonial model was instituted and enforced, it is said, for the benefit of the subjugated—to bring them God, education, progress, medicine, and now human rights. Billions have heard it so often that it almost sounds believable.

## Pluralistic

Following a pluralistic philosophical foundation, intangible resources are separate and disconnected from all others. Laws, statutes, tariffs, and so forth are implemented for their own particular purposes. There is little, if any, interest in identifying how these decisions affect any other resource area. Government passes laws and implements programs without input from any other sector of the society. The Ronald Reagan and George Bush administrations believed a group of U.S. economists when they advocated that the role of government was to get out of the way and let business prosper. Clinton's economists are suggesting the opposite. Of course there is another possibility: Government helps business.

### Unitary

Intangible resources are concerned with legal restrictions, proprietary restrictions, and import/export restrictions. These areas are combined with all others to block competition. I often tell my marketing colleagues, who continue to advocate customer needs and wants, that it does not matter what the customer needs and wants if competition is blocked. They then move to the idea that it is unfair to block competition and that what these businesses and governments are doing is evil. The simple truth is that hundreds of thousands of products are blocked from the U.S. market. They have been since George Washington was president and they will be after Clinton is no longer president. The question has never been whether the United States should block products. The question is whether the United States should block in the consumer sector. The United States blocks in the agricultural, military, government, and educational sectors.

### Summary

Intangible resources have the potential to provide market power to those firms that can apply those resources as a means to their ends. The acquisition and application of all resources working together under a common philosophy, philosophy (KSA), philosophy in action, direction, structure, process, and resources as required in today's global marketplace.

### FINANCIAL RESOURCES

There are five resources that have been identified that make up the unitary approach: marketing, human, physical, intangible, and financial resources. Financial resources are those resources that revolve around the use of money. These resources are not always specifically in the form of cash, but their value is considered to be more liquid than the other resources. Financial resources can be a great source of market power, and properly conceived, they are important to the success of a business. A word of caution: in pluralistic America, those who were and are involved in the area of finance have had a vise grip on corporations. Just as all those in the other functions do, those in finance departments view market power as coming only from their particular worldviews. Because of their control over the money, they have added to an environment that is incapable of applying different resources as a form of market power.

Financial resources are valuable, but only as a means to an end and not as an end in themselves. Other resource areas and power centers are working hard to convince anyone who will listen that *they* are the saviors of the company and that they alone can solve all of the firm's problems. When I hear any of them, I cringe for fear that someone may believe them.

**Pluralistic**

The pluralistic view of the financial resource is that it is a separate function within the organization. This function is responsible for overseeing and making decisions that will give the organization the best returns on its money and assets. The value of any asset is understood in relation to returns in financial terms. Because of the U.S. tax system and the way that organizations are financed (through the sale of stocks), these specialists have responded to a short-term, single-minded view of the organization. Those in finance have perceived themselves (as do those in all other resource areas) as the most important and critical component to achieve organizational success.

The financial resource area has been overly cautious for the last thirty years, a viewpoint that is well explained in David Halberstam's book *The Reckoning*. Unfortunately, there is no one functional area that has the market power to overcome the functional grip that the financial resource area has taken away from the other functional areas in the United States. I hear a lot of complaining but little evidence. It will take changes in the way that American business finances the expansion of business and in the tax laws to dislodge them from their functional power.

**Unitary**

From a unitary philosophical point of view, financial resources are valued tools in an organization's arsenal. They are no more or less regarded than any other means to achieve an end. Decisions made by people in financial areas are not considered any more a mandate of heaven because of their financial KSA than anyone else's functional decision. All members work together to achieve a common purpose. This common purpose has been determined by the CEO not by the chief financial officer (CFO). I have often argued that no organization should allow the title of CFO to exist within its firm. It sends a message to all that power is shared at the top. This cannot occur because there has to be one final authority and only one within a group (Theory "W"). That authority is the CEO. No army in the world has two final authorities. They each have only one.

From a unitary perspective, financial resources must be controlled by the firm. When a firm controls its own financial destiny, it has far more market power than a firm whose financial destiny is in the hands of an outside firm. The financial destinies of Japanese firms are linked through their *zaibatsu* networks. Financial institutions and the *zaibatsu* member firms are working together for their common success. In contrast, when financial institutions (as in the American model) work for their own success, this brings about a different type of decision making that may be detrimental to the organization that is being lent money. American financial institutions function in their self-interests not in the interest of the nation.

**Summary**

Financial resources have the potential to provide an organization with market power. This is accomplished when the firm applies all resources as a means to achieve its end. The acquisition and application of these resources—working together in unity under a common philosophy, philosophy (KSA), philosophy in action (market power), structure, process, and resources—is what is proposed.

## SELECTED READINGS

Baker, Michael et al. *Marketing theory and practice*. 2d ed. London: Macmillan, 1983.

Burke, James. *Connections*. Boston: Little, Brown, 1978.

Dixon D. F., and I. F. Wilkinson. *The marketing system*. Melbourne, Australia: Longman Cheshire, 1982.

Kotler, Philip. *Marketing management: Analysis, planning, implementing and control*. 8th ed. Englewood Cliffs, N.J.: Prentice-Hall, 1994.

Lamb, Charles W., Jr., Joseph F. Hair, and Carl McDaniel, Jr. *Principles of marketing*. 2d ed. Cincinnati: South-Western, 1994.

Monroe, Kent. *Pricing: Making profitable decisions*. 2d ed. New York: McGraw-Hill, 1990.

Morris, David. *Marketing as a means to achieve organizational ends*. 4th ed. West Haven, Conn.: University of New Haven Press, 1994.

Ries, Al, and Jack Trout. *Positioning: The battle for your mind*. New York: Warner Books, 1987.

### Human Resources

Cascio, Wayne F. 1986. *Managing human resources: Productivity, quality of work life, profits*. 2d ed. New York: McGraw-Hill.

French, Wendall. 1990. *Human resource management*. 2d ed. Boston: Houghton Mifflin.

Garfield, Charles. *Second to none: How smart companies put people first*. Homewood, Ill.: Irwin, 1992.

Milkovitch, George, and Jerry Newman. *Compensation*. 3d ed. Homewood, Ill.: Irwin, 1990.

Morris, David. Improving efficiencies: Selection and training related to the bottom line. *Performance and Instruction Journal* 25(10)(1987): 19–22, 25.

————. Meta-marketing needs assessment: Unifying organizational focus to achieve marketplace goals and objectives. *Performance and Instruction Journal*. 29(4)(1990):16-20.

Myers, Donald W. *Human resource management: Principles and practice*. 2d ed. Chicago: Commerce Clearing House, 1992.

### Physical Resources

Smith, Adam. *The wealth of nations*. Ed. Edwin Cannan. New York: Modern Library, 1965.

### Financial Resources

Downes, John, and Jordan Elliot Goodman. *Dictionary of finance and investment terms*. Woodbury, New York: Barron's, 1985.

# Final Thoughts

This book is a search to identify the importance of a common operating system for a business. From my own experience, I have been struck with just how much of my thinking has been developed and nurtured as part of a post–World War II, separating American worldview. I, like many of my colleagues in academics, found myself teaching with great authority the specialized disciplines that Western universities deemed to be important.

## CORPORATE OPERATING SYSTEM

When individuals and groups come together and form tribes, they must create a common underlying operating system from which all actions overlap. Operating systems, throughout the world, are generally organized into those that separate and those that combine. Because of America's diversified population, operating systems in the United States have searched for actions that separate knowledge, skills, and attitudes (KSA). This separation has been identified as individual and linear. A Western philosophical emphasis on separation is derived from the sixteenth-century European Enlightenment. Eastern philosophy never experienced a period of philosophical separation and continued to maintain its tribal operating system of combining KSA. This Eastern form of combining is circular and searches for overlapping relationships.

When the Christian white males ran corporate America, they separated the organization into job specialization. This new American approach successfully directed the attention of the workforce away from the issues of ethnicity and the different forms of Christianity. Europeans were killing each other over differences within Christianity. After the success of World War II, the social engineers in the

United States succeeded in extending the separating operating systems in business to include many more forms of separation and specialization. Gender, race, physical and emotional diversity, sexual preference, non-Christian religions, and different philosophical identities became new constructs of specialization. Power was transferred from one set of distinctive criteria (job specialization) to other forms of specialization.

Unfortunately, the postwar emphasis on these new forms of specialization have continued to weaken corporate America against more unified international competition. The age-old understanding of separation as a form of power against the "other" has never succeeded in the history of the world. To force people to work together is impossible if no mechanisms exist for combining operating systems. The war in the Balkans is a prime example of the failure of this understanding. The fact that American corporate membership is from a throng of backgrounds may be overcome only when a unified operating system is applied.

We all bring differences to any job, but the outcome of working together on a job becomes adversely affected when those within the corporation emphasize their differences rather than their similarities at the operating system level. When individuals, or groups, continue to focus on their unique operating systems, backgrounds, and experiences, other individuals and groups become excluded. Each person must selflessly bring to the corporation his or her particular accumulation of knowledge, skills, and attitudes, but that KSA must be understood and applied by all of the members to a common operating system.

The corporate challenge of the future will be to develop common corporate operating systems that can be applied by all who choose to contribute to the success of the whole. When individuals from diverse backgrounds and specializations are allowed to justify differences, it can and does lead to internal corporate warfare. This warfare must be avoided if the corporation is to prosper. If members from specialized backgrounds cannot adjust to the new corporate operating system, they should not remain within the corporation. If they prevail, they create many disjointed companies working toward disconnected purposes.

Those who wish to retain membership must work selflessly for the benefit of the whole. Diversity is only an organizational resource when it is applied to achieve a unified purpose. Diversity cannot be viewed as a benefit to a particular individual or group. Imposed advantages that are granted to individuals, or groups, sooner or later end up in conflicts between those who attain the benefit and those who perceive exclusion.

Organizations are fragile agreements between people to work together for the common benefit of all. A focus on separation that emphasizes job specialization, race, gender, and religion—we all see surface each day—will destroy all of us. We all have to find common overlapping operating systems that work to the benefit of the whole.

## DO ANY BUSINESSES TODAY TAKE A UNITARY APPROACH?

Most of the world, with the exception of the United States, takes a unitary approach. This may be because the United States is a new country in the history of the world. America has not experienced the long-term decline that most other nations have had as part of their historic consciousness. When resources are scarce, people are forced to develop operating systems to adjust to that reality. This compels individuals and groups to think in terms of combining rather than separating.

Almost all small-businesspersons are required to take a unitary approach to business. They simply lack the resources to separate their businesses into functions. If the owner decides that a function is necessary, he or she is forced to assume that responsibility.

Large corporations today in the United States are laying off millions of functional workers in an attempt to compete in a global economy. This is only a temporary solution to a much broader problem. Reengineering, thought to be the new corporate salvation, is proving to be useless at best. Technology is only one potential form of market power. If competition has the same application of resources, then there is no derived market power. Technology will be successful only when combined with many other resources to achieve a purpose. The optimal means of achieving market power is to conceptualize endless combinations through the creation of a common unifying operating system. There are four American corporations that I believe understand the principles as outlined in this book: Disney, McDonald's, General Electric, and Arthur Andersen. The continued success of these companies has occurred because of a Theory "W" leadership model as part of a combining operating system.

## TO THE ALPHA LEADERS OF CORPORATE AMERICA

If you intend to survive and prosper, you must begin to combine resources to attain market power. To continue to separate yourselves in the face of foreign competition that combines its resources puts the entire nation at risk. Begin with the idea of combining at the operating system level, as put forth in this book. Search for the similarities of life rather than the differences. Start to defunctionalize the company. Understand the positive aspects of market power. Develop a single, clearly defined direction and rid yourselves of the mission-statement mentality. Do not allow any present functional area to have its own philosophy in action. No more functions, resources only. For example, marketing's obsession with needs and wants, separates marketing from all other resources. Drive all resources on market power. Teach and develop your trusted followers. Force analysis, design, development, implementation, and evaluation (ADDIE) whenever there is a process application. Add direction to ADDIE and call it DADDIE. Reward those who can apply multiple resources to achieve a purpose. Avoid the trap of identifying a single resource solution to any challenge.

## THE MILITARY

Like it or not, most large businesses follow the lead of the military. The U.S. military understood after the war in Vietnam that a mechanized and functionalized military was incapable of defeating the enemy of the future. The military has taken steps to defunctionalize and change its resource configuration. I believe that the present military downsizing is not a downsizing, but rather a reconfiguration applying a unified operating system. The soldier of the present and the future will be a highly educated, highly trained, multiskilled problem solver. Selection, training, and upgrading will focus on similarities rather than differences. The submarine service is a prototype within the military for this approach. There is no functional specialists because of the danger to all if that person is lost.

## RED TEAM/BLUE TEAM

Select your best thinkers to compare operating system and resources with that of competition. Do not let ego stand in the way of strategy. Divide the group into two teams. Then play "move" and "countermove." Many in business fail to realize that the competitors will almost always, when they become aware of your actions, respond to your attack. Unprepared responses leave you much more vulnerable. Let the competitor team within your company do the best job possible to counter your strategy. Then, think though and counter their countermoves. The game never ends. It should be played on a regular basis. If you have prepared for an action then market power is with you. It is always better to be prepared than to think that the competition will not react.

## JACK OF ALL TRADES, MASTER OF NONE

This one statement expresses the obstacle in the United States to undertaking a unitary approach. It has been embedded in the minds of the society as a warning against those who put forth a unified approach. Specialization is a form of market power that all specialists wish to protect. The corporation of the present and future cannot afford separation and specialization as a means to attain market power. It is ridiculous to think that, as educated humans, we cannot do many things at a high standard of performance.

## SHOULD ANYONE BE A SPECIALIST IN THE CORPORATION?

No one individual should be a specialist within the corporation. This does not mean that a person cannot be working on a particular activity at a moment in time. This activity must be understood to benefit the whole. I understand the argument that it is those on the fringe of a group that bring the mass forward. This idea reinforces the linear position of separation and specialization. The mass never moves forward, but rather, the circle expands and contracts. This is not to suggest that the organization takes a short-term approach to its actions. Change is not as feared when we are assured that we will be a part of that change. Protection does not have to be within a specialization or the new right way. Protection comes from the ability to apply a common operating system to new applications of resources. All resources come and go.

## THE QUEST

The quest that is represented by this book began many years ago. I was not even aware that it had begun. I hope that my readers have begun their own quests for understanding. Many critics have asked me with great joy, "How do you know any of this to be true?" I respond that none of it is true, nor is it untrue. It is a worldview; a way to live your life. These are powerful movers of us all, and challenges to any ideas, even the most simple, have rarely been met with enthusiasm. We must begin the search for unity in diversity. Know yourself and know the other by combining and simplifying to achieve a purpose.

# Index

**About the Author**

DAVID JOSEPH MORRIS, JR., Associate Professor of Marketing at the University of New Haven, Connecticut, has received national and international attention for his theories of business and marketing. He has been a visiting faculty member of Trinity College, Dublin, and Cyprus College, Nicosia, and visiting Faculty Fellow at Yale University. Author of several other books and many articles, Dr. Morris is host of a radio interview program and heads an international consultancy, Market Power Institute, Madison, Connecticut.